Advance Praise for
The SRI Advantage

"*The SRI Advantage* takes this subject to a new level of exciting complexity, clarity, and horizon. ... With the collapse of self-discipline among the large accounting firms, the many conflicts of interest among management and shareholders and within the larger circle of investment bankers, brokers, law firms, and boards, the environment is now ripe for accelerating change."

> Ralph Nader, from the foreword

"Peter Camejo, always on the cutting edge, has created a compelling volume blending information on socially responsible investing with strong statistical evidence. This book should put anyone's fears to rest about combining their values and investments."

> Barbara Krumsiek, President and CEO of Calvert Group, Ltd.

"Peter Camejo describes the future of financial capital in America — when people learn how to get control of their own money."

> William Greider, National Affairs Correspondent for *The Nation* and author of *Secrets of the Temple* and *Who Will Tell the People?*

"Where to put your money in this Enron bear market? Now, definitive documentation by recognized experts on why and how socially responsible investing has beaten Wall Street's averages for over a decade. As a long-time environmental activist and SRI investor, I will be giving this book to all my friends!"

> Hazel Henderson, author of *Beyond Globalization* and partner, The Calvert-Henderson Quality of Life Indicators

The SRI Advantage

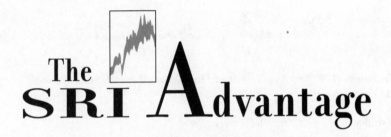

The SRI Advantage

Why Socially Responsible Investing Has Outperformed Financially

PETER CAMEJO

With Geeta Aiyer, Samuel Case, Jon F. Hale,
James T. Hawley, Steven Heim, Ian Chan Hodges,
Matthew Kiernan, Christopher Luck, James Nixon,
Steven J. Schueth, Stephen Viederman, and
Andrew T. Williams

Foreword by RALPH NADER

Introduction by ROBERT A.G. MONKS

NEW SOCIETY PUBLISHERS

Cataloguing in Publication Data:
A catalog record for this publication is available from the National Library of Canada.

Text design by Steven Hiatt, San Francisco
Cover design by Stewart Cauley / POLLEN

Printed in Canada by Friesens Inc., Altona, Manitoba

New Society acknowledges the financial support of the Government of Canada through the Book Publishing Industry Development Program (BDIDP) for our publishing activities.

Hardcover ISBN: 0 86571 477 0

Inquiries regarding requests to reprint all or part of *The SRI Advantage* should be addressed to New Society Publishers at the address below.

To order directly from the publishers, please add $4.50 shipping to the price of the first copy, and $1.00 for each additional copy (plus GST in Canada). Send check or money order to:

New Society Publishers
P.O. Box 189, Gabriola Island, B.C. V0R 1X0, Canada
1-800-567-6772

New Society Publishers' mission is to publish books that contribute in fundamental ways to building an ecologically sustainable and just society, and to do so with the least possible impact on the environment, in a manner that models this vision. We are committed to doing this not just through education, but through action. We are acting on our commitment to the world's remaining ancient forests by phasing out our paper supply from ancient forests worldwide. This book is one step towards ending global deforestation and climate change. It is printed on acid-free paper that is 100% old growth forest-free (100% post-consumer recycled), processed chlorine free, and printed with vegetable based, low VOC inks. For further information, or to browse our full list of books and purchase securely, visit our website at: www. newsociety.com

New Society Publishers

www.newsociety.com

To my grandchildren:
Daniel José and Andrew John

Contents

Acknowledgments   ix

Foreword *by Ralph Nader*   xi

Introduction *by Robert A.G. Monks*   xiii

1   The Case for SRI Outperformance   1

2   SRI Indexes, Risk, and Volatility   11

3   SRI Mutual Funds   23

4   30 Years of Studies: SRI Performance and Market History   37

5   Why SRI Has Outperformed   47

6   Pension Funds and Fiduciary Responsibility: 73
The SRI Imperative

7   Socially Responsible Investing for the Individual Investor   97

8   Socially Responsible Investing in the US   115
by Steven J. Schueth

9   Socially Responsible Investing: From the Margins   123
to the Mainstream *by Matthew Kiernan*

10   Seeing Stars: SRI Mutual Fund Performance   133
     by Jon F. Hale

11   Factoring Out Sector Bets   145
     by Christopher Luck

12   Can Universal Owners Be Socially Responsible Investors?   151
     by James T. Hawley and Andrew T. Williams

13   "Crossing the Black Waters": The International Dimension   173
     of Socially Responsible Investing *by Geeta Aiyer and Steven Heim*

14   SRI and Energy: Scenes from a Revolution   185
     by Samuel Case

15   Foundations and Mission-Related Investing   207
     by Stephen Viederman

16   The World of Community Investing Strategies   215
     by James Nixon

APPENDIXES

A   SRI Investment Consultants   241

B   CCCERA's Social and Environmental Issues Voting Policy   243

C   Progress Is Possible: A Year of Capital   245
     Stewardship in Hawaii *by Ian Chan Hodges*

About the Authors   253

Index   261

Acknowledgments

I owe a debt of gratitude to the many people who helped me prepare this book. I must start by thanking all the trustees of the Contra Costa County Employees' Retirement Board (CCCERA), who helped me understand how pensions and pension funds work. I especially want to thank trustees Richard Cabral, Bob Rey, and Brian Hast for all the time they spent answering my questions over the last three years; CCCERA's outstanding legal councel, Bill Sokol, for all his assistance; and Patricia Wiegert, the CCCERA's retirement administrator, and her staff for their kindness and patience.

I want to thank Kara Gifford, a student at Saint Mary's College, who worked on the book at each step of the way, resolving issues and checking facts for well over a two-year period. Steven Hiatt of San Francisco, an old friend and professional editor, did a marvelous job of turning my work into readable material. I'm grateful to the other contributors to the book, whose chapters helped broaden its focus and illuminate many aspects of socially responsible investing. I do want to clarify that they did not review the chapters I authored and that only I am responsible for their content.

My thanks go to Lloyd Kurtz for his stimulating discussions of SRI performance issues, which were of great help to me even though he was not in complete agreement with some of my arguments. Steve Viederman advised me throughout the project of this book. I must also mention Eric Leenson, president and CEO of Progressive Asset Management, and Catherine Cartier, director of PAM, because their many years of support made this project possible. Thanks also to Neal Stalling, PAM's director of research, for digging hard to find facts.

Lastly, I want to thank the two individuals who open this book. They are both inspirations to all people involved in SRI and whose lives have been dedicated to trying to make our nation and the world a better place for all: Robert A.G. Monks and Ralph Nader.

Foreword

by Ralph Nader

Books on socially responsible investing usually rival dry high school civics texts as cures for insomnia. Not this volume. *The SRI Advantage* takes this subject to a new level of exciting complexity, clarity, and horizon. With the brilliant introduction by Robert A.G. Monks foreshadowing potential transformations if owners act *as* owners and seek the rights and remedies of ownership of their companies, with the chapters by Peter Camejo elaborating what *outperform* means in terms of conventional returns on investment, and with the additional specific contributions by several veterans of this movement regarding unconventional returns that affect corporate behavior and impact, we can see the emergence of a new maturity about what SRI is and can become.

Part of this maturity is moving from SRI-by-deletion to an active engagement by individual and institutional shareholders in the governance of their corporations. Not governance as it is now conceived by the concentrators of power at the executive and board levels; but a governance where the owners control what they own in ways that make their companies absorb larger social values — some of which can become competitive edges while others avoid looming turmoil and costs. SRI has had two strategies, one being *exit* (sell or do not invest in troublesome companies), and the other *voice* (engage as owners in changing the companies). Robert A.G. Monks has been the leader in the latter strategy throughout his robust, independent career — often a voice in the wilderness and lately a leader of arriving voices. Peter Camejo, a successful investor, citizen advocate, and man of unusual foresight, brings together many of the voices in this volume that will, among other consequences, strengthen the obligations of trustees for institutional investors and redefine their role from passive-exit to active-engage. Of course, this outcome has been the hope for more than a few years. But with the collapse of self-discipline among the large accounting firms, the many conflicts of interest among management and shareholders and within the larger circle of investment bankers, brokers, law firms, and boards, perhaps the environment is now ripe for accelerating change.

Commercial tumult, massive loses inflicted upon beneficiaries and employees, a wave of corporate crime, fraud, and abuse regularly depicted in the mainstream business media (*Business Week, Fortune,* the *Wall Street Journal*), egregious self-dealing and breath-taking levels of greed all invite our thought, resolution, and action. These pages should help the vanguard advance and the rearguard diminish. Yes, you can put this book down, in order to collect your own stimulated thoughts and put together your own plans. Much work lies ahead for which Peter Camejo and the other contributors to this volume provide a most useful roadmap.

Washington, D.C.
June 2002

Introduction

by Robert A. G. Monks

People talk a lot about socially responsible investing (SRI). We need to talk more about who determines what constitutes SRI. Who sets the standards? Or, put another way, what is SRI? Let's start with what it is not. SRI cannot be the best-intentioned, most elaborately researched conclusions of the "best people," be they corporate executives, university professors, or philosophers. In a democratic society, only those whose authority derives from informed popular consensus can establish legitimate standards defining the balance between corporate and public interest. SRI must therefore focus on assuring that portfolio companies clearly obey the law. However, it is not quite that simple.

For the democratic process to work in a meaningful way, laws must be based on full information. The situation today is often otherwise. Not only are legislators dealing with imperfect information, in many situations they are legislating in areas where the information is deliberately withheld or distorted by the party they are seeking to regulate. In the United States over the last 25 years, this has conspicuously been the situation with respect to the automobile and power generating industries. W.R. Grace deliberately withheld information that its products contained asbestos well after it was scientifically established that asbestos injures workers. Responsible shareholders must ensure that the managements of portfolio companies disclose fully the impact of corporate functioning on society.

Ownership responsibility goes further. It is necessary in a democratic capitalist society that business and government communicate. In order to pass responsible laws, government must have full information about business' operations and their impact on society. There is a further need that business be restrained in its impact on elections, the making of laws, and their implementation. The perception that laws are being made and enforced not for the public good but for the interest of corporate money and power will surely destroy a free society. Where are we today?

Consider the recent example of Microsoft. When the Clinton administration filed its first suit against Microsoft in the fall of 1997, the company had a one-man lobbying shop with an office above a suburban Washington mall and company executives considered the Capitol as a largely irrelevant factor in corporate life. The company's political contributions were minimal. By early 1998, the Justice Department and 20 states filed their broad antitrust suit against Microsoft. Many observers came to believe that persistent lobbying by its competitors and adversaries, as well as senators from the states where they were located, contributed to the decision. As befits the premier enterprise of its time, Microsoft learned fast and reacted on a large scale. The company assembled the usual bank of lobbyists, spinmeisters, and political payoffs and, as they say, the rest is history. There is no hero in this story. It is a story of SRI gone badly. It is a model of too much corporate power over government, both in its beginning and in its end.

The only element in the corporate universe that can effectively restrain management in its dealings with government is the owners. What we are talking about is real socially responsible investing. It is the kind of SRI we must have if the concept is to have legitimacy — but it is not what we have today. Consider what that might mean. Real SRI exists when owners change their company in accord with sensitivity to social concerns. Indeed, as I will note in concluding this introduction, shareholder involvement is necessary in order to mitigate the most brutal negation of shareholder values — as dramatically evidenced in recent times by the collapse of Enron.

SRI has largely existed as a passive concept. The guiding principle has been that skilled individuals are capable of selecting certain companies that do not (the emphasis has been on excluding certain categories) have acceptable impact on society. Using modern technology to achieve diversification and analyze risk, it has been possible to construct portfolios that comprise "good" (in the sense that they are not bad) companies, which approximate the investment characteristics of the market as a whole — usually the S&P 500 Index. Peter Camejo devotes the first five chapters of this book to a careful analysis of the various modes of measuring stock performance over varying lengths of time. He usefully lays to rest any concern that SRI-indexed funds might not perform at least as well as the general averages over any relevant length of time. This is very important because the impression persists that social consciousness has an investment cost. So long as trustees, a species that incarnates risk aversion, have any reason to be inhibited by even a scintilla of potential liability they will decline to endorse a controversial investment mode.

This theme is picked up in Jon Hale's reference to the Department of Labor's Ruling 98-04A. The Pension and Welfare Benefits Agency (the "Agency") with authority over all US private employee benefit systems under the Employees' Retirement Income Security Act of 1974 (ERISA) is probably the most important explicator of fiduciary responsibility in the world today. The Agency has consistently maintained that SRI is not in itself illegal. A trustee must manage prudently with an "eye solely" to enhancing the value of the beneficiaries' interest. However, this investment may at the same time serve a parallel social purpose. An example is the investment by Prudential, as trustee, in mortgages on projects that are constructed only with union labor. Prudential's loan committee reviews all loan applications on a union-blind basis. Only after the committee has approved particular credits is the fact of union labor involvement in construction revealed. The Agency opined that there was no ERISA objection to a trustee selecting from the approved credits only those with union involvement. This is an essential legal foundation for the community-based investing referred to in Steve Schueth's article, which "allows investors to put money to work in local communities, where capital is not readily available, to create jobs, affordable housing and environmentally friendly products and services."

Matthew Kiernan's piece and the article by James P. Hawley and Andrew T. Williams raise the interesting question of whether SRI is correctly seen as an entirely passive activity. One can ask what useful purpose is served by declining to invest in "bad" companies. The theory is that if enough potential buyers decline to purchase a security its price in the market will drop, leading, one hopes, to appropriate remediation. The "creation myth" here is the long program of forced disinvestments in apartheid South Africa. It is occasionally cited that Nelson Mandela applauded those who demonstrated concern in this way; it is also widely cited that the great man applauded those companies who continued operations in South Africa while attempting to improve racial working conditions. There has never been any demonstration of adverse stock price movement among companies who continued to do business in South Africa. Horribly enough, the only financial consequences from this well-intended effort that can clearly be adduced are the huge losses of the companies who, in response to SRI clamor, divested their operations under "fire sale" conditions. It is also certain that divesting institutions suffered losses. Roland Machold, formerly the much respected investment manager (later, state treasurer) for the New Jersey pension funds, estimated his funds' losses at half a billion dollars. Philosophers have long taught that one cannot prove a negative. By analogy, it is difficult to imagine being able to prove that moving pieces of paper (this is the action required under traditional SRI) representing minor ownership percentages among classes of owners will have material effect on the conduct of a publicly owned corporation.

We need pause to reflect on the appalling economic consequences involved in the creation myth of the SRI movement. What do we learn? Unless the "social rules" requiring divestiture are universally agreed and universally enforced, passive noninvestment can be predicted to have little positive effect and, indeed, serious value-destroying consequences. Global enforcement of a universal norm that not everyone will necessarily agree to seems unlikely in the extreme. This same energy directed at changing companies from within offers a more promising route.

The idea that there is such a category as SRI certainly raises consciousness. Thus, from Geeta Aiyer and Steven Heim we learn that Novartis was retained in the favored index notwithstanding "a well documented, troubling legacy of product liability and environmental problems." The basis for this was the willingness of the company to change its internal environmental management systems and to have a dialog with its critics. The concept of informed and persistent involvement by the shareholder begins to appear a critical element for an effective SRI.

Williams and Hawley bring us tantalizingly close to a world in which the global investors, whom they identify and quantify, can have useful impact, but they content themselves with "… a universal owner has a fiduciary obligation to use a variety of means (including public policy advocacy and the corporate governance processes) to encourage firms to produce positive externalities, and to minimize or eliminate negative ones. 'Care' involves active and forceful engagement with the firms they own. Thus, they must engage." We are left to wonder how. But we can hope that that fascinating subject will be the subject of their next book.

Stephen Viederman concludes this useful collection with a most insightful list of the reasons why the finance committees and boards of directors and trustees of our leading institutions largely continue to refrain from considering social investing. The facts are discouraging — Harvard University teaches ethics, Harvard Management Company eschews active shareholding; the Ford Foundation grants hundreds of millions of dollars annually for well-conceived programs; Ford's investment committee declines to be involved in shareholder activism. This raises a most serious question: Is SRI a fringe activity, to be limited to the "true believers" who have always had a bit of trouble with the ugly face of capitalism?

Where are the "great and the good"? This question is slowly and patiently being addressed in the United Kingdom, where institutional investors are now required explicitly to adopt social and environmental policies with respect to their investments. The burden has been placed on institutions to become activist with respect to the companies whose equity securities are held in their portfolios if such is necessary to enhance value (the Myners Report). This has come about as a result of ten years of public dialog, starting with the so-called Cadbury Commission, involving managements, accountants, money managers, bankers, and government figures. No such high-level discussion has yet taken place in the United States, either in the public or private sector.

Who is opposed to SRI? There is, to be sure, legitimate concern by the pension and investment communities that fiduciary disciplines not be diluted. Are those who hold back genuinely moved by the imagined plight of the pensioners, or is something else at stake? Do companies worry that social consideration will decrease their competitiveness domestically and abroad? If all companies operate under the same rules, there should be no change in competitiveness. Is it a question of power? Is there something fundamentally unacceptable about accepting corporate wisdom from a group outside of management? The overarching reality is vast inertia from a community that is riddled with conflicting interests and which finds the present resolution of power and wealth satisfactory.

Over the next decade, I predict that sensitivity to societal and environmental concerns will be explicitly recognized as adding value to companies. I have patented a simulation BRIGHTLINE, available at www.ragm.com, for those who would like to probe this area further. We need to instill into the public consciousness the reality that only attention to sustainable values will allow corporations to achieve optimum value.

The Enron debacle, causing the destruction of value for hundreds of thousands of pensioners and investors, has turned attention at the presidential level to the need for corporate accountability: "Through stricter accounting standards and tougher disclosure requirements, corporate America must be made more accountable to employees and shareholders and hold to the highest standards of conduct." The pervasiveness of public outrage gives the opportunity to assure that "accounting standards" are defined spaciously so as to include fully the impact of corporate functioning on society. The possibility of fully legitimate legal standards raises the hope for a robust conceptual basis for socially responsible corporations. The certainty of loss in the absence of informed and effective activity persuades owners to be responsible themselves and to require it from their managers. This is the only formulation that can ensure the global sustainability of a corporate system.

1

The Case for Socially Responsible Investing

Yes, it's true. Socially responsible investing (SRI) has financially outperformed conventional investment strategies. And not only has SRI outperformed, it has also lowered risk. Most investment strategies require adding risk to increase performance or accept lower performance as the price of lower risk. SRI reduces risk *and* improves performance. This book is primarily about *why* that is true.

The empirical evidence for SRI's outperformance is overwhelming. In later chapters you'll see that socially screened market indexes have tended to outperform nonscreened indexes. You will find that socially screened mutual funds have received on average higher ratings that reflect their risk-adjusted outperformance. You'll also see reviews of some of the large number of studies that show either outperformance or equal performance by SRI.

By *socially responsible*, I mean investing with a concern for the social consequences of your investment. Popularly, *socially responsible investing* refers to investments that screen out companies that violate environmental or other laws, use child labor or sweatshops, discriminate in hiring, or in general, produce products detrimental to society or engage in practices deemed reprehensible by most people. (In Europe the term *sustainable investing* with a more narrowly environmental focus has been predominant. In England and Australia, the term *ethical investing* seems to have caught on to express a similar approach.) Obviously, there can be no exact agreement in our diverse society on what is socially responsible. For instance, some Catholic funds include social justice and environmental issues in their screens but also screen out companies that produce contraceptives. Other funds would consider producing contraceptives a positive social factor as part of family planning programs. But such controversial issues are minor compared to the consensus on what is today called socially responsible investing in the United States.

The mutual funds and other organizations that call themselves socially responsible also vary in the kinds of screens they use and how they use the information derived from their screens. For example, one fund may not be willing to invest in a company that has any relationship to nuclear power, while others may set a limit of no more than 5 percent of a company's business in such an area. Tobacco screens have usually been based on a 15 percent rule so as to exclude only corporations really based on the tobacco industry but not screen out retail firms that may sell cigarettes.

Investments, Values, and Performance

According to a 1999 Yankelovich study, 57 percent of people owning mutual funds were unaware that SRI funds existed at all (see Table 1.1). Socially responsible investing is still a completely new phenomenon to most investors. Ninety percent of investors cannot name any SRI mutual funds. However, interest in the basic idea of socially responsible investing is high. Yankelovich found that a majority of people said that they would prefer to invest in companies that are environmentally and socially responsible.[1]

But although many people want to invest in socially responsible ways, until quite recently most investors believed that they had to give up some measure of performance to do so. According to Yankelovich, however, awareness of SRI's higher performance is starting to spread. Their study indicates that 46 percent of investors who were aware of SRI funds believe that SRI mutual funds offer the same or higher performance, up from 36 percent in 1996. Nevertheless, a majority of 54 percent still believes that socially screened funds underperform, and the total amount invested in SRI mutual funds — while growing rapidly — remains a very small percentage of the total invested in all mutual funds.[2]

Table 1.1   Investors and Values

Issue	Women	Men
Companies that do no harm to the environment	73%	67%
Companies with good records of hiring/promoting women	69%	56%
Companies with good records of hiring/promoting minorities	69%	55%
Companies that are not involved in sweatshops	62%	51%
Companies not involved in tobacco	54%	45%

Megatrends Influencing SRI

This book cannot promise that SRI will continue to outperform indefinitely or for any specific period of time. However, the current conflict between economic forces destroying the natural world to achieve short-term profit gains and the inevitable countermovement to preserve natural equity and thus our economic well-being for the long term can lead to a multidecade period of superior performance for SRI funds.

In recent years the term *New Economy* has been used to describe the explosive microprocessor-driven rise in the importance of technology and innovation. This trend is not a short-term, cyclical phenomenon but one that characterizes a fundamental economic fact of the era we live in. There is no end in sight to the continued rapid and accelerating development of new technologies with their enormous potential for increased human productivity. And since SRI tends to push investments toward New Economy growth sectors such as high technology, SRI performance benefits as the technological revolution advances.

Parallel with these technological trends and in concert with them is another megatrend that is only in its early stages. Our world economy will be driven by the necessity of balancing economic development with restoring our civilization's harmony with nature — popularly referred to as "sustainability." This trend is explained in detail in *Natural Capitalism,* a powerfully argued book by Paul Hawken, Amory Lovins, and Hunter Lovins.[3] The trend toward sustainability will work to reinforce the outperformance of socially responsible investing for the foreseeable future. These two trends — adoption of SRI as a mainstream financial practice and the movement toward a sustainable economy — will pull in opposite directions in terms of financial performance for a period of time. As more and more people recognize that SRI outperforms they will begin to incorporate it in their financial practice. Wall Street will begin to imitate SRI screens to achieve performance, and the relative outperformance of SRI will decrease. In the end, SRI will cease to be a countertrend in the financial world, and will instead simply be the way things are done. It is unlikely that 100 years from now there will be socially responsible investing and non–socially responsible investing, and the performance comparison will have become a footnote in economic history.

The Forces Behind SRI Outperformance

The issue of SRI performance involves all the usual considerations of the discipline of investing and the mathematics of performance measurement. But it is an issue that is not approached by most people in the same manner as typical investment controversies, such as whether small-cap or large-cap stocks perform better over time or whether value- or growth-oriented investing will be successful over a particular time period. SRI touches on cultural and sociopolitical considerations and therefore stirs emotional reactions in addition to investment or measurement issues.

Part of the mystery of SRI's outperformance is precisely associated with the interrelationship between the investment community and its culture and sociopolitical outlook, and the rest of society. To put it simply, *SRI reveals a link between existing mass social trends and the financial performance of corporations.* The earliest example of this link is the abolitionist movement in the United States, especially its second wave from the 1820s to the 1860s. During this period mass social alliances developed in opposition to slavery and impacted the profitability of the slave trade. By the mid nineteenth century, shifts in production, transportation, and markets such as the opening of the Midwest corn and wheat belts reduced the importance of cotton to the US economy and challenged the sociopolitical support for slavery, leading in the end to the demise of plantation slavery as a business.

In the same manner, mass socioeconomic trends are under way and are in the process of altering the workings of the market. SRI reflects these currents, while mainstream Wall Street culture often fails to understand them or is in denial on such issues — or worse, opposes the direction of history like the Confederacy of yesteryear. The most obvious example is the tidal wave of environmental impacts now working to transform the economy. A recent historical example was the disastrous push to develop nuclear power in the 1970s. The SRI community refused to invest in nuclear power because of safety and nuclear waste disposal issues and correctly predicted its financial demise. By contrast, Wall Street championed nuclear energy. The result was one financial disaster after another for the firms betting on nuclear power.

A Conflict of Ideas

Truth in human society is determined through the conflict of ideas. In investment issues it is often essential to hear conflicting views as the best way to develop an opinion. It is the free flow of ideas, the interchange of advocacy and criticism, that allows the most accurate accounts of reality to surface. This book therefore does not claim to be the last word on the subject of SRI performance. I and the other authors welcome criticism, since efforts to argue against the positions and conclusions provided in this book can only help clarify reality. One of the points that we will outline here is how little exists in the form of studies, articles, or arguments to support the idea, widely believed and acted upon, that SRI underperforms. On the other hand, a wide range of studies show that SRI outperforms or at least does not underperform.

I suspect that some of those who have opposed SRI professionally, and this includes much of Wall Street, will find this book quite disagreeable and will look hard to find errors in our figures. I and the other authors in this book expect and welcome such comments. And undoubtedly no matter how hard we have tried to check all figures used in this book there will undoubtedly be some errors. We, of course, have had to rely on the published figures for performance by all kinds of sources from Morningstar to individual funds, and inevitably one or more will be wrong or incomplete.

Oddly enough, the issue of SRI performance is controversial even within the SRI community itself. As I'll discuss in more detail later on, many in the SRI community, though aware of SRI's outperformance, are hesitant to refer to it. They prefer to maintain only that SRI does not lead to any loss of performance. This leads logically to a powerful "why not?" argument to invest socially if there is a social benefit but no financial cost. This may be a politically wise position to take, since advocacy of SRI is not primarily based on short-term performance. In fact, SRI did not begin nor does its growth depend on financial outperformance. But obviously financial outperformance will lead to a rapid expansion of the SRI sector and recruit many new investors to SRI.

SRI tends instead by its nature to take the long-term view. One of the SRI community's critiques of mainstream investment concepts is that they are short term and involve inaccurate accounting and lack of accountability. A firm can appear to be profitable because it succeeds in externalizing much of its costs onto other sectors of society. The SRI community does not consider such an investment to be truly profitable and would see judging investments solely on the basis of their short-term profitability itself as suspect. Showing that SRI outperforms financially can be considered by some in the SRI community as missing the point: The goal of SRI is to create a sustainable economy that provides a good quality of life for all, not high short-term performance for a few.

For most investors who read this book, however, it will come as quite a surprise that they are sacrificing performance to invest in companies that pollute, violate the law, and discriminate. Trustees of pension funds, for example, have for the most part refused, in the name of "fiduciary responsibility," to even consider investing with SRI-focused managers. In doing so they have in fact unconsciously acted in a financially irresponsible manner, violating their fiduciary responsibility to seek the highest return at the lowest risk.

In fact, as I will argue later on, this issue is far more complex than it first appears. Part of the reality we face in the marketplace is that corporations are using their political power to force others to bear their costs, thus making their financial results appear far better than they actually are. Their use of externalities to reduce their costs goes all the way from outright grants of corporate welfare from the government to indirect subsidies as other consumers or taxpayers bear the costs of social or environmental damage. For example, just think how long tobacco companies would exist if they had to pay the costs of treating the health problems that tobacco use creates. The estimates, as you will read later on in this book, are that we subsidize the tobacco industry by $80 billion a year (not counting subsidies to tobacco farmers), while the tobacco companies register a profit of approximately $16 billion a year. By any realistic accounting, therefore, the tobacco industry loses $64 billion a year.[4]

The Evolution of Popular Mythology on SRI

Arguments against SRI investing have evolved slowly over the last few decades, reflecting the gradually developing impact of SRI as a financial trend. Milton Friedman, for example, expressed one of the most extreme points of view in the early 1960s. In his eyes the concept of socially responsible investing was un-American: "Few trends would so thoroughly undermine the very foundations of our free society as the acceptance by corporate officials of a social responsibility other than to make as much money for their stockholders as they possibly can. This is fundamentally a subversive doctrine."[5]

During the 1980s Wall Street's view of SRI moderated with the rise of a mass movement in favor of divestment from South Africa. A good example of what became the predominant point of view, and one still accepted in less sophisticated investment circles, is the definition by Bloomberg of SRI as "an investment that carries a lower rate of return, but that provides society with many benefits." By the late 1990s the growing evidence of SRI outperformance led more sophisticated opponents to see SRI in a new light. Michael Lipper put it this way: "It's underweighted in basic industries and energy, sectors with lower social standing ... and it emphasizes technology and services." These sectors were those that led the bull market of the late 1990s.[6] Lipper's argument is an effort to explain SRI's outperformance in terms of technical, not social issues, and thus dismiss SRI's outperformance as a temporary by-product of sector outperformance. In other words, SRI outperforms because it tends to favor investment in the New Economy instead of the Old Economy, in small-cap stocks instead of large-cap stocks, and so on. Since some of the best-performing sectors (growth and technology) in 1995–2000 were precisely those that SRI tends to favor, this theory would attribute SRI outperformance to something other than the actual social screens. I'll take up this issue in more detail later. Suffice it to say that it's true that SRI screens tend to overweight some sectors and underweight others. But as you will see, many studies have shown that removing this factor, either by adjusting sector weighting or by investing in only one sector, continue to show SRI outperformance, so the SRI advantage cannot be explained away in this manner.

So whether you're an investment professional, a pension fund trustee, or an individual interested in managing your own funds in a manner consistent with your personal values, this book will help you understand a phenomenon that is truly one of the great paradoxes of recent history in investing: the outperformance of socially responsible investing in the face of public and professional disbelief. But before we delve further into the *why* of SRI performance, let's review the empirical evidence that SRI does in fact perform better than conventional investment strategies.

Notes

1. Yankelovich Partners, survey conducted for The Calvert Group, April 1999.
2. Ibid.
3. Paul Hawken, Amory Lovins, and L. Hunter Lovins, *Natural Capitalism: Creating the Next Industrial Revolution* (New York: Back Bay Books/Little, Brown, 2000).
4. The estimate of about $16 billion a year for tobacco industry profits may be a little generous, but is based on Philip Morris's recent profits of about $8 billion a year; the company accounts for 50 percent of the tobacco industry. About two-thirds of the company's business is in tobacco. The figure of $80 billion for the cost of treating tobacco-related health problems is an extrapolation to the United States as a whole of the costs estimated by the California Health Department for the state of California.
5. Milton Friedman, *Capitalism and Freedom* (Chicago: University of Chicago Press, 1962), p. 153.
6. Joanne Legomsky, "Investing by Conscience Is Paying Off These Days," *New York Times,* January 24, 1999.

2

SRI Indexes, Risk, and
Volatility

Indexes are playing an increasing role in investing. Indexes are usually based on a group of stocks from a specific area, such as the largest 1000 companies, or from a specific industry, such as all energy or semiconductor companies. Indexes are useful because they allow us to compare the performance of managers to what the market or a market sector does, letting us determine if a manager is adding any value. The most famous index is of course the Dow Jones Industrial Average, but the one most commonly followed in the financial industry is the Standard & Poor's 500 Index (S&P 500), which includes 500 companies that account for about 71 percent of the total capitalization of the market. The performance of the S&P 500 therefore fairly accurately reflects the performance of the US equity markets as a whole.

The claim that SRI outperforms is backed by the results of SRI indexes and mutual funds and by specific studies of SRI performance. A wealth of anecdotal evidence tends to support the thesis. This chapter surveys the leading SRI indexes and their development and reviews some of the highlights of SRI performance as measured by indexes.

The beginning of the 1990s saw an important turning point in the history of SRI when Amy Domini, Peter Kinder, and Steve Lyndenberg, with quantitative assistance from Lloyd Kurtz, decided to launch the Domini 400 Social Index (DSI). Their idea was to remove 200 of the 500 stocks in the S&P 500 based on the application of social screens. They then added another 100 to help balance their new index by sector. They did not intend to try to outperform the S&P 500 but instead to establish a benchmark for SRI fund managers similar to the S&P 500. But of course everyone quickly realized that the new DSI's performance would be compared to that of the S&P 500. Some ten years later the Domini Index has clearly outperformed the S&P 500.

Through January 1, 2001, the annualized performance of the Domini 400 Social Index and the S&P 500 compared as follows:

Time Span	Domini 400 Social Index	S&P 500
Ten Years	19.01%	17.48%
Five Years	19.67%	18.37%
Three Years	12.80%	12.33%

Source: KLD, Inc.

As noted above the DSI outperformed the S&P 500 by 1.53 percentage points per year for a ten-year period. For the last five-year period it out performed by 1.3 percentage points. These figures include the year 2000. In 2001 the DSI and the S&P 500 ended the year with almost exactly the same performance: the DSI lost 12.07 percent while the S&P 500 lost 11.88 percent.[1] (See chapter 8, "The Growth of Socially Responsible Investing," by Steve Schueth for further details.) These figures might not appear impressive at first glance. The DSI, for example, outperformed the S&P 500 for the last five years by only 1.3 percentage points per year. But when you bear in mind that 82 percent of money managers failed to keep pace with the S&P 500 during that period, this performance becomes remarkable.[2] Any enhancement of the S&P 500 that can add 150 basis points to performance is rightly considered quite important.

The Domini 400 tended to outperform the S&P 500 by a greater margin in 1995–99, when New Economy technology and growth stocks outperformed value and Old Economy stocks. But during periods when New Economy stocks have performed more poorly and should have resulted in lower performance for an SRI index like the DSI, the S&P and the DSI turned in similar performances, with the exception of the year 2000. During 2000 the Domini Index did underperform the S&P 500, dropping 14.32 percent while the S&P 500 fell 9.01 percent. Inclusion of the year 2000 in our three-, five-, and ten-year comparisons in fact provides us with a more solid confirmation that SRI outperforms over time and over a range of market and economic conditions.[3]

Michael Lipper's sectoral critique of SRI (detailed in chapter 1), is thus partly correct in noting that SRI tends to change the focus of investment

Figure 2.1 Domini 400 Social Index
Comparative Performance Since Inception in May 1990

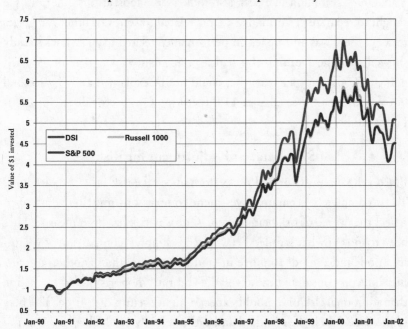

to different sectors, but SRI's outperformance does not appear to be the result of this factor. Sector performance will average out over a long period of time. During some periods growth investment strategies will outperform value investing, while other periods will show the opposite tendency, so the fact that SRI tends to push a portfolio toward growth stocks should not change its relative performance over the long haul.

Lorne Abramson and Chris Luck are two investment experts who have studied this issue in considerable detail. Abramson took on the issue of sorting out how the value stocks in the Domini 400 performed in comparison with value stocks generally. Abramson carefully rebalanced the value sector each year to achieve a clear value-to-value comparison. This study showed an outperformance against the accepted benchmarks (the Russell 1000 Value, S&P Barra Value, and the Wilshire Large Cap Value indexes) of 2 percentage points per year.[4]

Christopher Luck of 1st Quadrant, a Pasadena, California–based firm managing $26 billion in assets, also took a close look at this question. He sought to separate performance factors related to sector or other categories to see if there was an impact on performance related to SRI. Luck's study showed that the Domini 400 had a performance advantage of 77 basis points (.77 percent per year) that could not be explained away by sectoral or other theories. (See chapter 11, "Factoring Out Sector Bets," for Chris Luck's study.)

SRI, Beta, and Adjustment for Risk

But do these reports of SRI outperformance take risk fully into account? To be completely accurate, investment comparisons must be adjusted to reflect the degree of risk being taken. One way risk has been measured has been to look at what is called beta, which is simply a comparison of volatility. If one index tends to move up and down more than another, the former index is considered more volatile and thus more risky, and for taking that additional risk one should expect a higher return over time. The beta of the S&P 500 is the standard and is thus exactly 1. The beta for Domini 400 Social Index is 1.1, or somewhat higher than that of the S&P 500.

But are we comparing apples to apples when we say that the Domini 400 Index has a higher risk than the S&P 500? This is a crucial point in the debates about whether SRI's higher performance can rightly be called outperformance. SRI screens tend to move a portfolio like the S&P 500 toward the stocks of smaller companies with lower capitalizations. This factor tends to add to the volatility of the portfolio and thus results in a higher beta. The capitalization of the Domini 400 on a weighted average basis is 83 percent of that of the S&P 500, and its unweighted average capitalization is 66 percent of that of the S&P 500.

Company by company, what a social screen does is remove risk. Its overall impact is therefore to lower liability. Social screens will remove companies that tend to violate the law or market products that have questionable value or are most likely to lead to litigation, such as tobacco. Social screens knock out companies that engage in discrimination or are in conflict with their local communities or their workforce. Elimination of these companies reduces a specific kind of risk, what we can refer to as "company-specific risk." Wall Street does not measure such risk: it has instead used beta as its proxy for company-specific risk of all kinds.

However, volatility and risk are not exactly the same thing, especially over the long term. For short periods of time, beta is a useful indicator of the probability that something negative may happen, and in that sense beta describes risk. But over the longer term, SRI portfolios with higher betas may actually have lower risk — that is, a lower probability that they will run into economic problems resulting in unexpected financial decline.

Moreover, the beta of a stock is often different depending on the direction of the market. Upside beta measures volatility when the market is rising, and downside beta measures its volatility when the market is declining. Over a longer period of time, say, over several business cycles or a 15- or 20-year period, it is possible that SRI will show lower negative volatility — that is, SRI will show higher beta but lower downside beta. No studies have yet looked at this factor, but this theory is logical if SRI reduces company-specific risk while increasing volatility because it favors companies with lower capitalization. The Domini 400 may thus actually be outperforming on a risk-adjusted basis even more than it is given credit for because it really has lower risk than the S&P 500 — even though its beta alone does not reveal that relationship. If this is true, Wall Street analysts who downgrade SRI portfolios because they believe them to be higher risks because of volatility may be making an important misjudgment.

A Bond Portfolio Based on the Domini 400

A 1997 study by D'Antonio et al. compared investment in bonds issued by all the companies in the S&P 500 and those issued by the companies in the Domini 400 Social Index. Antonio and his colleagues discovered that bonds from the Domini 400 companies slightly outperformed bonds issued by the S&P 500 over the period covered by the study, May 1990 to March 1996. The average monthly return for the period was .89 percent for the Domini Index bonds and .84 percent for the S&P 500 bonds. Interestingly, the standard deviation was (just barely, 1.44 percent to 1.45 percent) lower for the Domini Index bonds, indicating less risk for SRI.[5]

However, the ratings on the bonds of the S&P 500 companies were higher. This makes sense, since SRI will screen out many of the largest firms with the highest bond ratings. This study shows us something rather unusual, a lower standard deviation from a lower-rated universe. It should show the reverse: a lower-rated universe should have a higher standard deviation. Could this mean that SRI is eliminating elements of risk not registered by the ratings? Clearly the higher beta stocks and lower rated bonds should have shown a higher comparative standard deviation.

The Domini Index has higher volatility (beta) than the S&P 500. It also tends to include smaller, more volatile companies, whose bonds therefore on average have a lower rating than the bonds issued by S&P 500 companies. (Most bonds are rated by ratings agencies like Moody's or Standard & Poor's. A high rating would be AAA or AA, while a very low rating would be CCC.) A portfolio whose bonds have lower ratings will normally be more volatile than one whose bonds have higher ratings. Standard deviation is simply another measure of volatility or risk. But, amazingly, the Domini 400 bonds have the same standard deviation as the S&P 500 (actually, a tiny bit lower). This can only mean that risk measurement is inaccurate for some reason: Even though the Domini 400 has a higher beta, it may really have lower risk!

D'Antonio et al. conclude, "On a risk-return level, these results correspond to an information ratio of 1.08. The information ratio provides a measure of the return-risk trade-off for the SRI portfolio."[6] Grinold (1990) suggests that an information ratio of over 0.5 observed over five years provides support for the position that an active (bond) management strategy is indeed providing a risk-adjusted excess return.[7]

The Dow Jones Sustainability Global Index

At the beginning of 1999 Dow Jones created a new index called the Dow Jones Sustainability Global Index (DJSGI). The Dow Jones Industrial Index is the best-known stock index in the world. Created in the nineteenth century, this index has lasted over a century and even though it is not used as a benchmark by institutional investors because of its narrowness (it includes only 30 stocks), it continues to be followed as a popular indicator of the stock market's performance overall.

The DJSGI was created by selecting out of a large universe what seemed to be the most "sustainable" companies. The index is made up of approximately 230 companies from 61 industries in 27 countries, with the goal of picking the top 10 percent of the most sustainable companies in the world. Dow Jones has back-tested this index against its Dow Jones Global Index. Figure 2.2 shows the results.

The increasing interest in socially screened products is apparent in the rapid adoption of the new Dow Jones index in Europe. According to David Moran, president of Dow Jones Indexes, "Since the launch of the DJSGI World index it has gained 59.2%, outperforming the MSCI World (58.4%) and slightly underperforming the DJGI World (60.0%). After just one year, 17 licensees in eight countries — ie, Belgium, France, Germany, Luxembourg, Netherlands, Sweden, Switzerland, and the United Kingdom – have issued a variety of DJSGI-based financial products, including active and passive funds, equity baskets and index certifications."[8]

Figure 2.2 Dow Jones Sustainability World Indexes

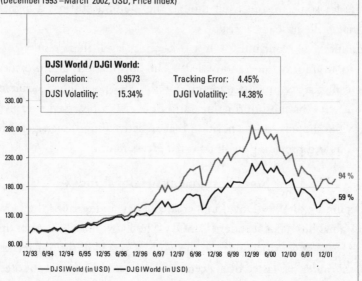

(December 1993 –March 2002, USD, Price Index)

DJSI World / DJGI World:

Correlation:	0.9573	Tracking Error:	4.45%
DJSI Volatility:	15.34%	DJGI Volatility:	14.38%

John Prestbo, chief editor of Dow Jones Indexes, offered this comparison: "The superior performance of companies integrating corporate sustainability in their business strategies is evidenced by some key financial parameters. In the first half of 2000, the average ROE [return on equity] of companies in the DJSGI World Index averaged 14.89 percent against 8.43 percent for those in the DJGI World Index. Likewise, for average ROI [return on investment], (DJSGI: 11.09 percent vs. DJGI 7.37%) and the average ROA [return on assets], (DJSGI: 5.8 percent vs. DJGI: 3.63%). Superior performance in 2000 is in line with the trend over the last five years, when the average DJSGI World Index's ROE was 14.73 percent against 9.87 percent for the DJGI World Index. During the same period the average ROI (DJSGI: 8.86 percent vs. DJGI: 6.97%) and the average ROA (DJSGI: 5.49 percent vs. DJGI: 4.77%) were also superior for sustainability-driven companies."[9]

In plain English, this means that (in terms of financial return) the more sustainable companies are beating the less sustainable companies, at least according to Dow Jones.

Prestbo concluded that the Dow Jones service helps "investors and industry, with a neutral, rigorous and transparent measurement of sustainability performance ... [I]t not only tells where they stand in terms of economic, environmental and social performance, but also how far they have come and how much further they have to go." Dow Jones has packaged its effort in 100 different indexes and currently produces "sustainability" indexes for North America, Europe, Asia Pacific and the United States and variations that include screens for alcohol, gambling and tobacco, separately or all three combined.[10]

The Walden International Index

Walden Asset Management, based in Boston, Massachusetts, launched the first socially screened international index. Geeta Aiyer, Walden's president and senior portfolio manager, sees no reason why Walden's index should fail to match or surpass its nonsocial equivalent in the same way that the Domini Index has outperformed in the United States. Although the Walden International index has outperformed since its inception, the index has existed only a little more than two years, so it is too early to judge its performance. Walden's experience in setting up its international index and its comparative performance is covered in chapter 13, "Crossing the Black Water," by Geeta Aiyer and Steven Heim.

New Indexes: The Vanguard and the FTSE 100

Two major organizations, Vanguard and FTSE 100 (Financial Times & Stock Exchange 100), have announced two other new socially screened indexes. Vanguard is a firm that specializes in creating index funds. It has come to an arrangement with the Calvert Group, which runs the largest family of SRI mutual funds, to screen the largest 1000 companies and create an index. The new Vanguard/Calvert index was launched mid-year 2000 and has so far underperformed its non-socially-screened equivalent benchmark, the Forbes 1000.

The FTSE 100 is the British equivalent of the S&P 500 index in the United States. The FTSE is jointly owned by the Financial Times and the

Stock Exchange in London. The FTSE has announced it will start new indexes for Britain, Continental Europe, and the United States, called the FTSE4Good. In a rather unusual move, it has agreed to donate part of its fees for the newly screened indexes to the United Nations Children's Fund (Unicef).   .

The Russell indexes have also joined in the new trend to establish socially screened indexes. In April 2001, it was announced that the Russell 1000 and Russell 2000 and therefore the Russell 3000 will all have socially screened equivalents. The screening is being provided by Kinder, Lydenberg, and Domini (KLD), a research firm based in Cambridge, Massachusetts.

Creation of new socially screened indexes by Dow Jones, Vanguard, Russell and the FTSE indicates the amazing growth of interest in SRI. But it also reveals the awareness of these firms that screened portfolios have turned in perfectly acceptable performance figures. There is growing demand from clients for socially screened investment products, and these firms, anxious to offer products to compete in all sectors of the market, are seeking to participate in the SRI sector — and avoid losing market share to the original SRI products.

The Citizens Index

A few years from now it will be interesting to examine the relative performance of these new indexes. At this writing we have only have a few to look at. One of the best-performing SRI indexes has been an index created by the Citizens family of mutual funds. This index finished its first five years by outperforming the S&P 500 by 700 basis points per year (7 percent per year). However, there is some question whether this index shouldn't be compared to a mix between a growth index and the S&P 500 since it has heavily emphasized technology although it is otherwise not too different from the S&P 500. Like all SRI portfolios it was underweighted in some industries such as oil. The overweighting in technology was reflected in its underperformance in the year 2000, though it has still outperformed the S&P 500 since its inception. Citizens has since decided to turn this index into a managed "growth" fund, so it is no longer considered an index. All the Citizens mutual funds that have existed for three or more years have outperformed their benchmarks.

The comparison in performance for SRI and non-SRI indexes is of great value. The Domini 400 Index stands out as the longest existing index and the Dow Jones Sustainability Group Index stands out since it has been back-tested for a longer period. These two offer the most important insights. The many new SRI indexes have not existed long enough to offer as much useful performance information. However, five or ten years from now a comparison of all these indexes will be of great value. Once the market has gone through a full cycle of bull and bear periods, we'll be able to use them to make a better judgment as to whether SRI adds performance — but these first two indexes seem to say yes.

Notes

1. Social Investment Forum, press release, January 17, 2002.
2. *Louis Ruckeyser's Mutual Funds,* newsletter, May 2001, p. 13.
3. Kinder, Lyndenberg, Domini & Co. (hereafter KLD). Performance comparisons are best if they cover periods when value and growth stocks outperformed. The DSI versus S&P 500 comparison now covers a long enough period that many factors are now included, not only value versus growth but also periods of large-cap versus small-cap outperformance and visa versa.
4. Lorne Abramson and Dan Chung, "Socially Responsible Investing: Viable for Value Investors?" *Journal of Investing* 9:3 (Fall 2000): pp. 73–80.
5. L. D'Antonio, T. Johnson, and B. Hutton, "Expanding Socially Screened Portofolios: An Attribution Analysis of Bond Portfolios," *Journal of Investing* 6:4 (1997): pp. 79–86.
6. Ibid.
7. Richard Grinold, "The Fundamental Law of Active Management," *Journal of Portfolio Management* 15:3 (Spring 1989): pp. 30–37.
8. Dow Jones SGI, Princeton, N.J., press release, September 6, 2000.
9. Ibid.
10. Ibid.

3

SRI Mutual Funds

According to the agencies that monitor mutual funds, SRI funds as a whole are outperforming risk-adjusted funds pretty much across the board. These figures are mathematically quite significant (see chapter 10, "Seeing Stars: SRI Mutual Fund Performance," by Jon Hale, and chapter 8, "The Growth of Socially Responsible Investing," by Steven Schueth). If, for instance, 25 percent of all funds fall into a particular ratings category and 30 percent of SRI funds place in that category, that would be considered significant. But what if a category fits 32.5 percent of all funds and SRI comes in above 50 percent? It would be quite difficult for anyone to claim that this was an accident. Yet these are exactly the kinds of figures we are starting to see.

The performance of SRI mutual funds has evolved over the short period that they have existed. As you will see, SRI fund performance seems to be improving, especially since 1995. During the last two years, 2000 and 2001, SRI funds have continued to do quite well even though we might easily have expected to see a lower performance for various reasons. Before we analyze the actual performance figures it may be of value to quickly review the history of SRI itself to place the development of SRI mutual funds and their performance in the proper context.

The history of socially responsible investing may give us some clues about why SRI outperforms and how it may develop in the future. The origins of socially responsible investing in what is now the United States can be traced to the Quakers and other abolitionists who before the Civil War refused to invest in human slavery or any business associated with slavery. Later, especially in the early twentieth century, various religious organizations applied an early form of social screening by refusing to invest in what they called "sin stocks." Most of their investments screened out companies involved in gambling or the production and distribution of alcohol and tobacco.

Socially responsible investing as we know it today has been shaped by the myriad of social forces that erupted in the 1960s. They include movements focusing on the issues of the environment, health, child labor, sweatshops, the military/industrial weapons complex, the rights of minorities and women, gay and lesbian rights, nuclear weapons and power, and racial discrimination, in addition to earlier concerns about morally reprehensible industries.

In the 1970s the nuclear power controversy swept the country, and the campaign against nuclear power became a success story for SRI as SRI investors avoided an industry sector doomed to failure. But it was the rise in the 1980s of support for the struggle against the apartheid regime of South Africa that began to transform the modern SRI movement, evidenced by the successful campaign for divestment of foreign capital from South Africa.

In the 1990s SRI began to penetrate the mainstream financial current and to mature in terms of financial sophistication. Most of what we call SRI today has come into existence since 1995, and SRI concepts are still novel and not well understood by many investors. Such misunderstandings are definitely evident in the institutional world of pension funds and endowments. Part of the driving force behind SRI's recent rapid growth is, of course, its financial outperformance.

Amazing as it may sound, in the last ten years there have been no research studies reporting that SRI limits investors to lower performance. Nevertheless, a number of newspaper or magazine articles have claimed this is the case. As noted earlier, Bloomberg defines a socially responsible investment as "an investment that carries a lower rate of return." However, during the 1980s campaign for divestment from South Africa some "studies" claimed that SRI underperformed. When the issue of South Africa was sweeping the nation, there was a natural tendency to focus on the difference between the untouched S&P 500 and the S&P 500 screened to exclude companies doing business in South Africa. At the beginning of the 1980s it appeared that a screened S&P 500 outperformed, but by the end of the decade this was no longer true.

What marked the 1985 to 1990 period was the decline of the US dollar, which favored companies with more international exposure. A South Africa–screened portfolio tended to remove large companies with significant international exposure and leave in businesses that operated strictly in the United States. This anomaly lasted only a few years. By the beginning of the 1990s, a South Africa–free S&P 500 no longer underperformed. This was, in part, because the dollar began to rise, as it did again dramatically in the last years of the 1990s. Nevertheless, the negative difference for a limited period resulted in articles about the supposed "cost" of SRI. The theme of these articles was that it cost 1 percent or more in performance per year to be socially responsible. As the fall of the dollar stopped and the trend shifted again, these journals ran fewer and fewer commentaries on SRI and performance. Today the belief that SRI underperforms persists, but without any basis in fact.

In SRI's earlier years, many of the original SRI money managers were less experienced than conventional money management firms. This factor also influenced the performance of SRI funds, but its importance has diminished with the increasing professionalism of SRI fund management. This shift can be seen in the performance of the Calvert Group of funds. Their performance has improved dramatically over the last five years as they changed their financial managers while strengthening their social research and screens, changes in good part due to the efforts of CEO Barbara Krumsiek. Portfolio managers like Daniel Boone with a multi-cap discipline, Eddie Brown of Wall Street Week fame with his GARP ("growth at a reasonable price") discipline, and James Awad in small-cap value investing have added to the professionalism of Calvert's management.

As late as 1997 John B Guerard Jr. noted in the Journal of Investing that Morningstar had reported underperformance for SRI mutual funds when Morningstar's comparison included only six SRI mutual funds with a five-year track record and only two with a ten-year track record.[1] The small number of SRI mutual funds and the lack of professionalism among some of the early funds led many people to assume that their temporary underperformance was rooted in the social screens themselves in spite of the evidence from comparisons in studies between socially screened and nonscreened stock universes.

Performance: SRI Mutual Funds

As the 1990s ended the number of SRI funds expanded rapidly and their ratings shifted dramatically upward. An argument can of course be made that these ratings are still too recent to be of much value. However, the degree of outperformance in these ratings has become sharp and hard to dismiss, and this outperformance is now based on a much larger number of funds than those marked by early underperformance.

Co-op America's newsletter *Real Money* gives a summary of the performance of many of the SRI funds. From this list it's clear that many of the funds are relatively new. If we consider only those funds with at least a five-year track record, we find many funds with fine performance. The Green Century Balanced Fund has grown at 23.08 percent per year, while the Aquinas Equity Growth Fund came in at 23.51 percent per year. Other funds surpassed even those figures. Some fund managers whose experience in SRI goes back many years, like Jerry Dodson of the Parnassus Fund, can claim long-term stellar performance. With its 15.33 percent per year return over the last ten years (through December 31, 2001), the Parnassus Fund has outperformed the S&P 500 by 2.43 percentage points per year.

Philip Johansson analyzed 25 SRI funds, based on only their last three years of performance. As he explains, there are so many new funds in SRI that it is hard to go much further back without excluding some excellent funds just finishing their first three years. But even some of the oldest funds, such as Dreyfus Premier Third Century Fund, called the "grand-daddy" of large-capitalization SRI funds by Johansson because it was launched in 1972, returned 27.21 percent for the last three years, beating the S&P 500's three-year return of 23.7 percent. [2]

A small ($6 million) fund called Bridgeway Social Responsibility reported a 34 percent per year return over a three-year period. IPS Millennium is a fund that almost doubled the S&P 500's performance with a 44.67 percent return over the last three years. The IPS Millennium Fund does not call itself SRI but does cover the entire usual basis for SRI screens. The fund has $400 million in assets and is managed by Robert Loest, who uses "complex adaptive systems" theory to select stocks.

The Green Century Balanced Fund, managed by Jack Robinson, who specializes in environmental issues, has had an exceptional record of performance, coming in with 76.39 percent for 1999. That was the highest performance for any balanced fund tracked by Lipper. However, the fund has a higher risk profile than usual, and in 1999 had a large position in one company whose sharp rise skewed its performance. But the Green Century Balanced Fund was not the only balanced SRI fund beating the balanced fund benchmark. The Pax World Fund and the Smith Barney Concert Social Awareness Fund also outperformed the balanced fund index. (The Smith Barney fund was transformed into an SRI fund in February 1997, so its performance over the full three years was not quite purely SRI.) The Pax World Fund has performed in the top quartile of its discipline (balanced fund) for years. This fund also goes back more then two decades. For the last twenty years (as of March 31, 2001) it has averaged a return of 12.53 percent. It has the highest — five stars — rating from Morningstar.

Studies of Comparative Mutual Fund Performance

The increase in the number of SRI mutual funds has stimulated curiosity about how well these funds have performed. John Hale, an employee at Morningstar, began keeping careful track of the performance of SRI funds. Morningstar rates mutual fund performance on a curve. The best 10 percent receive five stars and the worst 10 percent receive one star. Those in between receive, in descending order, four, three, and two stars. Hale's research showed that 20 percent of SRI mutual funds with at least $5 million in assets received five stars — double the ratio for nonscreened funds. In the bottom category the opposite was the case: Hale showed that SRI funds were four times less likely to have the lowest ranking of one star. An investor would run a far smaller risk of being in an underperforming fund if the fund were socially screened.[3] (A complete summary of Hale's research appears in chapter 10, "Seeing Stars: SRI Mutual Fund Performance.")

The Social Investment Forum (SIF) reports once a year on the relative performance of SRI mutual funds and the growth of the SRI in assets and products. SIF has repeatedly noted what Hale discovered at Morningstar. SRI funds are receiving on average higher ratings than nonscreened funds from Morningstar and Lipper Analytical services. (Details of the SIF reports are provided in chapter 8, "Socially Responsible Investing in the US," by Steve Schueth of First Affirmative Inc.)

The Big Test: The Year 2000 and the High-Tech Crash

The year 2000 was by far the most difficult for socially responsible investing since its inception, marked as the year was by a crash of 39 percent in the technology-heavy NASDAQ. If the drop is measured from the NASDAQ top of March 10, 2000, to its bottom on April 4, 2001, the drop was 67 percent — an all-time record for the NASDAQ since its inception and breaking the previous record drop set in 1973–74. In 2001 this drop continued, bringing the NASDAQ Composite after the September 11, 2001, tragedy to a low some 73 percent below its high of March 2000. Only the crash of 1929 saw a larger drop in a major index.

As a result, growth stocks dramatically underperformed value stocks in the year 2000. Certain sectors that are typically screened out of SRI portfolios rose sharply in the year 2000, especially tobacco and oil stocks. Therefore, SRI mutual fund ratings as of January 1, 2001 — which thus include the difficult year 2000 — give us a good test of SRI performance.

After the books were closed on the year 2000, investment professionals were quite surprised to see the Social Investment Forum report that the Lipper and Morningstar ratings of SRI mutual funds actually improved in 2000! Fourteen of the 16 SRI mutual funds with over $100 million in assets earned top marks from Morningstar and Lipper Analytical Services. That means that 88 percent of these funds received four or five stars from Morningstar and/or A or B rankings from Lipper. The 88 percent figure reflects an increase from 69 percent prior to 2000 — so in the hardest year for SRI from a sector point of view the largest SRI funds actually increased their ratings. By comparison, only 32.5 percent of all funds received four or five stars. These higher ratings also extended to smaller SRI mutual funds. Among all SRI funds existing for at least three years, the percentage of those with four- or five-star Morningstar ratings or A or B Lipper ratings increased from 57 percent to 61 percent — substantially higher than the ratings of nonscreened funds. (Note that we are combining all mutual funds that received either a Morningstar five- or four-star and/or A or B ratings from Lipper. Thus the comparison to 32.5 percent for all funds is somewhat skewed in favor of SRI. Nevertheless these figures do show strong ratings for SRI mutual funds.)

Although these performance comparisons favor SRI, they are not true apples-to-apples comparisons. On one side you have funds that call themselves socially responsible (and in most cases everyone would accept they are SRI), and on the other you have funds that do not call themselves SRI. However, many of the funds that do not claim to be SRI may in fact be invested only in companies that pass all the major social screens. These funds can therefore be considered SRI funds, even if they do not market themselves as such.

I've already mentioned the high-performing IPS Millennium Fund among a number of small-cap and technology funds. Despite the record drop in the NASDAQ during 2000–2001 many of these are still among the highest performing funds over the long term. Thus the category of non-SRI funds includes some of the highest performing funds that in fact belong on the other side of the ledger. How would the comparison between SRI and non-SRI funds look if all truly SRI funds were considered on the SRI side of the comparison, where they belong? That would give us an even more accurate measure of SRI's performance.

Case-by-Case Evidence

The Eco-Logical Trust

In 1991 I convinced Merrill Lynch to create the first socially screened fund ever launched by a major Wall Street firm. It was called the Eco-Logical Trust. I made my proposal after Merrill Lynch had launched two Environmental Technology Trusts, which we at Progressive Asset Management criticized because they were marketed as "green" even though these trusts included polluters like Waste Management Inc. and Browning Ferris Industries.[4] All of these funds were unit trusts launched by Merrill Lynch and sold by the five largest Wall Street firms. Hundreds of millions of dollars went into the funds with polluters, but a much smaller amount was invested in the Eco-Logical Trust. These unit trusts lasted five years, from 1990/91 to 1995/96. The two trusts that contained polluters both lost money, but the Eco-Logical Trust, which was screened by a team led by Progressive Asset Management, was the second-best-performing trust at Merrill Lynch, making its investors a larger-than-expected return. (It was unusual to see any major newspaper or magazine provide coverage of this development. The *New York Times* at one point prepared a front-page story on the Eco-Logical Trust for its business section, but the story was killed and never appeared.)[5]

During the years the Eco-Logical Fund existed I was periodically asked by Merrill Lynch executives why I thought the fund was outperforming their other two funds in a similar sector. One answer I gave repeatedly to this question is that removing companies like Waste Management Inc. in the end will add to performance — even though Waste Management Inc. and Browning Ferris Industries were among the darlings of Wall Street analysts in the early 1990s. But despite the analysts' affection for them, we rejected these firms because they kept getting felony convictions for all kinds of criminal activity. These included bribing city council members; deliberately polluting in order to lower costs in Chicago; taking cancer-producing toxic waste, mixing it with oil, and selling it back to burn in Cincinnati; and price fixing. Waste Management Inc. did all it could to try to silence its critics by donating more money than any other firm to environmental groups, and it succeeded in getting more then one environmental group to sing its praise.

In the end, though, Waste Management Inc. turned out to be a poor investment. In keeping with the company's history of criminal behavior, the SEC recently filed a civil fraud case against a big five accounting firm, Arthur Andersen, for colluding with Waste Management Inc.'s management in cooking the company's earnings figures to the tune of $1.43 billion! At least some criminals eventually get caught![6]

Business Week and the Wall Street Journal

We occasionally still see efforts in the media to claim SRI underperforms. Often these articles try to mix up a comparison between mutual funds of different asset classes to try to show that SRI underperforms. For instance, they compare the performance of funds that are in stocks and funds that focus on bonds and then compare them to a non-SRI equity or an equity-only index. Patrick McVeigh, senior vice president of Trillium Asset Management Corp., wrote a letter to the Wall Street Journal in April 1997 protesting just such an article:

> Even the most open-minded analysis ... should eliminate money market, bond and international funds.... If Mr. Glassman wanted to make a fair comparison, he would have compared the returns of only the socially screened equity and balanced funds to the performance of the S&P 500. If he had done this, he would have found that five of the 23 funds (or 22%) had outperformed the S&P 500 index. He might

have also pointed out the difficulty any fund had in beating the S&P 500 last year. According to Morningstar, only 517 of 2,644 stock, balanced and asset allocation funds (or 20%) beat the S&P 500 last year. Another measure would have been to point out that nine of the 18 socially conscious equity funds (50%) beat the Lipper Growth Fund Average.[7]

Another example of such "hit" comparisons appeared in *Business Week* in June 2000 in an article by Christopher Palmeri, who covers the California Public Employees' Retirement System (CalPERS). The focus of the article was a political attack on California State Treasurer Phil Angelides, claiming that his support for socially responsible investing would lead to losses for the retirement system. Palmeri also attacked Angelides for advocating that California divest its tobacco stocks and for supporting affordable housing efforts such as the housing program funded by the AFL-CIO. Palmeri's article reported as fact that socially responsible investing underperforms. He provided no figures to back up this view, but claimed that his evidence came from Morningstar. He also reported that an AFL-CIO SRI fund started after 1990 had failed to meet its performance benchmark.[8]

Jon Hale of Morningstar was surprised to see Palmeri's critique of SRI in *Business Week* and rechecked the Morningstar database. Hale used the same equity-diversified funds that Palmeri had mentioned and compared their performance for three and five years up to May 31, 2000, the date Palmeri must have used for his June article. But Hale's research again resulted in conclusions that were the reverse of Palmeri's. Mutual funds calling themselves SRI had returned 19.91 percent annually over five years compared to 19.34 percent for non-SRI funds. The three-year return for the SRI funds was 21.65 percent versus 20.13 percent for the non-SRI funds. "The *Business Week* article is misleading if not absolutely incorrect in its claim that SRI funds underperform. The article claims that 'according to Morningstar, the average socially responsible mutual fund under performed the average US stock fund in the past year, five years and in the year to date.' The pull-out quote highlighted on the page says something slightly different: 'According to Morningstar, the average socially responsible mutual fund underperforms the average diversified fund.'"[9]

Hale continued, "From this, I assume the writer compared all SRI funds with all diversified US stock funds. This is a frequent journalistic error when reporters write about SRI. It is most definitely an inappropriate comparison. 'All SRI mutual funds' would include SRI bond funds and international funds. Such funds, screened or unscreened, have underperformed US stock funds over the periods mentioned in the article." Instead, Hale argued, an accurate study would have to compare the performance of socially screened, diversified US stock funds with nonscreened diversified US stock funds. A few weeks after his article was published Palmeri apologized in his *Business Week* column for having gotten his figures wrong and admitted that SRI funds had in fact outperformed.

One of Palmeri's errors was his criticism of an AFL-CIO fund started after 1990 that had produced an "unspectacular 7% per year." However, no AFL-CIO fund has been launched since 1990. I called Palmeri and asked him where he got his information, and was told that he had gotten it from someone at CalPERS. He admitted that he had never checked the accuracy of this informant with the AFL-CIO itself. There are actually two AFL-CIO funds, one started in 1984 (reorganizing a previous effort started in 1965) and the other in 1988. I was quite interested in the facts of the matter because the pension fund on which I serve as a trustee is also invested with an AFL-CIO fund. In our review in June 2001 this fund was our best performing manager in its category of debt. Could the review have been wrong? After reading Palmeri's article, I checked with Aaron Prince, who represents the AFL-CIO fund in California.

Prince was quite surprised by Palmeri's charges: "In fact, for the past ten years, 7 percent would have beaten the 5.7 percent recorded by NCREIF, an equity real estate index comprising $65+ billion in assets. BIT's [the AFL-CIO fund] gross return was 8 percent. The Lehman Aggregate Bond Index, comprised of the $5+ trillion domestic, investment grade bond market, returned 7.7 percent. HIT's [the other AFL-CIO fund] gross return was 8.3 percent." Clarifying the goals of the two AFL-CIO funds, BIT and HIT, Prince added, "HIT is managed to provide a premium risk-adjusted return to the domestic, investment grade bond market. Our goal is to provide a relative outperformance to the benchmark. At year-end 1999 [the latest figures then available] HIT net returns exceeded our benchmark — the Lehman Aggregate Bond Index — for the last one-, three, five-, and ten-year periods by 25, 31, 69, and 11 basis points, respectively. We have provided extraordinary risk-adjusted returns in excess of our benchmark. Furthermore, we have done so with greater credit quality then the benchmark."[10] Not only have the AFL-CIO funds provided an above-average return, but they have helped also create affordable housing as well as commercial space and hotel rooms in California — a fine example of what SRI advocates refer to as the "double bottom line."

All in all, the evidence is powerful that something is happening in terms of performance and SRI in mutual fund ratings. It is true, though, that the time span covered by the studies I've cited has been relatively brief and that the comparisons lack some of the rigorous controls we would like to see. Such a study could be done. We could, for example, use an existing screen set or combine two or more — for example, we could take the screen set from Calvert's 1000 largest companies and KLD's study of the Russell 1000 and cross them for all companies eliminated by both screens. After creating this consolidated list, we would make a list of the 500 largest equity mutual funds and apply the list on, say, two days a year, such as April 15 and October 15. We would then rate the funds and check the performance comparisons. Such a study would tend to eliminate all secondary factors such as the ability of the manager and the size of the mutual fund to give us a realistic picture of SRI performance. Based on studies like this, ten years from now it will be easier to establish more accurate ratings. For the moment, though, it is clear that SRI mutual funds are outperforming!

Notes

1. John B. Guerard, "Is There a Cost to Being Socially Responsible in Investing?" *Journal of Investing* (Summer 1997).

2. Philip Johansson, "25 Sizzling SRI Funds that Beat a Tough Market," *Business Ethics* 14:4 (July/August 2000).

3. John Hale, speech delivered at a conference on socially responsible investing sponsored by Contra Costa County Employees' Retirement Association, December 6, 1999.

4. A study published by the *San Francisco Bay Guardian* using research by Progressive Asset Management exposed the problem of many so-called environmental funds invested in major polluters. (The article was written by Lew Tremaine, who is today the mayor of Fairfax in Marin County, California.) *Bay Guardian*, March 14, 1990.

5. My source for this story is Stanley Craig, vice president of national sales for the UIT department of Merrill Lynch.

6. The Arthur Andersen /Enron scandal came to public attention just as this book was going to press and confirms that Andersen's collusion with Waste Management, Inc. was not a fluke.

7. *Wall Street Journal,* April 25, 1997.

8 Christopher Palmeri, "CalPERS May Not Do as Well by Doing Good," *Business Week,* June 19, 2000, p. 218.

9. Jon Hale, letter, June 13, 2000.

10. Aaron Prince, letter to the author, August 2000.

4

SRI Performance and Market History: Thirty Years of Studies

The outperformance of SRI has been confirmed by a variety of studies made under very differing circumstances. The most important of these was a 1995 landmark book, *Corporate Responsibility and Financial Performance: The Paradox of Social Cost,* by Moses L. Pava and Joshua Krausz, two professors at New York's Yeshiva University. Pava and Krausz were the first academics to confirm what many people in the SRI community had suspected might be true about SRI and performance.[1] Prior to their work, possibly the first person to postulate that SRI outperforms was Milton Moskowitz back in 1972.[2]

Pava and Krausz looked at 21 studies to arrive at their conclusion that SRI screening enhances investment performance rather than reduces it, as had previously been assumed by most industry experts — thus their subtitle, *The Paradox of Social Cost.* Table 3.1 lists these 21 studies together with short summaries of their content by Pava and Krausz. Of these studies, 12 indicated that SRI outperforms, 8 indicated no loss or gain in performance, and 1 reported lower performance. It is interesting that throughout their work Pava and Krausz make few references to the then existing SRI mutual funds or to the Domini 400 Social Index, perhaps because they were considered to be too new or too small to be of value at the time of their study.

Table 4.1 Summary of 21 Empirical Studies

Authors/Date	Social Responsi-bility Criteria	Financial Perfor-mance Criteria	Results
Bragdon and Marlin, 1972	Council on Economic Priorities air and water pollution measures	Various measures of financial accounting returns	Lower levels of pollution were correlated with better financial performance.
Vance, 1975	Milton Moskowitz's social responsibility ratings	Percentage change in stock price	All but 1 of the 14 firms in the sample had performance records considerably worse than the NYSE composite index.
Bowman and Haire, 1975	Proportion of annual report devoted to social responsibility issues	Return on equity	Mean return on equity for firms with "some discussion" was 14.3 percent while the mean return for firms with "no discussion" was 9.1%.
Fogler and Nut, 1975	Three pollution indexes	Financial accounting earnings and stock price data	No significant relationship was found between pollution ratings and performance.
Belkaoui, 1976	Disclosure of pollution control information in 1970 annual reports	Market-based returns adjusted for risk	The 50 experimental firms, in which pollution control information was disclosed, outperformed the control sample in terms of returns on stocks.
Sturivant and Ginter, 1977	Milton Moskowitz's social responsibility ratings	Growth in ten-year earnings per share	Socially responsible firms significantly outperformed their non-socially-responsible counterparts in terms of EPS growth.
Alexander and Buchholz, 1978	Milton Moskowitz's social responsibility ratings	Market-based returns adjusted for risk	No significant relationship was found between social responsibility and market-based returns.

Authors/Date	Social Responsibility Criteria	Financial Performance Criteria	Results
Chugh, Haneman, and Mahapatra, 1978	Firms belonging to high-pollution industries	Market-based estimates of beta	Between 1970 and 1972, betas of "polluter" firms shifted up
Anderson and Frankel, 1980	Annual report disclosures related to social responsibility issues	Market-based returns adjusted for risk	In a six-month period following annual report disclosure there was no difference between disclosing and non-disclosing firms. Examination of March returns, however, suggests that there may be a positive impact.
Freedman and Jaffi, 1982	Council on Economic Priorities air and water pollution measures	Various measures of financial accounting returns	In general, there was no association between pollution measures and financial performance. However, evidence is reported suggesting that for very large firms with poor economic performance, pollution disclosures are more detailed.
Shane and Spicer, 1983	Council on Economic Priorities air and water pollution measures	Market-based returns adjusted for risk surrounding publication of CEP studies	The results indicated that the CEP firms experienced, on average, relatively large negative abnormal returns. Moreover, the returns for those companies revealed to have low pollution-control performance rankings were found, on average, to have significantly more negative returns than companies with high ratings.
Conchran and Wood, 1984	Milton Moskowitz's social responsibility ratings	Various measures of financial accounting–based returns and excess market valuations	Firms with older assets have lower social responsibility ratings. There is also a marginally significant positive association between social responsibility and financial performance.

Authors/Date	Social Responsibility Criteria	Financial Responsibility Criteria	Results
Chen and Metcalf, 1984	Two pollution indexes	Various measures of financial accounting based on returns, estimated betas, and price–earnings ratios	Controlling for firm size, there is no statistical association between pollution indexes and financial indicators.
Aupperle, Carroll and Harfield, 1985	CEO's concern for society as reflected in mail questionnaire	Return on assets adjusted for risk	No significant relationships were found between a strong orientation toward social responsibility and financial performance.
Freeman and Jaggi, 1986	A pollution index	Market-based returns adjusted for risk surrounding annual report data	The test results did not indicate any difference between investor reaction to extensive disclosures and investor reaction to minimal disclosures.
Baldwin, Tower, Litvak, Karpen, Jackson, and McTifue, 1986	Investment in South Africa	Market-based estimates of beta	Excluding firms that do business with South Africa from an investment portfolio produced a "minute" increase in risk.
Rockness, Schlachter, Schneeweis, 1988	*Fortune* magazine's annual survey of corporate reputations	Various measures of financial accounting–based returns, market-based returns adjusted for risk, and market-based estimates of beta	ROA and total assets showed positive relationships and operating income growth had a negative correlation. Accounting and stock market–based risk measures tended to be negatively associated with social responsibility.
Contrill, 1990	*Fortune* magazine's annual survey of corporate reputations	Market concentration, market share, industry	There was a positive association between market share and CSR. In addition, there was an industry effect as well..
Patten, 1990	Sullivan Principles (a code of behavior mandating equal opportunity for nonwhite workers in South Africa)	Market-based returns adjusted for risk and trading volume around the signing of the principles	No price reaction. Authors did report a volume reaction.

Authors/Date	Social Responsibility Criteria	Financial Responsibility Criteria	Results
Roberts, 1992	Council of Economic Priorities evaluations of social disclosure, dollars contributed by PACs, public affairs staff members, sponsorship of philanthropic foundations	Various measures of financial accounting based on returns, market-based estimates of beta, size, etc.	There was a positive association between CSR and economic performance.

Source: Moses L. Pava and Joshua Krausz, *Corporate Responsibility and Financial Performance: The Paradox of Social Cost* (Wesport, Ct.: Quorum/Greenwood, 1995), Appendix A. Reprinted by permission of the authors.

Although some of the earliest SRI funds like Pax World have for decades been in the top quartile of their category in performance, only a handful of such SRI funds existed in the 1980s. The last five years have seen such a rapid growth in SRI indexes and mutual funds that these are now far more useful for comparison studies. In addition, the professionalism from a financial point of view of these funds has changed dramatically from SRI's earlier days. What Pava and Krausz tried to do is explain *why* SRI seemed to outperform once they saw the trend in these studies indicating no loss of performance. Their views will be covered in chapter 5, "Why SRI Has Outperformed."

Another major figure in the study of SRI performance is Lloyd Kurtz, who maintains a list of SRI articles and studies on a website at www.SRIstudies.org. Part of the thesis in this book is that SRI is a parallel paradigm to that prevailing on Wall Street. This situation will change and is in fact already starting to change. Thus this current of thought is emanating from a different perception of the way the world works. It is the collision of these two worlds that is developing as the SRI current, which has its genesis in the religious community and in the environmental, labor, peace, and social justice movements, rapidly forces its way into the mainstream world of investing.

One has to consider whether in the long run there is some connection between this development and the massive rise of the pension funds as major concentrations of capital, a topic I'll examine in chapter 6, "Pension Funds and Fiduciary Responsibility." Certainly a major development in the history of capital is now under way with pension funds now controlling $10 trillion in assets, and the trade union movement is taking a new look at the possibility of exercising influence over this capital. There is growing coming together of the SRI current, the labor movement, and the environmental movement just in the last year or so.

Kurtz bridges the worlds of the SRI community and the traditional investment professionals. Based on his background in the world of traditional investing, he has tried to be precise in his mathematical evaluation of SRI performance. His position has been that there is no evidence to claim that SRI reduces performance, thus putting the "why not?" argument on solid ground. But Kurtz does not agree with my conclusions about SRI performance and instead takes the position that the outperformance of socially responsible investing has not been mathematically established. He is also skeptical that a clear, mathematically provable argument for SRI outperformance can be made.[3] I'll review some of his arguments in chapter 5.

The Innovest Studies

One of the most detailed and careful studies to establish whether environmental screens increase performance (in financial jargon referred to as *adding alpha*) has been carried out by a small firm called Innovest Strategic Value Advisors, led by Dr. Matthew Kiernan. Kiernan set out to remove any secondary factors influencing the returns of socially screened and nonscreened stocks. He did this in an innovative way by removing "the human factor." After all, it could be argued that socially screened mutual funds get better ratings because their managers are more talented or more experienced. By making his comparisons in a controlled universe, Kiernan produced a study that is exceptionally interesting.

Kiernan and Innovest kept the stock universe the same and simply altered the amount invested in each company. Innovest applied only one screen, focusing on corporate environmental performance. If a company received a good rating on its environmental performance, Innovest would invest a higher amount in that company. If the company received a poor rating, Innovest would invest less. No other judgment was involved. Innovest used over 60 environmental factors in its environmental measures. Companies were rated from the highest rating, AAA, to the lowest, CCC. Even within the technology sector, sharp differences appeared. Dell, for instance, received the highest rating of AAA, while Gateway got a CCC rating.

The result was outperformance based on the environmentally adjusted weightings. The performance improvement was 1.9 percent per year for a fully diversified, "eco-enhanced" S&P 500 portfolio. However, if one examines high-risk, high-impact sectors in greater detail, the outperfor-

Figure 4.1 EcoValue '21 Time Series Evaluation
Relative Performance Since 12/31/98 vs. S&P 500

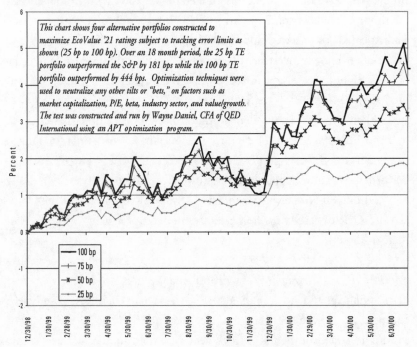

This chart shows four alternative portfolios constructed to maximize EcoValue '21 ratings subject to tracking error limits as shown (25 bp to 100 bp). Over an 18 month period, the 25 bp TE portfolio outperformed the S&P by 181 bps while the 100 bp TE portfolio outperformed by 444 bps. Optimization techniques were used to neutralize any other tilts or "bets," on factors such as market capitalization, P/E, beta, industry sector, and value/growth. The test was constructed and run by Wayne Daniel, CFA of QED International using an APT optimization program.

mance margins become much larger. In sector after sector, companies rated by Innovest in the top half of their industry sector outperformed those in the bottom half by substantial margins. (It should be noted that Innovest's top-ranking companies did not necessarily receive similar ratings from mainstream Wall Street analysts.) Nor was the outperformance restricted to Old Economy, "smokestack" industry sectors such as petroleum, chemicals, and forest products. For the year ending June 2000, for example, the top-rated companies in the telecommunications sector outperformed their bottom-half competitors by fully 10 percent. Even better numbers were achieved in the semiconductor (57 percent) and computer (25 percent) sectors.

Here no one can make a sector argument. There is only one sector under consideration at any one time. Nor can one argue that manager skill played a key role. There are no active managers.

Similarly promising results were achieved in a performance analysis of Innovest's EcoValue '21 model conducted in late 2000 by the independent quantitative analysis specialist firm QED. This study used an even more sophisticated "time-series" approach and, as in the Morgan Stanley test, all of the other known investment factor "bets" that could have explained the outperformance were "optimized" away. What remains is "pure" environmental-screen-driven outperformance.[4]

As Figure 4.1 illustrates, depending on how much emphasis was given to Innovest's EcoValue '21 factors, the outperformance margin ranged from 180 to 440 basis points (1.8–4.4 percent). Little if any of this outperformance can be explained by traditional securities analysis.

The Innovest studies have generated a wave of comments in the financial press. Below are two summaries by Innovest of articles printed about their studies:

Public Utilities Fortnightly: "Environmental leaders consistently achieve better financial and stock market performance than their less eco-efficient competitors. Of the S&P 500's 26 electrical utilities, the 13 utilities with the highest environmental ratings achieved stock market returns more than 600 basis points [6 percent] greater than the bottom environmental performers during 1998."[5]

Industry Week. "A new report released by Innovest Strategic Value Advisors, New York, shows that the top environmental performers in the computer sector have outperformed their industry rivals financially by 25% since the beginning of 1998. The report, *The Computer Industry: Hidden Risks and Value Potential for Strategic Investors,* calls into question the view of the environment as a cost center and presents evidence linking superior environmental performance with competitiveness and profitability. Citing Dell Computer Corp. as one example, the report says the company's energy-efficient initiatives already have generated cost savings of 37%."[6]

It's clear from the studies done so far that SRI indicates no loss of performance and may show a gain. It can be argued that those interested in doing such studies are sympathetic to SRI and that these sympathies have skewed their results. But the evidence is too overwhelming and consistent to be so easily dismissed. And in any case, where is the counterevidence? Given the skepticism and outright opposition to SRI on the part of many major firms and consultants, why has no evidence appeared with any pretense to objectivity that contradicts the large number of positive studies?

Notes

1. Moses L. Pava and Joshua Krausz, *Corporate Responsibility and Financial Performance: The Paradox of Social Cost* (Westport, Conn.: Greenwood, 1995).

2. Milton Moskowitz, "Choosing Socially Responsible Stocks," *Business and Society* (Spring 1972).

3. Lloyd Kurtz. "'Mr. Markowitz, Meet Mr. Moskowitz': A Review of Studies on Socially Responsible Investing," in Brian R. Bruce, ed., *The Investment Research Guide to Socially Responsible Investing* (Plano, Tex.: Investment Research Forums, 1998).

4. Cited in Robert A.G. Monks, *The New Global Investors: How Shareowners Can Unlock Sustainable Prosperity Worldwide* (Oxford: Capstone, 2001), p. 156.

5. Frank Dixon, "Wall Street Goes Green," *Public Utilities Fortnightly,* Septermber 15, 1999.

6. *Industry Week,* September 20, 1999.

5

Why SRI Has Outperformed

SRI has outperformed conventional investment strategies for a combination of reasons, but two stand out as the most likely explanations. First, SRI screens reduce company-specific risk and liabilities. Second, SRI screening helps discover firms with strong finances and effective management.

SRI reduces risk by screening out bad products, firms with legal difficulties or criminal records, firms with unpopular products or products that create social harm, firms with criminally inclined managements, firms that violate environmental regulations or in general are abusive to the environment, and firms that engage in discrimination on the basis of race, gender, sexual orientation, or national origin.

The term *backdoor financial screen* refers to two possible consequences of a positive SRI rating. One is that SRI research discovers well-managed companies that are careful to make sure their products will not run into problems, that have established good relations with their employees and community, and that in general have been able to manage their liabilities and risks well. Sturdivant and Ginter formulated this concept back in 1977: "It would appear that a case can be made for an association between responsiveness to social issues and the ability to respond effectively to traditional business challenges.... A company management group which reflects rather narrow and rigid views of social change and rising expectations might also be expected to respond less creatively and effectively in the traditional but also dynamic arenas in which business functions. Hence there is the stronger economic performance."[1]

The second is that SRI screens discover firms that are strong financially. Such firms are more likely to make sure to cover all their bases in terms of public relations, environmental issues, openness, and relations with employees. Thus, the high social rating may not reveal necessarily management commitment to social values but simply that a firm is financially strong enough to act appropriately. According to Kahneman, Knetsch and Thaler, "A realistic description of our economic system must include the fact that consumers, suppliers, and employees care about being treated fairly and treating others fairly. In addition, they are willing to resist unfair firms even at a positive cost to themselves. Satisfying the fairness constraint may lead to better long-run financial performance."[2]

Mass Social Currents

The reduction of risk and the indirect selection of strong financial and/or well-run companies are key factors, but they do not provide a complete explanation of SRI outperformance. There is an additional factor that has not been raised in the literature on this question. From my perspective, a broader understanding of this issue is rooted in the evolution of our society, socially, politically, and culturally. It is related to the appearance of large-scale social reform movements. Not all social screens have the same financial impact, because their impacts are directly related to the existence of public opinion and active mass social movements.

Mass social currents such as the anti-war movement in the late sixties, the women's movement, the labor movement, anti–nuclear power movement, or the environmental movement have an indirect impact on the financial performance of corporations. Social screens reflecting a mass social current will tend to improve performance because corporations that are in conflict with public opinion as expressed in such movements pay a price that is real though often difficult to measure. In the long run, however, the interrelationship between social movements and the success and failure of products and corporations is crucial to our understanding of the impact of social screens on financial performance.

The Relative Validity of Screens

The impact of a screen will be relative to the existence of avenues for popular pressure to exert itself. In the days of the robber barons of the 1880s, for example, SRI screens would probably have had a more limited impact. Likewise, in countries where crude forms of corruption are the rule, like Russia, SRI would probably underperform. Other examples might be certain US allies such as Saudi Arabia, a dictatorship where one family owns much of the country, or, until recently, the dictatorship in Indonesia, where the dictator's family siphoned off tens of billions of dollars from the country's treasury. It is the spread of the concept of democracy and the development of large-scale social movements for environmental and social justice that is changing the framework in which corporations must function.

Corporations are, of course, driven by profit. It is rare that their boards of directors or top managements consider the impact they are having on society unless they come under pressure from forces outside the corporate world. Those pressures may be reflected in the personal awareness of directors or executives, but often such pressures can alter the policies of a firm even against the personal views of management or the company's directors. The hiring of African Americans in the late 1950s and 1960s came as a by-product of the struggle for civil rights and the demands that government enforce the US Constitution; hiring practices were changed even where the managements retained their own racial prejudices.

Large corporations have enormous power because of the capital they control and the influence that capital permits them to assert. Top executives in major corporations are active in all kinds of organizations and in politics. Yet it is rare to see any corporate heads helping to form, lead, or build mass social movements such as those mentioned above. Why is this? Is there an underlying conflict between what is best for society and the drive by corporations to function, as Milton Friedman advised, as profit machines and nothing else?

The overwhelming growth in our awareness of the destruction of the environment and the spread of organized movements to fight to save our planet and our species from self-destruction exert pressure on corporations to stay within the law and avoid practices that damage the earth's eco-system. The rise of movements for women's equality, gay and lesbian rights, and the protection of our health have had a deep and irreversible impact on the world in which we live. It is the scientific knowledge of what tobacco does and the popular dissemination of that knowledge that has resulted in the campaign against tobacco, in turn leading to the poor performance of tobacco stocks over the last three years.

The increasing concern of unions in relation to globalization and the increasing use of child labor and sweatshops is another critical force today. Labor's new alliance with environmentalists in response to the growth of undemocratic world institutions like the World Trade Organization (WTO) is part of the framework in which sociopolitical factors are having an impact on the financial performance of stocks.

In 1995 a study by David Diltz discovered differing rates of alpha for differing social screens. Those that added the most alpha were the environment, military, animal testing, and South African operations. Those with negative alpha included charitable giving, community outreach, and family benefits. In general, the study showed environment, military business, and nuclear involvement screens as the strongest factors for a positive alpha. The different issues affecting alpha most likely change depending on events. Obviously, South Africa involvement is today no longer a factor. The environment has probably been a consistently strong screen for adding alpha. In general, Diltz's study showed about twice the normal variance for "excess return test results."[3]

Short-Term versus Long-Term Perspectives

Corporations in today's world are driven by a short-term perspective often directly associated with the price of their shares on the stock market. Economic policies for our nation and for the world are in turn often influenced by the decisions of corporations. But our economic needs are long term and corporate decision-making is short term: Yes, you can make a profit by clear-cutting a rain forest, but doing so strikes a long-term blow against the economy. Part of the root of the success of SRI is that it focuses on the long term and encourages policies that strengthen the economy's potential.

For example, in California only 4 percent of our natural ancient forests are left. Is it in the interest of our economy to remove this last remaining foothold of nature in our state, as is being done today, or to preserve it? Should it come as a surprise that Maxxam Inc., the corporation most active in destroying California's old growth forests, is one of the most hated firms in the state? Isn't it possible that Maxxam will pay a price in ways not so easily perceived precisely because it is working against the interests of the people of California and harming the state's economic future? Saying this does not mean that clear-cutting thousand-year-old redwoods may not be profitable in the short term and appear to Wall Street analysts to be a good business plan. But the logic of such a "good business plan" is to undermine the economy over the long term.

Isn't it obvious that these kinds of conflicts will eventually be reflected in the financial performance of corporations? Chapter 14 discusses the issue of energy and considers in more detail the dichotomy between a short-term, market-share orientation and a long-term economic orientation. The point is that when corporations work in a manner hostile to the best interests of the economy they create opposition. That opposition has an economic impact, but it is often registered outside the normal channels watched by Wall Street. SRI factors in this aspect of reality and thus gains an advantage financially because of its recognition of long-term economic factors.

Does SRI Reflect Inefficiency in the Market?

Robert Helliesen of Milliman USA, a San Francisco–based consulting firm, has raised an important question on the issue of performance and social screens. Theoretically, if the issues raised by SRI are recognized by the market, this recognition should be discounted in the price of stocks so that no financial gain can result from including or screening out stocks based on these issues. In posing this question, based on the theory of the efficiency of the market, Helliesen gets at the heart of the issue of performance and social responsibility. The answer to his question, I believe, is that the market registers a large inefficiency on social issues. In other words, investors have tended to miss the impact of environmental and social problems on corporations. This is due in part because of the great divide culturally between the financial community and the social currents among academics, environmentalists, health-oriented nonprofits and the labor movement.

If I am right and the outperformance of social investing becomes widely recognized, then the integration of these factors into the discounting mechanism of the market should gradually remove the advantage of socially screened portfolios.

Modern Portfolio Theory postulates that markets are efficient over time if they are transparent — that is, if all relevant information about a product or security is fully and freely available to all market participants. Market theory further assumes neutrality on the part of governmental or other manipulative forces and that the market exists in a nonconflictive society. Reality is far more complex. Ideology, culture, belief systems, and political structures all have an influence on the actual results of markets, so although market theory describes an important part of reality, it does not describe the reality of the market for any specific period of time. The market in fact tends to become by turns overvalued and undervalued. While the long-term trend is toward efficiency, the market is best characterized as permanently inefficient at any specific moment. Money managers see part of their job as understanding the inefficiencies or oscillations of the market in order to take advantage of them and provide alpha for their clients by outperforming benchmarks.

Free Trade and Market Efficiency

The same point applies to theories of free trade. In a pure sense, free trade has never existed. The nations with the most economic and military power have determined the framework for defining what is considered "free" when it comes to trade. The United States, for example, as it freed itself from British economic domination (especially after the Civil War) favored tariffs and opposed Britain's advocacy of free trade. When the United States became the dominant economic power in the world the predominant ideology in the US gradually shifted in favor of free trade. Most people forget, for instance, that the Republican Party was founded in support of tariffs (against free trade), higher national taxes, and greater government involvement in economic development. Today the Republican program is based on the opposite paradigm. In other words, the United States government and business community opposed free trade when tariffs seemed to favor US economic development, and the same forces are now determined partisans of free trade as they define it because they now see free trade as in their economic interest. As these secular historical shifts in viewpoint take place they create all kinds of social and economic changes and can lead to prolonged inefficiencies in the market.

The efficiency of the market is clearly influenced by conflicts of interest between currents within society, between countries, and among new macro social and political trends. We are living today amidst such tectonic social shifts. The struggle over the environment is a perfect example: Will human industry and agriculture destroy the economy through destruction of natural equity, upon which the existence of the economy depends, or will we rebase our economy on renewable and sustainable production? As interests and economic strategies based on short-term and long-term goals collide with each other, the market can easily fail over the short run to reflect all aspects of reality, thus creating market inefficiencies.

SRI injects a new element into the market equation that has not yet been recognized on a broad scale and therefore it is able to exploit such market inefficiencies. This divergence can be seen clearly on the issue of tobacco. Most Wall Street analysts see tobacco as a very profitable business. The SRI community sees it as a losing proposition, a business with a negative cash flow. SRI looks beyond the immediate ability of tobacco companies to externalize the costs they generate, while Wall Street does not. In that sense Wall Street is assuming a pro-tobacco culture and political framework as a permanent feature of our society. The SRI community, on the other hand, foresees the inevitable collapse of that framework because tobacco addiction is bad for people and for the economy, and because more and more people are coming to share these views.

The Wall Street analysts may appear to be correct, but over time SRI results in outperformance because its perception of reality is more farseeing. As you will see in chapter 15, Steve Viederman notes that the root of the word *prudent* is "farseeing." Socially responsible investors are the prudent investors.

Tobacco stocks rose quite sharply in 2000 and 2001 and therefore it is an excellent moment to examine this proposition looking a little deeper into the issue of investing in the tobacco industry.

Social and Financial Screening: The Case of Tobacco

Tobacco kills over 1000 people a day in the United States alone. People in California lose $10 billion a year due to medical costs and lost productivity because of tobacco.[4]

Tobacco companies can succeed only if they addict millions of young people each year. Since people who are 30 or 40 years old do not start smoking, the business plans of the tobacco companies must therefore depend on addicting 15- to 25-year-olds. One powerful advantage they have is that addiction to tobacco takes hold very rapidly: It is in fact a stronger addiction than cocaine. The tobacco industry is therefore a predator, seeking our teenagers in their difficult transition years from childhood to adulthood to turn them into addicts. It is hard to understand how anyone can invest in tobacco, just as it is hard to understand how anyone can deal in heroin or cocaine. They are, after all, exactly the same problem — addictive substances that damage our bodies and wreak havoc on our society. Moreover, only 3000 people a year die from cocaine, while tobacco kills that number in less then three days.

Although they have reluctantly had to accommodate the opposition to their business plan in the United States, the US tobacco companies are hard at work trying to addict every young person they can in China, India, and other countries. And in many Third World countries only a small percentage of women smoke — so the tobacco companies are making a concerted effort to addict them. Their worldwide search for new addicts is a crime adding to the burdens of people who have difficulties enough financially without the burden of tobacco addiction.

Tobacco has thus become one of the central divestment issues confronting society. Here we can clearly see the role of the SRI community as an extension in the financial markets of a mass social development, best characterized as concern about health and knowledge of health issues. Leadership in this effort starts with health organizations like the American Heart Association and American Lung Association and extends to all kinds of organizations that focus on the fight against cancer and on protection of our children.

The California Health Department estimates that treatment of tobacco-related diseases and lost productivity stemming from them cost $10 billion a year. Nationwide this translates into an $80 billion dollar loss each year. The tobacco settlement that the politicians accepted requires about $10 billion in annual payments from the tobacco companies to state governments across America. In this manner our state governments are now sharing in the profits from an addictive drug, and some state officials actually worry publicly about the loss in revenues if antismoking campaigns succeed. But despite the tobacco settlement, we as a society are still subsidizing tobacco addiction by $70 billion per year. The tobacco companies have simply passed on a good part of the settlement cost to the approximately 25 percent of the US public that is addicted to tobacco by raising the price of cigarettes.

If one considers the hidden tobacco subsidy that society pays, it is correct to conclude tobacco is not really profitable. In fact, tobacco has never been profitable. It can appear profitable only on the basis of a narrow accounting in which the true costs of tobacco are passed on to society while the revenues remain in the hands of the tobacco companies. The fact that we still also openly subsidize the production of tobacco with taxpayer money spotlights the clash of opposing cultures taking place in our country today. But is it really that hard to guess who will win out over time between knowledge and ignorance, between poisoning people and protecting their health? Already polls show that 76 percent of the public does not want tobacco stocks in their pension plans.[5]

What statement does it make to our society when a pension or a not-for-profit endowment invests in tobacco companies? That investment cannot succeed unless millions of youth become addicted to tobacco over the next decades. It is an agreement to seek profit at the expense of our taxpayers, our health departments, and the general quality of life in our nation. In contrast, what message is sent when a pension fund or endowment fund says no to tobacco? It reinforces the idea that tobacco is not a legitimate product or investment. While it may be best not to outlaw tobacco (12 states have done so in the past), legal sale does not make tobacco a legitimate source of financial gain. It is quite possible in the future that the legal system, while not criminalizing tobacco, may end its use as a source of profits.

Yet 95 percent of pension funds and not-for-profit endowment funds continue to invest in tobacco stocks against the interests and desires of the people the trustees are sworn to uphold. As a trustee for the Contra Costa County Public Employees Retirement Systems, I am proud that our board has voted unanimously to divest its tobacco stocks. San Francisco was the first county in California to divest; other counties have since joined the divestment current. Thanks to the leadership of State Treasurer Phil Angelides, both CalPERS and the California State Teachers Retirement System have also divested their tobacco stocks. Other states that have already done so include Massachusetts, New York, Vermont, and Minnesota.

Recently Florida voted to end its divestment policy and once again invest in tobacco stocks. The tobacco corporations are by far the largest corporate donors to the Republican Party, with Philip Morris being the single largest corporate donor. They also donate large sums to the Democratic Party. The case of Florida is clearly related to the more pro-tobacco position of the Florida Republican Party now in power in Tallahassee.

The pressure for divestment is clearly coming from the grass roots. It reflects the desire of the public, of the advocacy of doctors, nurses, teachers, and health advocates. The American Medical Association has asked the American people to divest from tobacco. This pressure is reflected among many of the pension fund trustees closest to the retirees and participants in their plans. It finds expression among elected officials who sense the will of the public and are becoming increasingly willing to challenge the tobacco companies as the pressure builds up from below. The greatest pressure comes, of course, from the families of the millions of victims of the tobacco companies whose lives were cut short by tobacco addiction. The anger that is building up in our nation against those who profit through the addiction and suffering of others will not be contained by any arrangement devised to save tobacco. Juries will increasingly return verdicts against the tobacco companies, and large damages will continue to be awarded.

In July 2000 the World Health Organization published *Report of the Committee of Experts on Tobacco Industry Documents,* which documents how tobacco companies, including Philip Morris, have been hard at work trying to destroy the World Health Organization. These documents show that the top management in these firms are simply unconcerned about the great harm they are doing the people of the world. A full reading of the report makes it clear that our society is dealing with organizations that can be correctly labeled criminal in their actions today as in the past. What is amazing is the leniency with which they have so far been treated.[6]

There are also other issues relating to the production and sale of tobacco, including the use of child labor to grow tobacco in the Third World, the companies' attempts to deceive Congress, lies to the public, and falsification of scientific studies to hide the dangers of tobacco to health. All these make one wonder how long the honeymoon with some politicians can last before stronger action is taken to break the influence of tobacco on our nation.[7]

In the late 1980s the White House handed the Bill of Rights (yes, the actual original document) to Philip Morris to tour US high schools. The occasion was the 200th anniversary of the Bill of Rights. At that time Philip Morris was running an advertising campaign trying to associate smoking and freedom. Obviously, in the last ten years, our culture's values have shifted. What happened at the end of the 1980s would be difficult to repeat today without a massive public outcry. The idea that the attitudes toward tobacco could be switched back to the 1940s or 1950s (a time of general lack of understanding of tobacco) is naïve at best. The tobacco industry will never recover its reputation in the face of the hostility of the public.

When the tobacco stocks topped out in 1998, *all* Wall Street analysts following Philip Morris had a buy recommendation on the company's stock. Philip Morris represents about 80 percent of the tobacco sector of the S&P 500 and accounts for 50 percent of the tobacco market. The stock was trading at almost $60 a share in 1998. It then collapsed to just below $20 before recovering back to about $50, still below its price of three years ago. Not one analyst on Wall Street could see what was coming. Most have a permanent buy recommendation on Philip Morris. With the ups and downs in the battle to end tobacco's influence on our society and to stop the spread of tobacco addiction, these company's stocks will rebound or fall as events appear to favor or hurt the tobacco companies.

Despite the strength of the case against tobacco, the industry still has its allies. Christopher Palmeri of *Business Week* recently went to bat for the tobacco companies with another attack on SRI. In June 2001 Palmeri again attacked California Treasurer Phil Angelides for his views on tobacco divestment, and he supported Florida's decision to return to investments in tobacco companies. Under the title "Politicians Should Butt Out of Pension Funds" he charges that pension funds have suffered massive losses because of their divestment from tobacco. Unlike his previous attack piece, this article does not hide his antipathy to SRI. But his new article repeated the mistakes of the 1999 one. He does not, of course, discuss the fact that since its top in 1998 the tobacco index has underperformed the S&P 500. Nor does he cover the exceptional risks of investing in tobacco or the external costs stemming from tobacco addiction. He simply jumps on a recent rise in tobacco stocks from an extremely depressed level to charge that divestment causes pension funds to forgo profits from tobacco. I suspect that we will not see Palmeri write articles about the losses of those funds that did not divest when tobacco stocks drop again. Palmeri could, of course, write articles every week on one or another polluter, criminally inclined firm, or manufacturer of defective products whenever its stocks make a run upward. But in any case he has trouble explaining why SRI funds that screen out these companies continue to outperform.

It was easy for the American Heart Association or the American Lung Association to see why tobacco would fail as an investment when the investment "experts" couldn't see it. That is why SRI outperforms. SRI sees an aspect of reality not included in the research of traditional Wall Street firms.

Discussions of risks in tobacco investing always leave one risk out: Tobacco as an investment is always one discovery away from total collapse. The day scientists discover how to overcome the chemical addiction from nicotine the tobacco companies will be financial basket cases. Whether such a discovery is around the corner or far off, its eventual success is quite probable. A cure for tobacco addiction will be found, either through scientific advances or successful social-educational efforts. Another possible outcome is increasing governmental repression of tobacco. Legal sanctions will not end the use of tobacco, just as they have failed to stem the use of cocaine and heroin. I believe, as do most anti-tobacco organizations, that criminalizing tobacco is not the answer. However, government action, such as taxes, withdrawal of subsidies, and educational programs, could reduce its use and lead to the collapse of the existing tobacco firms and their stocks.

Markowitz versus Moskowitz: Evidence and Performance

As Lloyd Kurtz has emphasized, the goals of the SRI community will not have been realized until people come to understand that caring about the impact of our investments is essential, even if it leads to financial under-performance. Performance at the cost of people's health or the environment is simply poor accounting. Kurtz, as I noted earlier, does not believe that SRI outperforms based on his strictly mathematical review of the evidence. In his 1999 review of studies of socially responsible investing, Kurtz addressed many of the critical issues in this discussion.[8] He does not rule out the possibility that SRI outperforms, and he even points to studies indicating outperformance, but he says that he would prefer to see a clear scientific basis for such a claim before endorsing it.

Can there really be a definitive proof on the issue of SRI and perfor-mance? I believe that it is possible to carry out far larger and better studies to help establish whether SRI screens have added to performance. But it is next to impossible to prove mathematically that this has to be true for any specific period because the financial impact of SRI screens is based on evolving sociopolitical realities. The issue of SRI and performance is a moving target, not a static equation.

The starting point of this book is the existing empirical evidence, and the argument is quite simple. Given normal probability, how can all the empirical evidence showing outperformance exist without some underly-ing foundation? My goal here is to examine possible explanations that logically explain the outperformance that we observe. This is not a math-ematical proof. Quite the contrary: It is a hypothesis.

The nature of SRI makes it difficult to prove outperformance math-ematically because it involves various screens and definitions. However, if we focus studies on a crucial and specific screen, such as corporate environmental policies, it becomes easier to show empirical evidence of outperformance and to analyze why this outperformance exists. I believe that the impact on performance is true for a broad range of screens, not just environmental issues, but it is not necessarily true for every screen that someone might call "social." Part of my thesis here is that a social screen that reflects widespread public opinion on an issue is most likely to have a positive impact on performance. An issue on which people are sharply divided or a screen representing views that many people oppose will not have the same impact.

To understand the discussion of SRI performance, it is important to review Kurtz's logic and the questions he poses. In his article Kurtz explains, "Although there is no simple definition of SRI, screened portfolios have strong family resemblances, and the generalizations that follow are true for most widely used definitions. I have sought to present rigorous studies of SRI performance, but must forewarn the reader that only a few such studies exist."[9] Kurtz then lays out two views, which he characterizes as "Markowitz" and "Moskowitz," referring to two men who developed concepts related to the theory of how the stock market behaves (Markowitz) and the issue of SRI and financial performance (Moskowitz). Harry Markowitz's view, first expressed in the 1950s, is that a subset of a universe of stocks cannot outperform the universe. Markowitz sees SRI as a subset of all investment choices, since SRI screens out stocks and thus reduces the size of the universe. In a pure sense, Markowitz would hold that a broad index would outperform any managers' attempt to outperform by selecting out a smaller universe of stocks based on financial criteria that would hopefully lead to higher performance.

Wall Street's point of view on this issue is not purely Markowitzian. Wall Street believes that you can improve performance by reducing the size of the universe. That is the service that brokers and fund managers offer the public. Money management firms suggest that by allowing them, for a fee, to manage your money they will provide higher performance than the broad universe, the "benchmark." Wall Street instead sees SRI as a method that reduces the broad universe from which the "best" financial selections can be made, and thus concludes that SRI screening should result in lower performance. Logically this makes sense. Reducing the size of the universe gives an advantage to any investment strategy having the larger universe as a *starting point*. Note, however, that phrase *starting point*.

It is also logical to think of an SRI screen as limiting the universe from which to choose stocks in which to invest. Certainly that was the original intent of people applying social screens. Social screens were not developed by financial experts seeking to add alpha (performance). Quite the contrary: they came into existence and continue to flourish because a large number of people feel strongly about the impact on society of their investments — often, independent of the financial impact. It is therefore quite understandable that social screens were not originally seen as financial screens. The mystery of SRI is precisely that these social screens are rooted in a reality with a strong financial impact.

In other words, the Markowitzian view may well be correct when a screen that is not financial is placed on a universe of investment possibilities. For instance, we could screen out all companies whose names start with *a, b,* or *c.* The subset of all companies whose names start from *d* to *z* will tend to underperform if one applies financial screens to that subset versus the entire universe.

The counter-argument to Markowitz reflects the underlying thesis of this book. SRI screens do not yield an externalized nonfinancial subset. They instead start with the same universe. SRI acts as a fundamental *financial* screen. SRI is *acting* on the universe, not *reducing the size* of the universe. There is an enormous difference in these two concepts. SRI is just another financial screen, and usually it is combined with a series of other financial screens when a money manager invests an SRI mutual fund or portfolio.

In that sense, SRI is no different then any other financial screen that covers the full universe of stocks. The argument against SRI therefore has to be posed either as "no screen can add alpha" or as "SRI does not add alpha." Markowitz believed that in a "perfect" world of free efficiency no subset of stocks could add alpha. Wall Street and reality seem to indicate this is not the case—precisely because markets are not efficient. Wall Street's traditional view is that you can add alpha, but that SRI does not because it uses screens that are external to financial performance. But Wall Street is wrong in this judgment, precisely because SRI *is* a financial screen.

Kurtz notes that Moskowitz in 1972 presented another view suggesting that SRI might outperform "because they [SRI portfolios] incorporate important information not widely understood by the markets."[10] I believe that events have confirmed Moskowitz's view. Lloyd Kurtz believes that the jury is still out on this point, or that there might be conflicting forces affecting SRI performance. Kurtz raises the possibility that SRI does both things — that is, it both reduces the size of the universe of investments and adds alpha. He thus holds open the possibility that both Markowitz and Moskowitz may be right: social screens may be reducing the universe somewhat but also having an effect that adds performance. Kurtz is quite perceptive in advancing this viewpoint. The underlying reality may be that some social screens really do act as externalities and reduce the size of the universe available for investment, while other screens have a more powerful financial effect.

Kurtz notes that social screens tend to result in investments in companies with lower capitalization, higher price-to-book ratios, higher price-to-earnings ratios, and better "excellence" ratios. This list confirms our view that SRI screens increase beta (volatility) through lower capitalization and higher price-to-book and price-to-earnings earnings. SRI screens move portfolios toward growth and away from value stocks, as the ratio on book value would indicate. But also they introduce the "excellence" factor, which lowers company-specific risk. According to Clayman such companies reveal a positive alpha (performance).[11]

In contrast to Chris Luck's study showing 77 basis points of unexplained outperformance by the Domini Social Index, Kurtz points to several studies — for example, DiBartolomeo (1996), D'Antonio, Johnsen and Hutton (1997) — who all arrive at the conclusion that the outperformance of the DSI can be explained by what Kurtz calls "fundamental factors." These arguments are congruent with Lipper's comments on SRI based on sector allocation and specific stock selection. Kurtz points out that until 1997, Luck, Pilotte, and Diltz were the only rigorous risk-adjusted studies to report positive returns for SRI screens. Since then he sees a series of new studies pointing in this direction.

Finally, Kurtz asks that if SRI outperforms why hasn't Wall Street taken it up? The question is a good one, but really not difficult to answer. First is the fear of the topic by Wall Street. In addition to assuming that SRI reduces the universe and creates a subset of stocks doomed to financial underperformance, Wall Street as a whole sees SRI as challenging the free market philosophy as a self-correcting mechanism that in the end results in the best possible outcomes. SRI has an interventionist element that implies the markets may not work that well and that investors must consciously intervene on behalf of society's long-term future even against trends in the market. Thus SRI is seen as a philosophical threat to Wall Street.

SRI threatens Wall Street firms in another way. If they become involved in SRI how will the companies that are screened out respond? Will General Electric, Monsanto, Philip Morris, etc. go elsewhere for their business if a Wall Street firm creates an investment product that screens out their stocks because of their products, criminal activity, or other policies? This was one of the issues we had to overcome when Merrill Lynch launched the first Wall Street product with a social screen. What overrode this fear was the overwhelming pro-environmental sentiment that drove their approval of the Eco-Logical Trust. In fact, a meeting was held with the CEO of Merrill Lynch and other executives to decide if the Eco-Logical Trust should be approved. One high-level attorney for Merrill stated in response to others pointing out possible reasons for not launching the fund that he could not go home and tell his wife that Merrill had refused to launch a pro-environmental fund. Those gathered laughed and the decision was made to launch the Eco-Logical Trust.[12] Here we see clearly one small example of how the outside world — in this case, public opinion favoring environmentalism — can alter how a firm acts.

Second, until very recently there has not been enough empirical evidence to draw on and, as Kurtz notes, few serious risk-adjusted studies. It was thus understandable that Wall Street has not been easily convinced to take on the risks they saw in SRI until some solid arguments and (even more important) a demand in the market persuaded them that they would lose business unless they developed SRI products.

Third, times have changed since Kurtz first asked the question, and almost despite itself Wall Street is now becoming intrigued by SRI and is beginning to adopt it. As mentioned earlier, Vanguard, Russell, Dow Jones, and the British FTSE are all jumping on the bandwagon with socially screened indexes. In addition to these indexes various major firms have either launched SRI mutual funds or are encouraging their brokers to look at SRI as a market that they must enter.

Fiduciary Responsibility

Texts on the issue of investing have all assumed that SRI inevitably leads to lower performance based on the "smaller universe" argument. This issue is of extreme importance when dealing with fiduciary responsibility, as I'll discuss in chapter 6, "Pension Funds and Fiduciary Responsibility." A good example is how Trone, Allbright, and Taylor express this idea in *The Management of Investment Decisions.* Under the heading of "Fiduciary Issues" they state, "Regardless of one's personal views of the merits of social investing, *a prudent fiduciary must recognize that any restriction on an investment program has the potential to reduce the portfolio's total return* (italics in original). Consequently, when social restrictions are adopted, the fiduciary must be willing to accept the potential for lower returns and plan accordingly. It is wishful thinking to imagine that such portfolio constraints will have no impact on performance."[13] Clearly Trone et al. assume that SRI has nothing to do with financial performance. Here is how they state it: "Socially responsible investors attempt to look beyond a company's financial statements and consider how a company serves society as a whole."[14] Isn't it curious how it does not cross these authors' minds that how a company serves society has a direct impact on its finances!

Notice how Trone et al. conclude that the impact of SRI screens can only be negative because they assume that we are talking about matters external to financial considerations and thus by Markowitzian logic a negative influence on financial performance. They conclude, "Therefore, the fiduciary is prohibited from using trust assets to further the fiduciary's own personal views of social or political issues."[15] They actually see considering social issues as a conflict-of-interest problem. No one seems to have noticed in the literature on this issue that trustees are also expressing or accepting a point of view when they agree to make investments in companies whose products they know will harm their retirees and participants, such as investment in tobacco stocks. If Trone et al. are correct, almost every pension fund trustee in the United States is in violation of his or her fiduciary responsibility! It is just that they believe that their personal views on social and political issues are the norm at this time — and, as sociologists have long noted, mainstream beliefs are invisible to those who hold them.

The decision that any investment should be considered if it is legal regardless of its impact is *a political point of view.* A true fiduciary looks out for the interests of the retirees and participants in the fund's plan and acts solely in their interests. Investing in a scheme that would destroy their jobs, homes, culture, or quality of life can easily be argued as not in their interests.

In today's world, investments that destroy the basis of our economy and society, such as clear-cutting our last remaining old-growth forests or projects that increase global warming, are not in the interest of our participants and retirees. Those who argue that it is acceptable to invest in companies that have a destructive impact are expressing a political point of view, just as are those who oppose it. The fiduciary must instead ask, "What is in the interest of the participants and retirees?"

What happens, however, is that trustees hide behind letting the money manager make the decisions for them. Doing so lets the manager impose the prevailing point of view without discussion of whether an investment hurts retirees or participants.

Pava and Krausz

Moses L. Pava and Joshua Krausz, as I noted earlier, laid out five possible reasons why SRI outperforms in their book *Corporate Responsibility and Financial Performance: The Paradox of Social Cost.* Pava and Krausz's book appeared in 1995, but the studies they looked at covered the period 1970–92. Unlike much of the evidence I present in this book, which compares the performance of indexes and mutual funds over periods varying from three to ten years, Pava and Krausz focused on controlled studies in which groups of companies having similar financial characteristics were compared to a parallel group with higher social ratings. Much of the research at that time was based on the work of the Council for Economic Priorities (CEP), focusing on a screened group of about 800 major corporations.

Pava and Krausz argue against A. A. Ullman's claim that studies of social performance reveal no trend.[16] They do not believe that SRI results in a "cost" — that is, in negative performance — and report that SRI appears, on the contrary, to outperform. For those seriously interested in this topic from a theoretical viewpoint their book is must reading. They provide five possible, though not exclusive, explanations for SRI's outperformance:

- Socially responsible firms are identical to nonsocially responsible firms.
- Experiments to test the association between corporate social responsibility and traditional financial performance have not been carefully designed or controlled.
- Conscious pursuit of corporate social responsibility goals causes better financial performance.
- Only firms with stronger finances can afford a conscious pursuit of corporate responsibility goals.
- A conscious pursuit of corporate social responsibility goals can result in better financial performance.

Their first two explanations question the methodology of studies claiming that SRI underperforms: the results may be affected by weaknesses in the studies or fail to discover much of value because there is little real difference between socially acceptable and not socially acceptable firms and thus their performance will be similar.[17]

The third and fifth possible explanations hit at what I consider an interesting point to be developed further later in this book. That is the concept that there is one bottom line. SRI advocates have traditionally argued that there are two bottom lines, one financial and one social. SRI pays attention to the results on both bottom lines and thus is superior. The argument for one bottom line, by contrast, insists that a firm's social performance cannot be separated from its financial performance. In other words, there is a "cost" to *not* being social, not the other way around. The fourth answer in their list is perhaps the most obvious one: Strong financial companies are simply best positioned to act in a socially responsible manner.

Pava and Krausz state it is "premature to conclude that, in general, socially responsible firms perform better over time." They continue, "The issues involved in assessing socially responsible actions and measuring financial performance are too complex and nuanced to expect definitive answers. However, based on our results to date and to the extent they are corroborated by additional studies using alternative samples and even longer testing periods, Explanation 5 becomes more plausible." In conclusion they write, "[T]he consistency of the results reported here and the persistent findings across numerous studies that socially responsible firms certainly perform no worse and, perhaps, better than non-socially responsible firms is an important and intriguing finding that demands additional attention."[18]

SRI and Diversity

SRI is also pushing the financial services industry to broaden the diversity of its employees. At least in terms of the inclusion of women, the SRI current has been ahead of Wall Street. The financial industry has in fact been one of the last to stop discrimination based on race and sex. Back in the 1930s Jews were excluded from many firms. African Americans could not become brokers until the late 1960s, with a few exceptions such as the Lehman Brothers branch in Harlem. The number of women in the industry was minuscule until recently.

In spite of its ideological commitment on these issues, the SRI current to some degree still reflects the past of the broader industry. However, we can see rapid growth, not only in the involvement of women and the beginnings of broader participation by people of color, but also in the appearance of women as key leaders of a number of major SRI firms. The largest SRI mutual fund firm, the Calvert Group, is headed by Barbara Krumsiek, while the Calvert Foundation, which has played a key role in the development of community investing, has been led by Shari Berenbach. Amy Domini, whom the leading SRI index is named after, wrote one of the earliest books explaining SRI and has become an important figure recognized internatonally for promoting and defending SRI. Another woman heading a major SRI firm is Geeta Aiyer of Walden Asset Management (see her discussion of international SRI in chapter 13). Joan Bavaria, who heads Trillium, played an important role in the development of SRI, as did Alisa Gravitz, who currently heads Co-op America. Joan Shapiro, originally with the South Shore Bank of Chicago, was a central leader in the development of community investing. The list could go on and on — for example, to Susan Davis, who through her firm Capital Missions has done extensive conference work that has introduced thousands to socially responsible investing. At our own firm, Progressive Asset Management, 31 percent of out brokers are women — a sharp rise from even five years ago. While the individuals I've just noted have played outstanding roles in the development of SRI and show the deep involvement of women in the industry, there is still much to be done to overcome the legacy of past discrimination. That legacy is even more pronounced in terms of the people of color.

There are few leaders in the SRI field of African American, Latino, or other people of color descent, although some have appeared. Marx Cazenave, while not exclusively involved in SRI, made a major breakthrough in helping to include African Americans in institutional investing. Back in 1987, when Cazenave set out to champion the involvement of African Americans, few thoughts his efforts would succeed. He persevered, however, and built a firm that blazed a trail for a long list of African American money managers. While this process is still in its early stages, the door has finally been opened by the efforts of people like Marx Cazenave.

I can personally testify to the difficulities involved in effecting change and to the possibility of progress. When PAM was first started only a handful of firms in the broker/dealer business were headed by Latinos, and I was the first to head a firm in the SRI field. However, when I studied the list developed by Lloyd Kurtz of articles on SRI performance, I was struck by the large proportion of male authors, almost all of them European American. Hopefully the progress we have made will continue, and we will see broader representation of all sectors of society both in the financial services industry as a whole and within the SRI community.

Wall Street Versus SRI

The opposition to SRI from Wall Street institutions like the *Wall Street Journal* is rooted in their belief that if markets are left to themselves they will over time solve social problems on their own. Any perusal of the world today should make us at least question the concept of automatic market correction of environmental or social abuses. The reliance on the "free market" as a solution to social problems is in conflict with the interventionist concept of SRI investing, which seeks to withdraw capital from firms violating the law, destroying the environment, using sweatshops or child labor.

The fact of SRI outperformance enters this debate in an embarrassing manner for Wall Street, because it appears to put its opponents in conflict with their own belief system on several levels. The interventionist view of SRI is supposed to lead to a cost — that is, lower performance. Wall Street in general favors deregulation and privatization, allowing the markets to work their "invisible hand" magic. Wall Street is ideologically committed to the highest risk-adjusted return on any investment the government allows (tobacco, prostitution where that is legal, polluters, gambling, whatever). But when confronted with an outlook that factors in social impact and then leads to financial outperformance at lower risk, Wall Street finds itself in an ideological bind. Deep down, SRI is a threat to Wall Street's traditional philosophy.

Notes

1. F.D. Sturdivant and J.L. Ginter, "Corporate Social Responsivness," *California Management Review* 19:3 (1977): p. 38.

2. D. Kahneman, J.L. Knetsch, and R.H. Thaler, "Fairness and Assumptions of Economics," *Journal of Business* 59:4 (1986): pp. 285–300.

3. J. David Diltz, "Does Social Screening Affect Portfolio Performance?" *Journal of Investing* (Spring 1995).

4. California Health Dept., 2000.

5. American Heart Association.

6. World Health Organization, *Tobacco Industry Strategies to Undermine Tobacco Control Activities at the World Health Organization* (Geneva: WHO, 2001).

7. For details, see the website www.bigtobaccosucks.com, which documents ongoing issues related to the tobacco companies and tobacco issues. The website is run by the Campaign Against Transnational Tobacco, a project of the Council for Responsible Public Investment.

8. Lloyd Kurtz, "'Mr. Markowitz, Meet Mr. Moskowitz': A Review of Studies on Socially Responsible Investing," in Brian R. Bruce, ed., *The Investment Research Guide to Socially Responsible Investing* (Plano, Tex.: Investment Research Forums, 1998).

9. Ibid.

10. Moskowitz, cited in Kurtz, "'Mr. Markowitz, Meet Mr. Moskowitz.'"

11. Michelle Clayman, "Excellence Revisited," *Financial Analysts Journal* (May/June 1994).

12. This account was relayed to me by Stanley L. Craig, vice president of national sales, Merrill Lynch & Company Unit Investment Trust Department.

13. Donald Trone, William R. Allbright, and Philip R. Taylor, *The Management of Investment Decisions* (Chicago: Irwin, 1996).

14. Ibid., p. 287.

15. Ibid., p. 286.

16. Pava and Krausz, *Corporate Responsibility and Financial Performance: The Paradox of Social Cost* (Westport, Conn.: Greenwood, 1995). pp. 33–34.

17. Ibid., pp. 23–39.

18. Ibid., p. 56.

6

Pension Funds and Fiduciary Responsibility: The SRI Imperative

Pension fund trustees must act in the best interests of the retirees and participants of their retirement plans. If, as we argue in this book, socially responsible investing reduces risks and increases financial returns, trustees must ensure that SRI techniques are used when fund managers make investment decisions. Investing in an SRI manner will be crucial to the long-term perspective that pension funds must consider, as we explain throughout this book.

Trustees thus have a fiduciary obligation to study SRI to verify for themselves if the claim of higher performance is correct. The overwhelming majority of trustees, however, have never considered SRI, and the advisors around them counsel against doing so. Consultants for pension and endowment funds in almost all cases know little about SRI and simply assume that SRI must result in lower performance. However, insistence on investing in corporations that pollute, violate the law, or use child labor while achieving a lower return for one's pension or endowment fund is a clear violation of fiduciary responsibility. This would seem obvious to most people. But even if SRI performs only as well as non-SRI investments the case for requiring pension trustees to move in the direction of SRI can be argued quite effectively.

The Universal Owner

The question of SRI and fiduciary responsibility has been investigated by a handful of pioneers who have seen the logic of a megatrend that could massively change the way pension funds invest money over the coming decades. That trend is the rapid growth of pension funds into majority owners of many large corporations, making them *universal owners*.

Robert A.G. Monks has played a visionary role as the originator of a conceptual trend advocating corporate accountability that could revolutionize how our economy functions. Monks was appointed by the Reagan administration to enforce the Employee Retirement Income Security Act (ERISA) as the Department of Labor's pension administrator. From that position Monks saw with shocking clarity a corporate world that was not guided by the interests of its titular owners or the needs of society. Starting from the framework of corporate governance, Monks began a campaign to make the corporate world accountable and law-abiding. His message: corporations are out of control, pursuing management's own short-term goals in conflict with society's needs and against the interests of their shareholders. Monks has written several books arguing his position, starting with his first and best-known work, *The Emperor's Nightingale: Restoring the Integrity of the Corporation in the Age of Shareholder Activism*; his latest work is *The New Global Investors: How Shareholders Can Unlock Sustainable Prosperity Worldwide*.[1]

It is an interesting coincidence that Robert A.G. Monks sat next to Ralph Nader at Harvard Law School when students were seated in alphabetical order there in the 1950s. Monks began his career as a Republican politician and business executive while Nader became a consumer advocate fighting to protect the public from corporate abuses, but some 50 years later their paths have again converged in the defense of democratic rights. Coming from completely different directions they are both coming to the same conclusion: One way or another, corporations must be held accountable to their stakeholders. Two other thinkers, James P. Hawley and Andrew T. Williams, have recently entered center stage in this discussion with their book *The Rise of Fiduciary Capitalism: How Institutional Investors Can Make Corporate America More Democratic.* Chapter 12 in this volume, "Can Universal Owners Be Socially Responsible Investors?" outlines their views on the logic of the universal owner and socially responsible investing.[2]

The concept of the universal owner, based on the work of Monks, is carefully defined in *The Rise of Fiduciary Capitalism.* Pension funds have become so large that they are in effect owners of the whole economy. According to *Pensions and Investments,* pension funds reached just under $10 trillion in assets at the turn of the millennium. About half of that amount, or $5 trillion, is invested in equities. Pension funds as a group therefore cannot sell their stocks: There is no one else capable of buying them.

All financial assets in the United States in 1997 amounted to approximately $67 trillion. The capitalization of US publicly traded equities obviously changes as markets rise and fall, but has been calculated between $11 trillion and $16 trillion in recent years. Pension fund investments are somewhat concentrated in the largest US companies, and thus control about 33 percent of existing equities. But when combined with other institutional investors such as mutual funds they own 60 percent of each of the largest 1000 US corporations on average and about 50 percent of all firms.[3] This is an enormous shift from the ownership patterns that prevailed 30 years ago.

While many believe that society benefits when firms compete with each other, leading to higher productivity and more efficient allocation of resources, it is absurd for pension funds to compete with each other. Quite the contrary: it is in their interests that they all survive and meet their obligations. Nothing can be gained when one pension fund sells a stock and another pension fund buys it. Pension funds considered as a group simply cannot sell all their equity positions: who could buy them? Equities are historically the most advantageous class of securities, and pension funds own them as a whole, a proxy for the economy. For example, when a pension fund sells a stock, it is often to another pension fund. Sometimes one manager makes the sale while another manager in the same fund is the buyer. I have noticed on occasion at the Contra Costa County Employees' Retirement Fund that when one of our money managers sells a stock another is buying the same company. Thus the fund sees no net change in its asset position, but incurs two transaction fees and a small loss in the bid and ask. On a large scale this phenomenon is being noticed indirectly. Most money managers are unable to beat their benchmarks after fees, so, the funds conclude, why not just index? Trustees have consciously or unconsciously recognized that pension funds are universal owners and that their well-being goes up and down with the market as a whole, or, better put, with the economy as a whole. As of 1996 the largest 200 defined-benefit pension funds had 34.6 percent of their total equities indexed, a percentage that has increased sharply since then.[4]

Often money managers who are hired for their capabilities in a specific discipline become closet indexers because they know that their jobs depend on not underperforming their benchmark for any period of time. The fees paid to managers are astronomical when one considers that the decision process used to manage one account is the same as for all the accounts they are managing. The name of the game is not to get fired once hired. Managers trying to gain accounts will take more risks and open themselves to tracking error to try to outperform for a period in order to replace managers who have fallen below their benchmarks ("tracking error" means the degree to which holdings can be expected to act differently from an index). The logic of universal ownership is thus to index, or at least to use enhanced indexing strategies.

The implications of these facts are profound. As Hawley and Williams explain, "To begin with, because they own the economy as a whole, universal owners should care about the overall health of the economy, not just the economic health of individual firms. In the long run, the performance of their large, diversified portfolios will depend more on the overall performance of the economy than it will on the performance of any individual company in their portfolio." They continue: "Consequently, a universal owner that really wants to maximize the shareholder value of its portfolio would need to develop public policy–like positions and monitor regulatory developments and legislation on a number of key issues to the economy as a whole."[5]

How Can Universal Owners Exercise Their Rights?

The question of how universal owners can exercise their stakeholder/ownership rights is quite complex and will be addressed shortly. But obviously SRI enters here as a step in the direction of maximizing portfolio performance by setting standards that limit negative externalities. This means making investments in companies whose actions do not hurt the broad economy.

Maximizing Corporate-Specific Short-Term Profits

When a company or several companies are able to make exceptional profits at the expense of the economy as a whole (by externalizing their costs), a pension fund's portfolio loses rather than gains *even if it owns stock in the "successful" corporation(s)*. Consider, for example, the case of the energy companies Enron, Calpine, Reliant, and El Paso, which benefited by manipulating energy supplies in California in 2001and in the process caused immense losses to the California economy. These firms actually hurt *their owners*, as well as collaterally hurting the participants and beneficiaries of pension funds, who must pay higher and unnecessary energy bills. Why didn't the owners act to protect their interests? Here is the great failure of pension funds to act as fiduciaries. In most cases pension trustees are not even aware of the issue, much less considering ways they could exercise their power to protect their funds and stakeholders.

Unfortunately, no one has suggested the obvious remedy regarding such firms. The owners, especially the pension funds, could simply remove the directors of, say, El Paso Natural Gas or Enron and replace them with law-abiding, responsible directors who would retain a management that would respect the law and act responsibly as a fiduciary for the owners. Instead, we have seen all kinds of legal negotiations and finger-pointing as politicians and executives in California and across the country try to shift the blame, and expense, to someone else. The power of the pension funds as owners is never mentioned. The only figure who has even dared to approach this topic is Phil Angelides, California's state treasurer.

Comically — if it weren't real money — California Governor Gray Davis rushed to buy long-term energy contracts at exactly the top of the market. He then turned around and in mid 2001 started selling contracts almost exactly at a low after the price of natural gas dropped sharply. In this manner he achieved about an 80 percent loss of the taxpayers' money on some of his purchases. In the process the artificial energy "crisis" destroyed the state budget surplus, depriving local governments of needed funds and weakening California's economy.

The price of natural gas jumped over 400 percent from mid 2000 to late 2000. The amazing artificial price spike in 2001 led Governor Davis to buy long-term commitments to sell natural gas to the state at absurd prices. He made no effort to hedge the state's position, as one would expect when going long into a position several standard deviations off a trend line. The result has been massive financial losses for the taxpayers.

Although the utilities blamed the energy crisis on environmental regulations and increasing demand, the use of electricity in California during the crisis was actually well below its highs (see Figure 6.1). We might well ask how California could have had enough electricity when demand was high but blackouts when demand was much lower.

This is the kind of damage El Paso, Enron, and others created when they sought to make as much profit as fast as possible regardless of the cost to others. Such a policy is held up as exactly what management should do by the "free market" advocates who dominate the landscape in today's world. This point of view prevails among the leadership of both major political parties and provides a self-serving rationale for the managements of companies looking for the largest possible immediate rise in their stock prices so that they can maximize their stock options.

With the purchase in 2001 of Investors Shareholder Services (ISS) by Proxy Monitor there is now a firm that coordinates the voting of $2 trillion

Figure 6.1   California Electricity Usage, 1999–2001

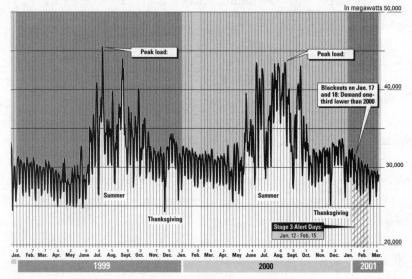

Chart by Christian Berthelsen and Scott Winokur. ©2001 The San Francisco Chronicle.
Reprinted by permission.

of institutional funds. While still at an early stage, the work of ISS and the Interfaith Conference for Corporate Responsibility (ICCR) and similar organizations could lead to the formation of a voting block of owners that could force management in large firms to obey the law and act in an accountable manner to their shareholders and stakeholders. Most pension fund trustees are not even aware of their potential power, or are heavily influenced by a procorporate culture that argues for letting management do whatever it wants.

Corporate Crime: Why No Three Strikes for Corporations?

A study of the 582 largest US corporations covering just a two-year period, 1975–76, revealed that 63.7 percent violated the law.[6] Why this propensity to criminal activity on the part of the foremost economic actors in our nation? The key is the potential profitability of corporate crime and the lack of law enforcement.

It is quite rare for any management personnel or directors of corporations to be imprisoned for criminal activity. Corporations can have felony convictions year after year, and no one goes to jail, no one loses the right to vote or suffers any personal financial penalty. When corporations are caught, they usually suffer a minimal financial penalty, which they consider to be a cost of doing business. Robert A.G. Monks explains the process in these words: "The short-term economic gains from some bad behavior (such as paying less than a living wage) are often higher than the cost of refraining from them. Either the odds of getting caught are low, the fine is less important than the profits from bad behavior, or a combination of the two."[7] In the short term, antisocial behavior often pays.

Mokhiber summarizes his research on the causes of corporate crime in this way: "Since corporate crimes are easy to conceal and all indications are that rates of apprehension are exceedingly low, most major corporations will not be deterred by the types of fines that federal sentencing officials currently are imposing." Those fines according to one study were under $5000 for 80 percent of the cases and only less then 1 percent were over $1million.[8]

Over the last two decades many politicians have run for office and have been elected on a law-and-order platform. Why then has the government been so lax in enforcing the law? Why no "three strikes" law for corporations? The answer is obvious, even though we may not like to acknowledge it. Corporations have been able through their enormous financial power to influence government, including controlling who is elected to such an extent that they are becoming above the law. According to Monks, "The inherent weakness of government in trying to regulate one of its largest sources of revenue is evidenced by the growth in both lobbying and campaign financing by corporations. Government efforts at 'reform' of these processes range from the ludicrous — lawyers weren't 'lobbyists,' for example — to the genuinely tragic escalation of campaign costs to the level where noncorporate involvement is virtually irrelevant." The problem lies in corporations being treated in the legal system as citizens. "Corporate citizenship is a great fallacy. The founding fathers of the American Republic did not contemplate that corporations would be citizens. Indeed, the word 'corporation' is not mentioned in the constitution."[9] The United States is rapidly losing its democratic principle of one person, one vote.

Political action committees (PACs) originated as a way for citizens to combine to promote a common point of view, but this mechanism has been totally distorted by corporate PACs. For instance, the structure of a labor union PAC depends on one person, one vote. Union leaderships may abuse democracy, but the underlying structure is based on people. The same is true for all kinds of citizen organizations. But corporations don't make decisions on the basis of one person, one vote. Corporate PAC contributions are not based on the view of the employees but on shareholder voting, where one person may simply have a majority or a million times more votes than another shareholder. Such PACs should of course be banned, since elections must be based on democratic debate among people, not the influence of money.

Monks quotes a beautiful example of the corruption of democracy through corporate campaign financing from an article in the *Wall Street Journal*. "On the day the Senate killed comprehensive tobacco legislation, Sen. Mitch McConnell stood up at a closed-door meeting of Republican senators to deliver good news: The tobacco industry would mount a television ad campaign to support those who voted to knock off the bill. Such ads, Mr. McConnell says now, 'would be generally helpful to people who decided to kill this bill as a big tax increase on working Americans.'"[10]

Corporations function in a world where the overwhelming majority of people believe in democracy, favor respect for law, oppose corruption and support fairness and equal opportunity, oppose poverty, and want a society with economic stability and a high quality of life. In spite of corporate power, "the market place appears to penalize companies whose functioning affronts societal standards. This raises the cost of capital and tends to make those companies uncompetitive."[11] This last statement is key. SRI is based on a fact that is often underestimated: the power of people, of labor, of environmentalists, of the overwhelming majority who have begun to develop a negative view of corporate power. Antisocial actions and criminal activities on the part of corporations, while possibly profitable in the short run, lead inevitably to negative financial consequences.

The appearance of the universal owner will intensify this process. The long political struggle now beginning around this issue will change the way pensions and other institutional investors act. A battle for fiduciary responsibility is now under way. At this moment there is little understanding of these issues in the world of institutional investment. But as social forces in our nation become increasingly aware of the increasing assets of the pension funds and their potential power, a struggle to use that power to ensure the well-being of society will be unleashed.

Who Owns the Money?

It may seem obvious that pension fund money belongs to the people whose benefits it guarantees. Unfortunately, this is not the view of many. In the state of California a Republican Governor, Pete Wilson, actually raided the state pension fund to balance the state's budget, arguing that since the state guarantees the defined benefit plan it is perfectly reasonable to use any surplus money in that fund for other state needs. The argument is not without a basis. If in the end the state of California guarantees pensioners' retirement benefits, why should it not be considered the owner of the pension funds?

But how real is the state's guarantee? The danger with that position is that the "guarantor"—a state or other government entity, or a corporation—may not be able to cope when a crisis occurs. An economic crisis that could cause a pension fund to default would also weaken the guarantor. Thus using surpluses to protect a fund for rainy days in the future is most likely the prudent course to take respecting the ownership rights of the participants and retirees of those funds. Corporate or governmental guarantees are abstract guarantees because in the end the financial ability of the guaranteeing entity itself cannot be guaranteed. If a financial crisis crushes a pension fund there is little chance a county, city, or state could or would raise taxes to honor its guarantee. This is especially likely if the crisis were national in scope.

As assets accumulate in pension funds, these balances should be used to guarantee payment of pensions to future retirees and, in the case of public funds, to help taxpayers by reducing the subsidy provided by the city, county, or state. In California, this issue of who in the last analysis really controls this money took the form of a new law. The voters adopted an initiative, Proposition 62, that prohibits the kind of action taken by Governor Wilson.

Corporate Pension Fund Raids

Corporations can make changes in their pension funds that on paper reduce their obligations to the funds — for instance, by raising their estimates of future performance. Such moves give the appearance of better financial results for the firm than it would otherwise be able to report. Another kind of manipulation of pension funds by corporations is associated with corporate takeovers. The 1980s saw many corporate takeovers whose advocates argued would improve shareholder value by increasing operational efficiency. But in many cases the purpose of the takeover was really to get a quick profit by scuttling labor contracts, breaking a union, or raiding a pension fund. And these antilabor takeovers were often financed by the money of working people through their own pension funds!

In California such a raid by Texan Charles Hurwitz, with the assistance of Michael Milken, succeeded in taking over Pacific Lumber, now Maxxam Corporation. Hurwitz and Maxxam are probably the most hated person and corporation, respectively, in California, since their objective is to clear-cut our last precious old-growth forests. One of Hurwitz's targets was Pacific Lumber's pension fund. He came close to destroying the entire fund by investing all its assets in Executive Life, a sort of fake insurance company tied to Milken's junk bond business that eventually collapsed financially.

Hurwitz's next target was a $60 million surplus in the workers' pension fund. Hurwitz is still in the courts on that one. He would probably have easily made off with the $60 million if he hadn't violated so many laws to get control of Maxxam that the employees of Pacific Lumber have a chance to save their pension funds. (An excellent book on this battle called *The Last Stand* by David Harris covers part of this story.)[12] The powerful San Francisco law firm Morrison Foerster LLP has represented Hurwitz at every step against the workers' pension fund. On the other side, the employees of Pacific Lumber have the help of local lawyers with far fewer resources.

In mid 2001 leading congressional Republicans proposed to raid the federal employees' pension surplus of $400+ billion to enable them to fund tax cuts proposed by President Bush. Such a proposal would of course be Robin Hood in reverse: The funds set aside for working people would be taken and given in great part to the wealthiest people in the land.

Theories also abound that pension funds should be seen only as loaners of capital to corporations and not as actual owners. All such theories are intended to dispossess working people of what is clearly theirs. If in the future the suggestions of Robert A.G. Monks are implemented and the pension funds begin to exercise their ownership rights we will undoubtedly see corporations try to issue nonvoting shares or engage in other maneuvers to prevent the owners from actually controlling their own firms.

Voting Shares

Today, however, most pension funds pay no attention to how they vote their shares. According to *Institutional Investor*, 72.3 percent of pension funds simply let their money managers vote their shares. Obviously, few if any of these managers will go out of their way to defend the environment or oppose child labor. On the contrary, they simply tend to support current management as part of their corporate culture. *Institutional Investor* reported that only 13.5 percent of funds vote their own proxies. The problem is not time: only 17.6 percent of respondents cite time as an issue. More than one-third of the funds believe that "voting doesn't make a difference." But if that is the case, why not vote for the environment and for social justice?[13]

Only 1.6 percent of pension funds have voted their shares on behalf of social issues. There thus is an incredible opportunity for advocating environmental stewardship and social justice that is being ignored. Appendix C reprints part of the policy my county's pension fund has adopted making support for social and environmental justice our default policy. As our trustees stated, such a policy is "in keeping with [our] fiduciary responsibility."

A Right Without a Remedy

In his book *The New Global Investor,* Robert A.G. Monks accurately characterizes the dilemma that pension fund beneficiaries face: "While the letter and the spirit of the law both require fiduciaries to act exclusively for the benefit of plan participants, the reality is that beneficiaries *have a right without a remedy*" (italics mine). Monks develops this point by noting how difficult it would be for an owner to seek remedy in the courts: "Lawmakers have taken ownership away from the individuals and put it in the hands of trustees, passing trust laws to support this new status. Unfortunately, however, government has failed to enforce those laws and has failed to make a suitable provision for individuals to enforce."[14] Trustees are simply in violation of their fiduciary responsibility, and the laws that require them to carry out their fiduciary responsibility are never enforced. As Michael Calabrese notes, "The Department of Labor has repeatedly stated that ERISA requires pension fiduciaries to regard shareholder voting rights as plan assets and manage them accordingly." But little is done, even though such strategies "have been shown to increase returns to large public plans that pursued" voting their shares.[15]

When Monks refers to a failure to enforce the law he is referring to the duty of trustees to exercise ownership rights on behalf of the owners they represent—that is, on behalf of retirees and future retirees. Criticizing trustees on this issue is easy, but finding solutions to the problem will be quite difficult. To be true fiduciaries, trustees need expert assistance. Smaller pension funds especially find it next to impossible to exercise their ownership responsibilities in a fiduciary manner without outside expertise. No institutions currently offer this kind of consulting service to pension trustees. Such services do not exist in part because there has been no demand for them. Foundations that could help initiate them have not stepped forward because of their own lack of expertise on this issue.

Most trustees are not even aware of the problem. There is a real breakdown in terms of using the power of ownership. Most have not thought about it, while those who have see no solution. Except for very large funds with large staffs it seems impossible to get involved. But funds with large staffs tend to be so heavily influenced by corporations that they will not take the lead on these issues. A vacuum exists in terms of the power of ownership of $10 trillion.

In the epilogue of his book *The Emperor's Nightingale*, Robert A.G. Monks refers to the future as though it were the past and tells the story of the appearance of special purpose trust companies (SPTCs).[16] Such for-profit firms would help institutional investors carry out their fiduciary responsibility. In England, for example, a $55 billion money manager, Friends Ivory & Sime (FIS), has begun offering a service to its institutional investors called Responsible Engagement Overlay (REO). REO is a program through which FIS will interact with the companies their clients own to make sure these corporations act in a manner beneficial to their owners in respect to environmental laws and other similar issues. Recently, FIS has been approached by pension funds that are not their clients but wish to subscribe to the REO service. This is the only service existing today that is somewhat similar to Monks's concept of a special-purpose trust company. As mentioned earlier, the new and combined ISS is voting shares for institutions as a service following guidelines determined by pension funds or other trustees.

Joseph Keefe in New Hampshire has established a firm called New Circle Communications (NCC) to act as a consultant to help corporations pass SRI screens. In California a group of elected officials that I helped bring together into a coalition around the issue of responsible public investments led to the formation of the Council for Responsible Public Investments (CRPI). The council has received funding from the Health Department of California to help educate the public on tobacco divestment issues (see the website www.bigtobaccosucks.com). The CRPI Board of Directors includes representatives from the Tobacco Free Coalition, American Heart Association, American Lung Association, Social Investment Forum, labor and foundations. If one combines the kind of services offered by NCC, ICCR, CRPI, ISS, and REO, one can see the embryo of organizations that offer services to help trustees be effective fiduciaries.

The Coming Battle for Fiduciary Responsibility

The conflict between the drive of corporations to seek short-term maximization of profits, if need be by externalizing costs or violating the law, and the need of the world economy for long-term planning to protect natural equity, create a sustainable economy, and protect the quality of life on the planet will be partly played out in terms of pension and endowment funds exercising their ownership power.

As large concentrated ownership declines and pension funds with their highly disbursed and indirect ownership begin to dominate, corporate managements have begun to feel quite independent of the owners. They have increasingly begun to simply expropriate profits for themselves. Pension funds are slowly becoming increasingly concerned as this process grows more and more extreme.

Working Capital, the quarterly newsletter of the Center for Working Capital (a pro–working class nonprofit group), reported startling figures in its summer 2001 issue on CEO compensation: "As stock prices tumbled last year, executive pay packages at many public companies scaled new and dizzying heights. According to the *New York Times,* the average CEO took home a record-breaking $20 million — nearly 50 percent more in stock options and 22 percent more in salary and bonus than in 1999.... As another measure of comparison, according to *Business Week,* CEO salaries were 531 times the average blue-collar worker's salary in 2000, up from 85 times in 1990."[17]

This is an abuse of shareholders and other stakeholders. Most of this compensation is through stock options. Top executives know precisely when to sell since they have the best information on when the performance of their firm may be topping out. Executives will often maneuver to position their firm's stock for a sharp upward run in earnings for a 24-month period or so. The stock share price rises in response to higher earnings, and they sell their holdings and cash out their options. Then the company returns to a lower, more normal level of growth, and the share price falls back, sometimes significantly. The effect of this exercise is a transfer of wealth from shareholders to the top management. Managers clearly violate their fiduciary responsibility to the shareholders by engaging in such maneuvers, but most compensation packages for top executives in effect encourage such conduct.

A recent example is the collapse of Enron. As it turns out, Enron was faking its figures and balance sheet to a point that has led to the total collapse of this once-huge firm. Its stock price has declined from $90 a share to less than $1. But its top management had their hands in the till, taking out hundreds of millions of dollars in "bonuses" in the weeks before the firm declared bankruptcy. CEO Kenneth Lay, a close friend of President Bush and advisor to California, made off with $300 million in stock options while 75 Enron management "traders" were each being paid $5 million a year.[18] Charges have also been made that $1.1 billion was taken through insider trading. Loses in Enron run as high as $100 million for some pension funds.

When one combines the confiscation of profits by management with their short-term focus and efforts to externalize costs, it becomes clear that a deep conflict is brewing due to the lack of fiduciary oversight of ownership. One rough estimate of the total externalities created by corporations puts the figure at $2.6 trillion a year in 1994 dollars.[19] Speaking of this issue, Hawley and Williams state, "This is particularly true for public pension employee retirement funds. Here, the cost of a narrow focus on profit maximization may not only reduce long-term portfolio returns, but may affect beneficiaries as citizens either directly as a result of the action or indirectly through its effect on their tax bill." SRI by its very nature acts as a partial control mechanism against such abuses. SRI focuses on investing in corporations with good corporate governance, respect for shareholders and stakeholders, and long-term business plans.

The labor movement is one player in this drama that is rapidly coming to realize just how high the stakes are. Labor unions have recently taken increasing interest in the influence they could wield on the pension funds of their members. A remarkable book titled *Working Capital: The Power of Labor's Pensions,* edited by Archon Fung, Tessa Hebb, and Joel Rogers, covers many of these issues for the labor movement.[20] As we begin the new century an alliance is forming among the labor movement, the SRI community, health advocates, environmentalists, and others around these issues. I foresee a political struggle in the years to come as more and more people become aware that shareholders and stakeholders are becoming one and the same. Increasingly the people who own corporations are the same people who work for corporations, so seeking profits at the expense of employees is for them as owners self-defeating. The concept of the universal owner will make the labor movement and the trustees influenced by it more aware of their fiduciary responsibility to protect the long-term well-being of society.

Although it may not yet be evident, this issue will be expressed politically. As Robert A.G. Monks puts it, "Short of declaring pension and securities laws a massive fraud perpetrated on American workers and shareholders, only one solution seems feasible: the government must act to enforce those laws for the good of all."[21] Sooner or later this issue will become part of a political battle, because in the end politics is nothing but concentrated economics.

Corporate Governance

Shareholder activism on corporate governance started with the largest pension funds some years ago but is now beginning to spill over into dealing with social and environmental issues. At first the administration of these large funds considered corporate governance issues only as they related to the financial performance of their funds. They mistakenly failed to see the connection between social and environmental issues and bottom-line performance. For example, CalPERS CEO Dale Hanson announced this position on corporate governance: "At CalPERS, corporate governance is about making money, not changing the political or social environment."[22]

The failure to see social and environmental issues as an aspect of corporate governance with important financial impacts remains a problem at many of the larger funds. However, pressure from their trustees has forced the staff at CalPERS to consider adopting the Sullivan Principles to apply to their investments in the Third World as well as other social issues, including sending trustees to visit corporations such as El Paso that have questionable policies.

In general the bureaucracy at pension funds, the "administration," is backward on these issues. Pension administrators as a whole were strongly opposed to divestment from South Africa. Today most oppose divestment from tobacco. The fear of change is part of the problem. More important is the predominance of what Hawley and Williams refer to as corporate co-optation: "The problem of the potential co-optation of fiduciary institutions by the corporations they are supposed to monitor does represent serious problems."[23]

The battle for the owners, working people, to exercise their ownership in their own interest will require trustees willing to be independent from the corporate world and willing to retain an administrative staff sympathetic to the interests of the retirees and participants. The pro-corporate culture is deeply entrenched today, but working people have many of the needed vehicles to regain control of their own money and make sure it is invested on their behalf. The Social Investment Forum, the labor unions, and major health and environmental organizations should seek to educate trustees, train trustees, and help get trustees elected or appointed who will act in a fiduciary manner on pension funds. Up to now the education of trustees has been primarily in the hands of procorporate forces.

As a trustee I have been shocked to see how the privatize-everything, short-term-profits, globalization-is-great ideology dominates even the world of public pension funds. In California, 20 county public pension funds function under a law called the 1937 Act. These 20 funds have an association called State Association of County Retirement Systems

(SACRS). The association has conferences twice a year to educate trustees and provide them with a forum where they can discuss the issues before their funds. At one SACRS conference, however, two speakers, attorney Virginia Gibson of Baker & Mckenzie and Chris Cesare, a consultant from Barra Roger Casey, were invited to speak as experts on socially responsible investing. Chris Cesare, who works as the financial consultant for San Diego County, informed the trustees that the Domini Social Index had underperformed the S&P 500 — though anyone with the most minimal knowledge on SRI knows that exactly the opposite is true. For her part, Virginia Gibson quoted the inaccuracies that had appeared in Palmeri's *Business Week* article (see chapter 3) as proof that SRI underperforms. She further argued that if a fund divests tobacco stocks it could be sued or loose its tax-exempt status. The truth, of course, is that trustees will not be sued or lose their tax-exempt status on the basis of the tobacco divestment issue regardless of whether they divest or not. If there were a danger, however, it would be for *not* divesting, based on the possibility that the tobacco companies might collapse because of legal action or a medical discovery that cured nicotine addiction.

This kind of scare tactic is typical in the pension world. Gibson never referred to the major studies on the legal issues around tobacco divestment—for example, the study carried out by the Investors Responsibility Research Center (IRRC) and another by the Technical Assistance Legal Center (TALC). IRRC is a major research group in Washington, D.C. that specializes in researching such issues. TALC provides legal advice on tobacco issues for the California Health Department. Neither study, of course, supports the claim that funds that divested tobacco stocks would be legally liable in any way.

I should add that Chris Cesare called me after the conference to apologize for getting his figures wrong, and I believe in the future he will try to educate himself on SRI before offering to speak on the topic. Both Cesare and Gibson are quite knowledgeable on other issues. What is typical in this example, however, is how socially responsible investing is considered something to be dismissed out of hand. Fortunately, at that meeting several people protested the inaccuracy of this information, including a representative from the AFL-CIO funds. Interest in SRI increased, since for once the typical dismissal of it was challenged, and a workshop on SRI, which I helped organize, was held at the May 2001 SACRS conference with speakers from the SRI industry — the first time that any formal US pension fund association had invited pro-SRI firms to speak to trustees in a formal setting as a legitimate investment current.

Earlier in December 1999 I helped launch an all-day educational meeting on SRI attended by trustees from several funds. This was to my knowledge the first-ever educational forum of its kind in the United States. Since that first effort I have helped organize educational conferences for trustees in Vermont at the request of the city of Burlington, and in Hawaii working with Ian Chan Hodges of Responsible Markets and several indigenous leaders. At both meetings a group of professional representatives from the SRI community made compelling presentations on all the issues regarding SRI, including its financial performance. In Hawaii the conference led to the state's legislature adoption of a resolution in support of SRI as the guiding principle of public investment in Hawaii. The lieutenant-governor of Hawaii, Mazie K. Hirono, has assisted in forming the Hawaii Capital Stewardship Forum to advise on implementation of the pro-SRI resolution. These steps make Hawaii the first governmental entity to declare its public support for SRI as an investment goal. (See Appendix D outlining these developments in Hawaii.)

Labor and Environmentalists

There has been an increasing convergence of the labor movement and environmentalists. As the labor movement has come to understand that jobs depend on the environment it is starting to reject its original stance that one had to balance the two. Meanwhile, environmentalists are starting to see the labor movement as an ally in the struggle against rapidly developing international institutions like the World Bank, the World Trade Organization, and NAFTA that roll back environmental protections.

Adoption of this new perspective remains uneven, however, as can be seen in the case of a mutual fund launched by prolabor forces in Massachusetts called the Massachusetts Financial Services Union Standard Equity Fund. A labor advisory board was set up to help guide the fund, which requires that 65 percent of the companies selected be "labor sensitive." The fund has grown to over $100 million in assets. But a closer look at this fund shows that when it was launched its largest holding was Philip Morris. More recently, among its five largest holdings were General Electric, Exxon, and Philip Morris.

Mitchell Dynan, the portfolio manager of the fund, appears to see these firms as labor-friendly. Such a view is, however, myopic: these are not labor-friendly firms. Exxon is currently being accused by labor organizations of working with and funding Indonesia's military to repress workers' organizing campaigns, including the use of torture and murder. Exxon's long history of disregard of environmental laws is legendary, with all its negative impact on the economic well-being of working people. Philip Morris is out trying to addict teenagers throughout the Third World to tobacco and using child labor in many countries to produce its addictive drug.[24] General Electric is one of the most criminally inclined firms in the world, with a criminal record that goes back decades. In the US alone it has successfully stolen millions of dollars from the taxpayers. These crimes include overcharging the US government by falsifying time cards, accepting bribes and repeatedly overcharging in sales of military equipment, faking a simulated crash test, hiding faulty parts and thus risking people's lives, and violating patents. In a few cases some of its management ended in jail, but most of GE's crimes are so carefully calculated that even if it gets caught the fines amount to less than the company's gains.

It is not surprising the MFS Union Standard Equity Fund is not considered socially responsible by most everyone in the SRI community. Moreover, the fund's performance has been terrible: it has received the lowest Morningstar rating possible, a one-star rating— something quite rare for an SRI mutual fund.

A group of Canadian venture capital funds that are truly social provides an opposite example to the MFS Fund. In a complex process through which certain advantages are given to trade union–backed venture funds in Canada several such funds have come into existence. Only five of them are truly prolabor and social, while the others were launched by corporate venture funds renting-a-union to meet legal requirements.

The prolabor funds engage in social audits that "screen out ... poor labor relations, dangerous environmental practices, and disregard for consumers and communities."[25] Procorporate funds see these screens as obstacles to achieving the best possible returns. But the financial results according to Tessa Hebb in *Working Capital* say otherwise. The five prolabor environmental funds came in with an average return 785 basis points (7.85 percentage points) higher than the procorporate funds — once again confirming the superior performance of SRI. The MFS Fund reflects how labor looked at these issues 30 years ago, while the five Canadian venture funds mentioned above reflect today's outlook, which emphasizes the unity of labor, environmental, health, and other social interests.

Mission-Driven Investing

Stephen Viederman, the former executive director of the Jesse Smith Noyes Foundation, has argued that foundations should adopt the concept of mission-driven investing. This concept is quite straightforward: foundations, like labor unions and pension funds, should invest in harmony with their objectives. For example, an environmental organization that asks people to care about the environment when they make purchases or political decisions should also care about the impact of its own investments on the environment. Surprisingly, most environmental organizations with endowment funds do not care where their own investments go. I have personally met with many of the major environmental organizations (I won't mention their names here to avoid embarassing them), but have failed to convince them that they should place an environmental screen on their own portfolios. Their resistance to making their own investment decisions in concert with their missions has been amazing. Sadly, they have also given up financial performance by bending to Wall Street's prejudice against SRI.

Viederman has toured the nation repeatedly, speaking at conference after conference and everywhere noting the simple fact that no loss of return should be expected or suffered by those who have followed the example of the Noyes Foundation in adopting a mission-driven investment policy. As a result of his work there has recently been a pickup of interest in mission-driven investing in the foundation world. Once awareness sets in of the interrelationship between SRI, performance, and our long-term goals for the economy and environment there should be a growing trend among foundations to adopt SRI. (See chapter 15, "Foundations and Mission-Related Investing," by Stephen Viederman.)

Steps Trustees Can Take Now

There are several steps trustees who recognize the importance of understanding SRI and the issues of universal ownership can take to help begin the process of educating their boards on these issues. Trustees should try to attend educational conferences on SRI — though they may have to look for such conferences on their own since administrators tend to exclude SRI conferences from the choices they present to trustees for their attendance. This certainly was the experience our firm went through as we tried to notify trustees who might have wished to attend the quite successful "Bottom Line: The Future of Fiduciary Responsibility" conference held in San Francisco in April 2001.

Encourage your board to hold a special educational afternoon and have a panel of experts from SRI firms make presentations. Try to learn from them about the changes now taking place in England and Australia. In those two countries all pension funds have been requested by the government to establish SRI policies in writing. A majority of the funds have done so in the UK. Several countries in Europe are discussing adoption of similar policies.

Voting your shares in support of what will benefit your retirees and participants as well as taxpayers and society as a whole should not be such a difficult decision. There are firms with quite reasonable fees who can handle the voting of your shares.

Notes

1. Robert A.G. Monks, *The Emperor's Nightingale: Restoring the Integrity of the Corporation in the Age of Shareholder Activism* (Reading, Mass.: Addison-Wesley, 1998); and *The New Global Investors: How Shareholders Can Unlock Sustainable Prosperity Worldwide* (Oxford: Capstone, 2001).

2. James P. Hawley and Andrew T. Williams, *The Rise of Fiduciary Capitalism: How Institutional Investors Can Make Corporate America More Democratic* (Philadelphia: University of Pennsylvania Press, 2000), p. 167.

3. Ibid.

4. Ibid., p. 7.

5. Ibid., p. 170.

6. Russell Mokhiber, *Corporate Crime and Violence: Big Business Power and the Abuse of Public Trust* (San Francisco: Sierra Club Books, 1988), p. 18.

7. Monks, *New Global Investors,* p. 47.

8. Mokhiber, *Corporate Crime,* pp. 30, 31.

9. Monks, *New Global Investors,* p. 45.

10. Ibid., p. 57.

11. Ibid., p. 59.

12. David Harris, *The Last Stand: The War Between Wall Street and Main Street over California's Ancient Redwoods* (San Francisco: Sierra Club Books, 1996).

13. "Passing the Buck II," *Institutional Investor,* October 2000.

14. Monks, *New Global Investors,* p. 6.

15. Michael Calabrese, "Building on Success: Labor-Friendly Investment Vehicles and the Power of Private Equity," in Archon Fung, Tessa Hebb, and Joel Rogers, eds., *Working Capital: The Power of Labor's Pensions* (Ithaca, N.Y.: ILR Press of Cornell Univ. Press, 2001), p. 117.

16. Monks, *The Emperor's Nightingale,* pp. 195–217.

17. *Working Capital* 4:3 (Summer 2001), p. 1.

18. *Barron's,* Dec. 3, 2001, p. 3.

19. Monks, *New Global Investors,* p. 149.

20. Archon Fung, Tessa Bebb, and Joel Rogers, *Working Capital: The Power of Labor's Pensions* (Ithaca, N.Y.: ILR Press of Cornell University Press, 2001).

21. Monks, *New Global Investors,* p. 133.

22. Hawley and Williams, *Fiduciary Capitalism,* p. 103.

23. Ibid., p. 175.

24. For additional information on the international tobacco companies and their practices, see the website www.bigtobaccosucks.com.

25. Tessa Hebb and David Mackenzie, "Canadian Labour-Sponsored Investment Funds: A Model for US Economically Targeted Investments," in Fung et al., *Working Capital,* p. 142.

7

SRI for the Individual Investor

The outperformance of SRI provides individual investors with opportunities on three levels. Using SRI mutual funds both lowers your risk and increases the long-term return on your money. Moreover, when they vote their shares SRI mutual funds help push corporations in a law-abiding and environmentally responsible direction. The funds will vote against abuses of pay for top management, demand respect for environmental laws, and insist that firms pay a living wage and respect unions. By becoming an SRI investor you help to create the kind of world we all want to live in — and you do so without sacrificing return or taking on additional risk.

Asset Allocation

The key for you as an individual investor is to make sure that your asset allocation is appropriate for you based on your personal situation. This point cannot be overemphasized. Asset allocation means placing the funds you have in a manner that diversifies your holdings. Nothing lowers risk more than an appropriate diversification, especially if your asset allocation includes assets that do not correlate. (Note that SRI is not a kind of asset allocation. It is a screening overlay on your investments.) Noncorrelating assets are those assets that do not act in the same way in the market. For instance, stocks and Treasury bills do not correlate. Treasury bills do not move up or down with stock prices, but instead more or less gradually appreciate as they earn interest.

Asset allocation means considering what percentage of your funds should be in stocks, real estate, bonds, or other investments, as well as diversification within each type of investment. Your stock investments may include what are called "growth" stocks or "value" stocks. They may also include large-, mid- and small-capitalization stocks. You may want to own some stocks that are focused in one specific area, such as alternative energy or technology. The key is to diversify your investments and to make them long term.

Professional Advice

In recent years investing has become almost a national mania. The development of the Internet has led to an enormous amount of advertising suggesting that anyone can learn how to invest just by opening an account with an online service. Unfortunately, most of this publicity focuses on the idea of trading. Millions follow CNBC not to learn how to make a ten-year investment but how to discern an investment that can be flipped three days later for a quick profit. The appearance of "day trading" is only the most extreme form of this mania. On the one hand, you have people incorrectly thinking that they are going to succeed by trading online based on very limited knowledge, and on the other you still have large numbers of people who see investing as something too complicated to learn.

Most people remain a bit intimidated by the topic of investing — which is why some of them look for quick, easy answers. Like medicine, you do not become a doctor by reading a few books. It is not wise to try and treat yourself if you are sick based on hearsay or minimal knowledge. But the truth is that the basics of investing are not so complicated. Our educational system has failed to provide education on investing for the public. For decades investing was considered something only for the children of the rich. But the fact is that one way or another a very large percentage of the population faces investment decisions.

Time and Value

A person who earns a salary of $70,000 a year and suddenly inherits $300,000 often does not understand the issue of money and time. They will work 40 hours a week for 50 weeks a year for $70,000. That amounts to pay at $35 an hour. Their $300,000 invested at 7 percent will earn them $21,000 a year, but will they spend even 40 hours a year working on earning that $21,000? That would be making over $500 an hour. Most people do not take the time to learn the basics of investing, and they should do so for self-protection — primarily protection from themselves.

Here's some simple advice, based on my 17 years of experience as a broker. Learn the terminology of investing from a good book on the basics, and in particular study the concept of asset allocation. A good book to start with is Samuel Case's *Investing for Beginners*.[1] Learn what terms like *mutual fund, closed end fund, stock, preferred stock, bonds, notes, futures,* and *options* mean. Learn the basic principles of asset allocation. Once you have a general understanding of asset allocation you should work with a professional who has learned both through study and experience how to set an appropriate asset allocation for you and how to adjust it over time, as well as how to implement your asset allocation plans.

Patience

The next most important aspect of being successful with your investments is to avoid letting your emotions take over. Patience is the key. Unless you decide to give up return by investing only in CDs or Treasury bills you are going to suffer from the twin dangers of investing, fear and greed.

Everyone involved in the industry has suffered from both and made mistakes because of them. That's because it is very hard to learn that most of the time you must do the opposite of what your emotions tell you.

The best time to buy stocks is when they are down, when everyone is panicking and selling them. With few exceptions, investors tend to want to sell when stocks are cheap. When the market is running up and you are doing well few people want to sell. The single greatest error I personally have made has been not to take profits. Do not let it bother you after taking profits that your investment continues higher. Look at the chart of any stock over a long-term period and you will realize how volatile stocks are. After a major move up, almost all stocks will offer you another opportunity to invest within two or three years. The key is to sell part of your holdings in a timely manner because there is another basic concept you should also respect and that is to follow trends. Let your winners run, but only partially.

No advisor you work with will always be right — or they would not be working for you as your advisor. No one can buy at the bottom and sell at the top all the time. Those who attempt to time the market more often than not end up getting it wrong. Therefore long-term investing with patience is the key. But there is a way to adjust your portfolio to take advantage of rises and drops in the market.

Market Timing

There are hotlines offered by people who claim to tell you whether the market will go up or down each day. But think about it: If they really knew what direction the market would take they would be so rich that they would not need (or want) to let anyone else in on the secret. But there is a simple way for you to ensure that you buy when stocks are down and sell when they are up. The answer is the same as our first point in investing. Establish a clear asset allocation. Let me explain why this program works.

Let's say you invest $100,000 as follows: 40 percent in bonds and 60 percent in stocks. This ratio is often referred to as a balanced account. (There are mutual funds, called balanced funds, that follow such a policy. Two excellent SRI balanced funds are Pax World and Winslow Balanced Fund.) What happens to your portfolio of 40 percent bonds and 60 percent stocks when stocks go up? Your funds are no longer 40 percent bonds and 60 percent stocks. For argument's sake, let's say that the value of your stocks doubled while the value of your bonds rose by only 10 percent over a period of time.

Your portfolio has grown and its allocation is now 27 percent bonds and 73 percent stocks. Your $40,000 in bonds is now $44,000. Your stocks have doubled in value, so they are now worth $120,000, for a total portfolio value of $164,000. The market is up and you are happy about your investments. Everyone you talk to is happy (and driven by greed in anticipation of further investment gains to come, not by fear that their investments might fall in value).

When you do your annual review with your investment advisor, you point out that your account is not 40 percent bonds and 60 percent stocks, as originally planned. To reset your portfolio to its original asset allocation you will have to sell stocks and buy bonds. A good advisor will suggest that you reduce your investment in stocks and increase your holdings in bonds. But at this point, many people are inclined to do exactly the opposite. The stocks are working fine — why not increase them? Greed takes over, and you set yourself up for a major mistake. Keeping with your original asset allocation will protect you from yourself.

What happens if the market drops sharply — as it did starting in March 2001? Let's say that your stocks drop in value by half while your bonds have increased by 10 percent. You now have $44,000 in bonds and only $30,000 in stocks, for a total of $74,000. You are now 59 percent in bonds and only 41 percent in stocks. When you review your account, you find that you need to readjust it by selling bonds and buying stocks. Now you will be buying stocks when they are low and doing so prudently by making only an adjustment. You are still keeping 40 percent of the value of your portfolio in bonds.

At the moment you adjust your asset allocation to buy stocks most people are filled with fear. Their account is dropping in value. Their emotions drive them to want to increase their bonds because bonds are "OK"; their value is not declining. Remember: Your emotions always point you in the wrong direction. If you stick to an asset allocation you will tend to do the right thing over time.

Again, note carefully in the above example that if you follow your asset allocation you will be selling stocks when they are up and buying when they are low. You do not need to try to time the market; the market will do that for you.

Letting Winners Run

Most people have heard the Wall Street advice to "stop out your losers" and to "let your winners run." In general this advice is correct. Making adjustments as outlined above will overall allow winners to run. When you sell stocks that run up in value you do not sell all your position, you just readjust your position, the amount of your holdings, down. If you are using mutual funds, you assume that the mutual fund manager will follow a policy of letting your winners run. However, if you have a portfolio of specific stocks and you need to lower your allocation in stocks you should sell those that are not working out and partially lower your position in those that are working well for you. That is the most prudent manner to invest. For highly volatile stocks, it is almost always prudent to lower your position whenever a major rise takes place.

If I had to classify when clients are most upset about their portfolio it is, of course, when an account is down. It may be surprising to know that clients also become upset when advisors try to sell winners. The kind of advisor you want is one who is always trying to buy when the market is down and sell when it is high — essentially the opposite of what you will feel emotionally and the advice you will receive from friends.

It is well known that the public tends to buy near tops and sell near bottoms. This tendency is so pronounced that a recent study shows that the average mutual fund investor gained only 5.32 percent per year from 1984 through 2000 — a period when the S&P 500 had a return of 16.3 percent and the average mutual fund came in only about 1 percent below the S&P 500.[2] The key to avoiding such a disparity in performance is have a clear discipline based on an appropriate asset allocation — and to stick to it.

Age

Your age is a key variable in determining your asset allocation. Most advisors will offer more aggressive advice to a 25-year-old than to a 65-year-old. Conversely, someone who is 65 years old should be heavily in safer income-oriented investments as compared to a 25-year-old. That approach is fine, but my experience has led me to believe that it is smart to create a conservative portfolio sector for any investor regardless of his or her age. Having a conservative sector in your portfolio can help you get through unexpected financial problems. Adjusting an asset allocation works very well over time. If a 25-year-old has no safe sector, the volatility of the market will tend to be terrifying and thus lead to errors in judgment. The danger of buying at tops and selling at bottoms is a common mistake among young and inexperienced investors.

Hybrid Asset Allocations

Some investments combine the best qualities of different asset classes, and these hybrids can be of great value when designing a portfolio. A good example of a hybrid is an index note. Index notes are actually corporate debt, not a stock, and therefore would appear in your asset allocation as bonds. Index notes are bond-like instruments that are called notes because they are issued only for durations of five to ten years (bonds are debt instruments with longer maturity periods).

Instead of paying interest, index notes return only your original investment and roughly whatever a stock index did for a period of time. For example, let's assume that the S&P 500 is at 1200. A corporation like Merrill Lynch might offer the public an index note with a term of, say, five years and sell it like a stock at $10 a share. Merrill Lynch would guarantee that five years later you will receive at least $10 for this index note. Merrill Lynch would also offer to pay as interest when the note matures an amount equal to how much the S&P 500 rose during those five years starting from 1250.

An index note like the one in our hypothetical Merrill Lynch example gives you an advantage. If the market tanks and the S&P 500 drops to 600 (a 50 percent drop) you still get all your money back. If the S&P 500 rises to 2400 (a 100 percent increase) you will receive a gain of about 95 percent. You have eliminated the risk to your principal unless Merrill Lynch as the issuer goes under, a rather unlikely event. Your gain in most cases is not the entire rise of the market but it is a large portion of it.

Are index notes socially responsible? That's a good question. At Progressive Asset Management, we analyze them as debt instruments of the issuing firms. Most of those firms pass light screens. Some SRI investors might not be so generous with some of them. The indexes themselves of course include stocks that any screen would eliminate, and if index notes are defined as a basket of those stocks they could not pass a social screen. We would love to have an index note based on one of the SRI indexes like the Domini 400 Social Index but they do yet not exist. Such SRI index notes can be issued once long-term options on the SRI indexes exist.

Let's go back to our example of asset allocation of 40 percent in bonds and 60 percent in stocks. The market has dropped. We want to sell bonds and buy stocks, but we are apprehensive. (As I write this chapter we are in this exact situation.) So we sell some of our bond holdings, but instead of increasing our exposure to stocks by investing in a stock mutual fund or specific stocks we buy an index note. Now we have dissolved the tension between fear and greed. When the market is down, we know that we should buy stocks, but our fear tells us to stay in bonds. So what do we do? We buy a bond-like instrument (thus protecting our principal), but we will get a stock-like return if the market turns upward. This is the kind of situation where working with a professional can make quite a difference. Most people become paralyzed as the value of their portfolio declines in a market drop and they cannot handle the pressure to take advantage of the situation. Index notes make it easier to move your asset allocation toward stocks.

Another example of a hybrid is a convertible bond. These are in some ways even better than index notes in terms of their upward potential, but they usually have higher risk since they are not what is called "investment grade." Convertible bonds are bonds with a special kicker. Here's an example. Wind River, a software company specializing in embedded software, issued a convertible. The bond is due to mature in August 2002 and has a total maturity of about five years. The bond paid 5 percent. If you invested $10,000 in this bond you made 5 percent each year on your money or $500 per year. But you also had the right to change your mind after you bought the bond and say, no, I want to spend the $10,000 buying Wind River stock at $32 a share. The offer to convert remains in effect until the bond matures.

Wind River is at $15 a share as I am writing this, so you would just hold on to your bond and you would receive your principal plus your interest in August 2002. But if Wind River ran up to $60 or more — something it did for a period while the convertible bond existed — you could have turned your bond ($10,000 worth in this example) into stock at $32 and immediately sold it for over $60 a share, receiving on top of that the 5 percent the bond was paying while you waited to convert into the stock – an almost 100 percent profit. Is there any risk involved? If Wind River went out of business you could lose everything — in this example, all $10,000. Like any corporate bond, the corporation must be able to pay the bond off, so your real risk depends on the credit worthiness of the issuing corporation.

Managed Futures

The word *futures* generally scares people. It sounds like something quite risky. Most people find it surprising to learn that at least some managed futures companies offer quite high returns, higher on average than the stock market, and have less volatility (read risk) than the stock market. For example, the largest of the managed future companies, Campbell, claims on its website a return of over 15 percent per year over a 28-year period.

One of the most interesting aspects of managed futures is that they have zero correlation with stocks. There is no relationship between the motions of the stock market and the ups and downs of managed future accounts. Thus, if over time you make money combining the two you lower risk and reduce volatility. Managed futures companies are in the business of following trends in currencies, interest rates, and other futures contracts. The role they play in the economy is to act as insurance companies to help create liquidity where companies are hedging their business. For instance, a US company that wants to do business in Germany will hedge the euro to protect its German investments. Managed futures companies will take the other side of this trade. In effect, they are insuring the US company so it can do business in euros.

There are many other examples that could be raised. In developing an asset allocation it is important to look at many of your choices and design a portfolio that offers advantages and protection for a long and consistent potential. Using SRI in your choice of mutual funds and working with financial advisors knowledgeable in SRI will add an elemental advantage as mentioned above. Before I show you some examples of putting together an asset allocation and what a portfolio might look like using SRI mutual funds, let's look at another important question you may want to consider when determining an appropriate asset allocation.

A Long-Term Bull Market

Over the long term, the US stock market has been a bull market. You would always have made money in the market if you held all stocks over a 40-year period. Most theories of investing work on the premise that the future will be at least somewhat like the past. Will this pattern ever change? No one knows for sure, of course, but many people suspect that some day it may indeed shift.

Pension funds aim to exist for 100 years or more — in effect, indefinitely — and assume that asset classes will continue to provide the kinds of returns they have on average in the past over long periods of time. The SRI community is concerned that if we do not begin to shift our economy back toward harmony with the environment (which supports the economy by offering all kinds of services for free, such as converting CO_2 back into oxygen), we could one day see the economy, and therefore the stock market, suffer a long-term decline. Discussing this issue is beyond the scope of this book. What we emphasize here is that investing in companies that are moving the economy in the right direction on this issue gives an investor an advantage. (See chapter 14, "SRI and Energy: Scenes from a Revolution," by Samuel Case.)

But we must take into account long-term market trends even assuming that overall things remain the same. Although I do not believe you should try to time the market when you set up your asset allocation it may be of value on the margin to note whether we have been in a bear market or bull market and for how long. The pattern is that macro bull markets last longer then bear markets. And there are short-term counter-patterns within any major trend.

The last third of the twentieth century was marked by a macro bear market from 1966 to 1982, followed by a macro bull market. Adjusted for inflation, the Dow, for instance, dropped over 70 percent during the 1966–82 bear market. Since 1982 there has been a strong bull market during which the Dow has risen from about 770 to over 10,000. But amazing as it may sound, the inflation-adjusted Dow did not return to its 1966 value until 1996! Most people are unaware of this simple fact.

This fact would imply that it is highly unlikely that this bull market is over even though since March 2000 we have had a strong bear market. The bubble in Internet stocks and the overvaluation of technology stocks have now corrected. But are we in a macro bear market that will last ten years or more like the 1966–82 bear market? No one knows for sure, of course, but I do not believe so.

In any case, the important point is that we are not at the beginning of a bull market: The bull market kicked off in 1982, almost 20 years ago. Thus, in designing an asset allocation you might want to be a bit more conservative than you would have been in the early 1980s after a 16-year bear market. In his book *The Roaring 2000s,* Harry Dent argues that demographics are influencing this bull market. He points out that whenever there is a bubble in the population of an age group the market tends to rise as they reach a certain maximum earning age. These figures top out in 1966, bottom in 1982, and then top out 2008–10 as the post–World War II baby boomers reach their career maximum in earnings.[2]

Attempts to find simple solutions like this for market trends almost always prove wrong. But given how well this hypothesis has worked it would be prudent to become a bit more cautious as we approach the end of this decade. The point is to set up a reasonable asset allocation. Do not base it on your guesses as to when bull and bear markets will start or end, but keep in mind where you are in the big picture. As we prepare this book we are in a 20-year-old macro bull market going through a strong short-term bear market that has led to the largest drop ever in NASDAQ stocks. Probably this is a good buying period, because even if I am wrong and we are in a macro bear market there will be many bull runs within the bear run and your asset allocation adjustments will help you lock in profits after each major move up in the market.

Examples of Asset Allocations

Let's create three example asset allocations to give you an idea of what they might look like and some of the variables involved. We'll use some SRI mutual funds to help us design each allocation, in this case for a hypothetical 45-year-old couple earning between them $100,000 a year and having $250,000 to invest. In the real world, of course, these examples would need to be adjusted for a range of specific information about this couple, such as how many children they have, whether they own their home, how much equity they have in the home, whether they will inherit money, and when. The answers to any of these questions can make us want to make shifts in the asset allocation.

Table 7.1   Asset Allocation

Cash reserves		5 percent
Bonds		25 percent
Equities		50 percent
Large caps	25 percent	
Mid & small caps	15 percent	
International	10 percent	
Managed futures		10 percent
Special situations		10 percent

It's usually good to have a healthy cash reserve. Most people separate their cash reserves from their portfolio and keep cash in their bank account to deal with unexpected needs so they do not to have to disturb the long-term goals of their portfolio.

Bonds could be a mixture of government agency paper, maybe using closed-end funds, CDs, corporate bonds, or bond mutual funds such as the Calvert SRI funds. You might want to consider a more aggressive sector investment such as Diane Keefe's high-yield bond mutual fund from Pax World for a part of the portfolio. In equities (stocks) we could use for large caps the Domini 400 Index, Calvert Social Equity, or many other excellent SRI funds that are outperforming their benchmark and their competitors. We might, for instance, pick Pax World Balanced with its wonderful long-term performance and have it cover part of our large-cap allocation and part of our bond allocation, since as a balanced fund it will include both.

For mid caps we could use the Calvert Capital Accumulation fund run by Eddie Brown, who you may have seen on TV as a regular guest of *Wall Street Week*. Eddie Brown developed the concept of "growth at a reasonable price" or GARP, a concept now quite commonly followed on Wall Street. For small caps we could use the Calvert New Vision fund run by James Awad, who also appears regularly on CNBC. (There are many other good SRI choices in all of these categories.)

In the international area we could use the Citizens, Calvert, or MMA Praxis international funds. For managed futures, we could use or combine Campbell, John Henry or St. Lucas. An excellent source is a firm called Everest, based in Fairfield, Iowa, that combines the best managers into funds.

For special situations we might consider Jack Robinson's Green Growth Fund, which includes 25 percent in alternative energy and other fast-growing sectors of great interest to socially conscious investors. If the investors do not own their home we may want to consider REITs to provide some real estate exposure with large dividends.

If an individual's or couple's funds are much larger we could use actual money managers rather than mutual funds for some of these positions. The difference between money managers and mutual funds is simple. Mutual funds are a way for smaller investors to hire money managers. Larger investors who can meet certain minimums use their own manager, who can offer somewhat lower fees and more tax advantages, since they can be careful to minimize the tax consequences of individual investment decisions compared to mutual funds.

The asset allocation for a person already at retirement age needs to be substantially more conservative and income-oriented, but should not be completely devoid of equities. An asset allocation for a 70-year-old retiree might look like this:

Bonds	65 percent
Index Notes	15 percent
Equities	15 percent
Managed Futures	5 percent

The key would be an increased level of safety in the bond allocation. The equity position would focus more on a value approach, emphasizing dividends but not completely eliminating growth stocks. Index notes would best be focused on the S&P 500, with the issuers chosen to assure the safety of principal.

It's important to realize there is no one-asset allocation correct for everyone at any age. It depends on many questions related to the retiree's situation, such as whether the retiree has income from pension plans independent of his or her portfolio. And, of course, each individual seems to have a different level of tolerance for market volatility.

For a young person without children it might be appropriate to be far more aggressive. Here the issue of time works in favor of the investor. An example would be seeking out investments in alternative energy precisely because over time these may well become rather successful as a whole. However, we should keep in mind that a young person may face a 16-year bear market during his or her life, much like the one from 1966 to 1982. Even for young people a sector in bonds and other nonequity holdings is appropriate. An annual adjustment should lead to some outperformance as funds are shifted when markets act in a volatile manner. Below is an example of a more aggressive asset allocation:

Bonds	25 percent
Equities	60 percent
Alternatives Investments	15 percent

The major difference in this more aggressive portfolio lies in the sectors one would chose within equities. The ratios should shift toward more aggressive mutual funds or some direct investments in companies with great growth potential. A larger commitment to small-cap growth and technology would be appropriate. And regardless of whether one is being conservative or aggressive, using SRI as a screen will tend to lower risk and enhance performance.

The Schwab Program

The brokerage firm Charles Schwab has established a special program for financial advisors. They offer a huge number of mutual funds, including . most SRI funds. As a client you pay your advisor a set fee, and the advisor will prepare an asset allocation and work with you using no-load mutual funds. The value of this approach is that the advisor's compensation is not associated with transactions and is thus arms-length.

Getting Help

There are financial advisors all over the United States who can work with you as socially responsible investment experts. The largest concentration of SRI advisors is in the Progressive Asset Management Inc. (PAM) network, which has offices in 16 states. (The list of its representatives is available in Appendix A.) I founded PAM in 1987 with seven people in San Francisco. PAM works closely with many of the SRI firms because it does not have its own products but instead acts as your advisor in choosing from the large number of available SRI investments. PAM does not require its clients to agree with any particular SRI policy. Many of the PAM advisors began their careers in major Wall Street firms. Quite a few, if not all, are active in environmental organizations, religious groups, community associations, and other similar groups. There are also many brokers at the major firms who have specialized in SRI and who can also be of assistance to you. A list of these brokers is available from the Social Investment Forum.

In Colorado a firm called First Affirmative Financial Network is offering special help to clients and financial advisors to prepare asset allocations and design portfolios. PAM is one of many affiliates of First Affirmative. They can help you find an advisor in your area who can work directly with you while receiving assistance from First Affirmative.

Trillium Asset Management Inc. is a long-established money management firm specializing in SRI with offices on both the East and West Coasts. Joan Bavaria, one of the early advocates of SRI, has headed Trillium for many years. Bavaria was also a founder and leader of Coalition of Environmentally Responsible Economies (CERES), a nonprofit that since 1989 has championed improvements in environmental policies at major firms. Harrington Investments, another manager focusing on SRI, is based in Napa, California.

Hundreds of money managers now offer SRI services in various disciplines. These are firms that are not focused on SRI per se but are financial experts who will also invest using social screens. In the early 1990s PAM established a special campaign to encourage money managers to learn about SRI and offer their services so that full asset allocations would become possible for SRI investors. Prior to that time only a few managers offered SRI services, but in the last five years the number has multiplied dramatically.

For a book that will give you a full description of the SRI community and many insights for an individual investor I recommend *Investing with Your Values: Making Money and Making a Difference* by Hal Brill, Jack A. Brill and Cliff Feigenbaum. *Investing with Your Values* is an excellent companion to *The SRI Advantage*.[3] Think of the amount of time involved in reading a few books and the expected return on what savings you may have. Isn't it worth it to focus for a few evenings on books that are not exactly fun reading but that will give you many insights that can help you achieve your financial goals?

Community Investing

There is another category of SRI known as community investing. In general, these are high-social-impact investments that often offer below market returns to maximize their social purpose. In chapter 15, James Nixon discusses these investments and describes a range of successful community investment organizations. Many socially responsible investors set aside a portion of their portfolio to invest in this area.

The Calvert Social Investment Foundation, for example, created an investment called Calvert Community Investment Notes. These direct capital exclusively to local organizations for community development. Investors in Calvert Community Investment Notes receive lower rates of return than they would from many other investments, but benefit from the knowledge that they make a difference in the lives of thousands of people struggling to break out of poverty.

The Calvert Foundation, a nonprofit 501c(3) organization, has structured its investments with major foundations standing in front of investors to lower the risk should loans fail to be repaid. Participation in community investing through such an arrangement diversifies your risk among many different loans. (The Calvert Foundation is an entity separate from the Calvert Group. It has received generous support from The Acacia Group, Ameritas Companies, and the Calvert Group, as well as from the MacArthur and Ford Foundations.)

Notes

1. Samuel Case, *The First Book of Investing: The Absolute Beginner's Guide to Building Wealth Safely* (Roseville, Calif.: Prima/Crown, 1999).

2. Harry S. Dent, *The Roaring 2000s* (Carmichael, Calif.: Touchstone,1999).

3. Hal Brill, Jack A. Brill, and Cliff Feigenbaum, *Investing with Your Values: Making Money and Making a Difference* (Gabriola Island, B.C.: New Society, 2000, rev. edn.).

8

Socially Responsible Investing
in the United States

by Steven J. Schueth

The socially responsible investment industry in the United States is a young phenomenon. Even referring to it as an "industry" ten years ago may have been a bit of a stretch. While it has grown dramatically in recent years, it is an area of work, study, and practical application that continues to evolve in many significant ways. The language used to describe SRI reflects the ongoing development of the field. A wide array of terms are used by different industry players: socially conscious, green, natural, values-based, stewardship, and mission-related. These terms describe very similar approaches to investment decision-making within a socially and environmentally responsible context.

A Brief History

The origins of what has become known as socially responsible investing (SRI) date back many hundreds of years. In biblical times, Jewish law laid down directives about how to invest ethically. In the mid 1700s, the founder of Methodism, John Wesley, noted that the use of money was the second most important subject of New Testament teachings. For generations, religious investors whose traditions embrace peace and non-violence have avoided investing in enterprises that profit from products designed to enslave or kill fellow human beings. It is likely that Methodist and Quaker immigrants brought the concept of social responsibility in investing with them to the New World. The Methodists have been managing money in the US using what are now referred to as "social screens" for over two hundred years. Similarly, Quakers have never condoned investing in slavery or munitions.

The modern roots of this phenomenon can be traced to the impassioned political climate of the 1960s. During that tumultuous decade, a series of themes served to escalate sensitivities to issues of social responsibility and accountability. Concerns regarding the Vietnam War, civil rights, and equality for women broadened during the 1970s to include management and labor issues and the use of nuclear power. The ranks of socially concerned investors grew dramatically through the 1980s as millions of people, churches, universities, cities, and states focused investment strategies on pressuring the white minority government of South Africa to dismantle its racist system of apartheid. Then, with the Bhopal, Chernobyl, and Exxon Valdez incidents and vast amounts of new information about global warming and ozone depletion coming to the attention of the American public, the environment moved to the forefront of the minds of socially concerned investors.

Most recently, school shootings and issues of human rights and healthy working conditions in factories around the world producing goods for US consumption have become rallying points for investors with a dual objective for their investment capital.

Two Investor Motivations

The motivations of investors who are attracted to socially responsible investing tend to fall into two, often complementary, categories.

Some wish to put their money to work in a manner that more closely reflects their personal values and social priorities. Investors who are primarily motivated by this desire are sometimes described in the modern media as "feel good" investors. Others have a strong need to put investment capital to work in ways that support and encourage improvements in quality of life in society as a whole. This group is more focused on what their money can do to catalyze movement toward a more economically just and environmentally sustainable world that works for all its inhabitants. They tend to be interested in the "social change" strategies that are an integral part of socially responsible investing in the US.

Three Dynamic Strategies

Socially responsible investing can be defined most succinctly as the process of integrating personal values and societal concerns into investment decision-making. The process considers the social and environmental consequences of investments, both positive and negative, within the context of rigorous financial analysis.

Screening involves selecting companies for a portfolio based on social or environmental criteria. Socially conscious investors seek to own profitable companies that contribute positively to society and to avoid those perceived as harmful. They ask their advisors to overlay a qualitative analysis of corporate policies, practices, attitudes, and impacts on the traditional quantitative analysis of profit potential. This double-bottom-line approach can result in the inclusion of enterprises with outstanding employee and environmental policies that make and sell safe, useful products and demonstrate respect for human rights worldwide.

Reality check: Social investors know that there are no perfect companies. The qualitative research and evaluation known as social screening seeks to identify better-managed companies. The result is investment portfolios that meet investors' social criteria and produce the returns needed to achieve their financial goals. Screening decisions are rarely simple. Tough choices, informed by careful research, are part of the process.

Shareholder advocacy describes the actions many socially concerned investors take in their role as owners of corporate America. These efforts include engaging in dialogue with companies and submitting and voting on shareholder resolutions. Advocacy efforts are aimed at positively influencing corporate behavior. Social investors often work cooperatively to steer management on a course that they believe will improve financial performance over time and enhance the well-being of all of the company's stakeholders: customers, employees, vendors, communities, and the natural environment, as well as stockholders.

Community investing provides capital to people in low-income, at-risk communities who have difficulty accessing it through conventional channels. Many social investors earmark a small percentage of their investments to community development financial institutions that provide financing for affordable housing and small business development in disadvantaged communities.

Over $2 Trillion Under Management

The Social Investment Forum published its most recent *Report on Socially Responsible Investing Trends* in November 2001.[1] The forum's research found $2.34 trillion under professional management in the United States involved in one or more of the three primary socially responsible investment strategies. That total is nearly four times the $639 billion the forum identified as SRI in 1995. The overall social investment industry in the United States, as measured by assets under professional management involved in social screening, shareholder advocacy, and community investing, grew nearly 1.5 times faster than all professionally managed investment assets in the US between 1995 and 2001: 266 percent growth in SRI versus 184 percent general market growth during the same six-year period.

The growth of screened investments has been even more dramatic. Socially screened portfolios grew from $165 billion in 1995 to over $2 trillion in 2001 — up over 1153 percent in six years. It is clear that social investing has gained significant market share. Late in 2001, socially responsible portfolios accounted for nearly one in every eight dollars (12 percent) under professional management in the US, up from almost one in every ten dollars (9 percent) in 1995.

Grassroots Pressures

Note that the social investment industry's impressive growth is primarily consumer-driven. Wall Street did not come up with this one. The vast majority of the hundreds of investment management firms in the US who now manage socially screened portfolios had no interest in the field ten years ago. Evidence strongly suggests that most of them got into the business to avoid losing clients. Brokers, financial planners, and investment advisors tend to be nonbelievers and at least somewhat reluctant to offer socially responsible investments to their clients. Often, clients must ask for socially responsible options; then, more often than not, the investment professional will try to talk the client out of investing in a manner that reflects that client's values.

Similarly, it is not unusual that an institutional investor seeking to put money to work in a manner that reflects the values of the organization and its constituents is forced to seek investment management through alternative channels. However, more and more consultants are beginning to understand both the implications and potential of providing services in this area.

What Is Fueling the Growth of SRI?

There are many partial answers to the question of where the growth of the socially responsible investment industry is coming from. Here are some of the most significant reasons.

Information. The first and possibly most important factor is information. US investors are better educated and informed today than at any other time in history. Social research organizations are far more capable and are providing much higher quality information than ever before. Most important, the better-informed investors are, the more responsible their actions tend to be.

Sustainability. The dramatic growth in SRI goes hand-in-hand with the interest in and maturing of sustainable industries in the US over the last three decades. Growth in industries such as alternative energy, natural foods and products, sustainable building and alternative healthcare provides new opportunities for socially conscious investors. The coming of age of these industries also promotes a broader awareness of the potential for sustainability in the US culture at large.

Spirituality. A massive yearning for spirituality is beginning to infuse itself into many areas of life. Everybody seems to have a different term for it: "spiritual revival" in the Protestant churches; "renewal of basic values" in the Catholic Church; or a "new age" for people with other spiritual constructs.

Availability. As of late 2001, there were 230 mutual funds designed for socially aware investors.[2] Employers are increasingly offering socially screened options within retirement plans and employees are increasingly moving assets into them. Over 800 independent asset managers identify themselves as managers of socially responsible portfolios for institutional investors and high-net-worth individuals. The broad range of competitive socially responsible investment options now permits the development of a diverse, well-balanced portfolio for nearly every socially aware investor.

Women. A large part of the answer may lie with women. As they have moved into the work force — filling the ranks of MBA programs, working their way up the ladder within large organizations, starting their own companies, taking seats on boards of directors, and assuming roles as fiduciaries — women have brought a natural affinity to the concept of socially responsible investing with them.

Performance. Maybe most significant is the growing body of evidence that dispels the myth of underperformance. Investors no longer need to separate good fortune from good will and need not sacrifice performance when investing in a socially responsible manner. Academic studies and real-world results have shown that socially screened portfolios do not necessarily underperform conventional nonscreened portfolios. Many investors are realizing that responsibility can now walk hand-in-hand with prosperity.

Mutual Fund Performance Highlights

The Social Investment Forum assesses the performance of socially responsible mutual funds quarterly by looking at data from two objective and unrelated third-party sources: Lipper, Inc. and Morningstar, Inc. As of December 31, 2001, social funds continued to exhibit strong relative performance characteristics.

Of the 46 mutual funds tracked monthly by the Social Investment Forum with a minimum three-year performance record, 25 (63 percent) received top rankings in one or more of the independent analyses reviewed.[3] Twenty-one funds were ranked A or B by Lipper within their investment categories for one- and/or three-year total returns. Twenty funds earned four- or five-star ratings from Morningstar for three-year, risk-adjusted performance. A number of funds were recognized for top performance by both organizations, and 81 percent of the largest socially responsible mutual funds (those with over $100 million in assets) got top marks.

It is important to note that statistically only 40 percent of all mutual funds receive A or B rankings from Lipper, and only 32 percent receive four- or five-star ratings for risk-adjusted performance from Morningstar. As a subset of the much larger mutual fund universe, socially screened funds are generally above-average performers no matter which ranking or rating process is used. Top-performing socially responsible mutual funds are found in all major asset classes, including global, international, domestic equity, balanced, and fixed-income categories.

Investing to Create a Better Future

All investing is future-oriented; socially responsible investing is even more so. Socially conscious investors are not only looking to secure their own financial futures, they are also looking for ways that their money can work to improve our collective future.

The three strategies that together define socially responsible investing in the US allow investors to choose their level of involvement. Screening provides an opportunity for investors to align their values with their financial goals while earning competitive returns. Shareholder advocacy efforts facilitate direct communication with management and boards of directors about desired changes in corporate policies, practices and impacts. Community-based investing allows investors to put money to work in local communities where capital is not readily available to create jobs, affordable housing, and environmentally friendly products and services.

For most, socially responsible investing is about achieving one's financial goals while catalyzing positive change in corporate behavior. Thus, socially conscious investors put capital to work within traditional market mechanisms to help create a more just, sustainable, and healthy society — and to enhance the quality of life for all. Socially conscious investors know that business is the most powerful institution on the planet today. It is clear that the reach and impact of business have far surpassed the influence of either religion or government. More important, it is painfully obvious that if we are going to get a grip on many of the issues that threaten our quality of life, business must shoulder a large share of the responsibility.

Many investors are consciously casting a ballot with every consumer purchase and investment decision. When it is perceived that a company is exploiting workers in unsafe foreign factories, for example, informed consumers stop buying that company's product and informed investors sell that company's stock. Socially aware investors, no matter how large or small, are most satisfied with investments that reach beyond purely financial goals to address a need to make a difference. Fortunately, making money and making a difference with our money has never been easier.

Notes

1. Social Investment Forum, *2001 Report on Socially Responsible Investing Trends in the US*, available at http://www.socialinvest.org/areas/research/trends/2001-Trends.htm.

2. The 230 socially screened mutual funds identified in the Social Investment Forum's *2001 Trends Report* represent an increase from the 168 socially screened funds identified in 1999. This number does not include multiple share classes of the same fund.

3. The SRI funds involved in this analysis include all mutual fund members of the Social Investment Forum that were at least three years old on December 31, 2001, except money market funds. Only A-shares of funds with multiple classes of shares were included in the analysis.

9

SRI: From the Margins
to the Mainstream

By Dr. Matthew Kiernan

Much has been written about the presence or absence of a robust, positive relationship between companies' environmental and social performance on the one hand and their financial performance on the other. This book demonstrates, I believe, that the balance of available evidence strongly suggests that such a relationship does indeed exist. Even more important, there are compelling reasons to believe that this relationship will get even stronger before it gets weaker. Most important of all, the major institutional investors are beginning to pay close attention.

One watershed event occurred in the summer of 2001, when the $130 billion Dutch pension fund ABP, after a year's detailed consideration, created two $100 million "demonstration" SRI portfolios for the express purpose of testing and demonstrating the "SRI alpha" hypothesis. Given ABP's influence, particularly in Europe, we can anticipate further moves in this direction from other major institutional investors. And where the institutions lead, major industrial corporations will inevitably follow.

Mainstream institutional investors have previously accepted unquestioningly the conventional industry "wisdom" that excellent environmental and social performance can be achieved only at the cost of lower financial returns for investors. An important corollary of this argument held that, since environmental and social factors are, at best, irrelevant to the risk/return equation, prudent fiduciaries are actually precluded from considering them. It turns out that both the conventional wisdom and its corollary are, quite simply, wrong. Recent pension reform legislation in the United Kingdom has implicitly acknowledged this fact, and other countries such as Sweden, Germany, France, and Switzerland are actively considering similar moves. The "prudent fiduciary" equation is — quite rightly — now being turned on its head: since there is now incontrovertible evidence that superior environmental and social performance does in fact have positive effects on the level of risk, profitability, and stock performance of publicly traded companies, fiduciaries can now be seen as derelict in their duties if they do *not* consider using environmental and social screens.

One of the most critical drivers of this new, stakeholder-led paradigm shift is a deep-seated shift in public attitudes that is surprisingly consistent around the world. The respected survey research firm Environics International recently completed a "Millennium Poll on Corporate Social Responsibility." That unprecedented exercise included interviews with roughly 25,000 citizens in 23 countries on six continents. The study was supported by, among others, PricewaterhouseCoopers and the Conference Board. Among the study's most portentous findings:

The average investor's opinions of companies now depend much more heavily on perceived "corporate citizenship" (56 percent) than on either brand quality (40 percent) or even business fundamentals (34 percent). Fully 20 percent of the respondents had actually rewarded or punished companies financially within the past year on the basis of their environmental or social performance. A further 20 percent actively considered doing so.

The bar is being raised continually: what was considered leading-edge environmental and social performance only a few years ago is now both commonplace and a *minimum* entry ticket for companies that want to stay in the competitive game. By the same token, what once may have been acceptable performance is now considered substandard and is likely to provoke a consumer backlash.

An even more recent global survey by Edelman Public Relations Worldwide in early 2001 confirmed these findings and added another that gives them even greater potency: in virtually every country in the world, the best-known NGOs are much more credible than even the most respected corporation, sometimes by a factor of four or five!

In short, it's a brand-new ballgame, an unprecedented test not only of companies' environmental and social management skills but also of their strategic management capability in general. Indeed, I would argue that companies' ability to handle the complex, ever-changing kaleidoscope of SRI issues is an increasingly robust — but heretofore neglected — proxy for its management quality, period. And, as any Wall Street analyst will confirm, management quality is already viewed as the single most important determinant of companies' ultimate competitiveness and financial performance.

Figure 9.1 Central Concerns in Evaluating Companies

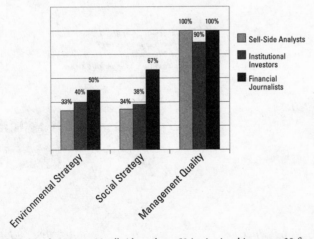

Source: MORI, March 2001 — 93 sell-side analysts, 50 institutional investors, 30 financial journalists. Respondents judging factors "fairly" or "very" N.B.

Sadly, however, most financial analysts and institutional investors have not yet made the connection between management quality in general and the ability to manage social and environmental issues in particular. A recent MORI poll in the UK of over 140 sell-side analysts and institutional investors in the City of London confirms this sobering reality. While 100 percent of the analysts and 90 percent of the institutional investors surveyed cited "management quality" as a central concern when evaluating companies, not even half that number mentioned environmental and social factors. In the case of the analysts, the figure was nearly *one-third*. We would, of course, argue that they are one and the same thing, but that is clearly not the City's view. When one stops to consider that investment professionals in London are if anything *more* sensitized to social and environmental issues than their North American counterparts, the true scale of the cognitive and cultural challenge facing SRI becomes apparent.

Figure 9.2 Key SRI Drivers of Competitive Advantage

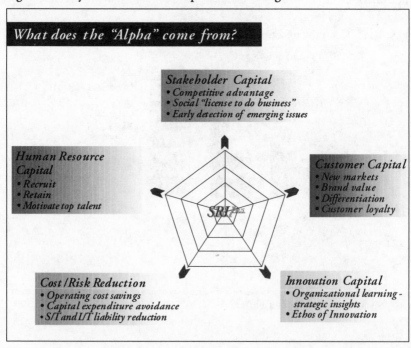

But why *should* superior SRI performance create better financial returns? For most of Wall Street, this is — believe it or not — profoundly counter-intuitive. The vast majority of mainstream analysts continue to believe that the pursuit of social or environmental performance objectives is an unadulterated "cost-center" — one without redeeming or offsetting financial and competitive advantages.

While I am unaware of any studies that conclusively prove a direct *cause-and-effect* relationship between SRI factors and financial performance, it is possible to postulate a reasonable hypothesis: superior SRI performance helps generate financial outperformance by contributing to at least five well-recognized drivers of competitive advantage, profitability, and superior share price performance. These drivers include shareholder capital, customer capital, innovation capital, cost/risk reduction, and human resource capital (see Figure 9.2).

Old Versus New Economy Performance by Sector

As we have already seen, these competitive weapons tend to produce superior share-price performance, even in a broadly diversified index such as the S&P 500. But things get *really* interesting for investors when we "drill down" from aggregated, marketwide data and focus in on the financial outperformance potential in individual high-impact sectors. Let's look at examples from three different industry sectors: mining, integrated oil and gas, and semiconductors. First, for the "Old Economy" sectors. Figures 9.3 and 9.4 show share-price performance in the oil and mining industries, respectively. In petroleum, the top half outperforms by 16 percent, while in the mining industry the top half outperforms by 23 percent.

One can already anticipate the response of the "flat earth" — that is, the dominant — ideologues on Wall Street: ah, but that's strictly for yesterday's sectors — the "smokestack" industries. Surely it's a different story with "New Economy" stocks?! Well, actually, no. If any sector epitomizes the contemporary, knowledge-driven economy, it's the semiconductor industry, whose performance is shown in Figure 9.5. Here the outperformance margin is, if anything, even larger: 27 percent.

Figure 9.3 Sector Performance: Petroleum

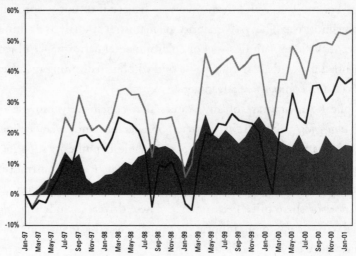

Figure 9.4 Sector Performance: Mining

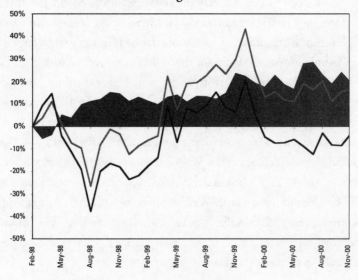

Figure 9.5 Sector Performance: Semiconductors

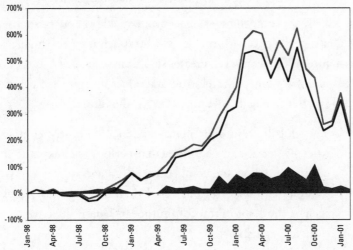

It may not be intuitively obvious why superior environmental performance in the semiconductor industry would create competitive and financial dividends. Well, it turns out that semiconductor fabrication plants
are huge consumers of water — an increasingly scarce resource. Building
a fabrication plant in, say, New Mexico, can have a major negative effect
on the local water table, thereby creating significant problems for a variety
of external stakeholders in the community. Those stakeholders can, with
relative ease, impede the necessary government regulatory approvals by
anywhere from six months to forever. This can cost some very serious
money when a billion-dollar facility is involved, whether measured as
additional interest cost, diversion of senior management time, or most
critical of all in a fast-paced industry such as semiconductors, the loss of
time, and therefore precious points of market share to competitors. Thus,
the company's ability to manage this set of issues becomes a very tangible
proxy for the quality of its strategic management and, rather quickly, for
its *financial* performance.

From the Margins to the Mainstream

As we have seen, compelling evidence from a wide variety of sources now exists that superior SRI performance is *already* helping drive financial out-performance. Of perhaps even greater significance, however, is the conflu-ence of a number of macro-level structural forces that give every indication of creating an even larger "SRI premium" in the future:

- The globalization and intensification of industry competition, whereby social and environmental performance become sources of differentiation and competitive advantage
- Tightening global, regional, and domestic regulatory pressures, such as the Kyoto Protocol, European Union directives, and US clean air regulations
- Changing consumer/investor demographics, with many younger, "greener" consumers and investors
- Growing institutional shareholder activism
- Growing CEO/CFO awareness of the competitive and financial benefits of superior environmental performance
- Global population/resource consumption pressures
- The increased transparency and velocity of company informa-tion
- Greater pressure from nongovernment organizations armed with better information and growing credibility

Each of these megatrends is powerful enough to expand the "SRI pre-mium" all by itself. Taken together, they form a virtually irresistible force that seems certain to transform the global competitive landscape for at least the next decade.

So what does all this add up to? In my view it adds up to an unprec-edented competitive environment for investors and their professional advi-sors. The arguments for corporate social responsibility thus start to move well beyond the roughly 5 percent of the global capital markets currently driven by "socially responsible" considerations. Companies' environmental and social performance starts to have more and more traction with the other 95 percent — the *mainstream* institutional investor. What we are currently witnessing, therefore, is the transmutation of SRI considerations from a marginal, "vertical" niche position to a much broader, "horizontal" analytical overlay brought to bear across the full spectrum of the mainstream capital markets.

Now we can finally begin to talk seriously about the capital markets playing a significant role in moving corporate behavior and strategy toward a more progressive trajectory. And it will not be before time.

10

Seeing Stars: Socially Responsible
Mutual Fund Performance

By Jon F. Hale

Socially responsible investing has often been criticized by traditional investors because it places social and environmental factors alongside conventional financial considerations in its investment decisions. From the standpoint of maximizing investment returns, social screening is said to place unnecessary restrictions on the investment opportunities available.

Socially responsible investors typically respond in one of two ways to this critique. Most argue simply that individuals and institutions should practice and promote social and environmental responsibility in their investment decisions just as they do in other spheres of their lives.[1] Some go further than that, arguing that the explicit attention paid by social investors to social and environmental factors actually helps them identify better companies and avoid risky ones (those not involved in potential social controversy or litigation, for example), which should result in better investment performance over the long run.[2]

Of course, the actual performance of socially screened portfolios is of great importance in helping to settle this debate. If it were found that socially screened investments systematically underperform, then these arguments would be difficult to sustain; it would be hard to convince average investors that they should apply their social conscience to their investments if the result were sure to be a smaller college fund or retirement nest egg. While institutional investors may consider a socially responsible investment, a 1998 Department of Labor advisory opinion counseled that institutional fiduciaries may do so only if the socially responsible investment's returns are commensurate with alternative investments having similar risks.[3]

This chapter examines the question of SRI performance by analyzing the risk-adjusted returns of socially responsible mutual funds. Using the Morningstar Principia Pro database, I identified 48 socially responsible mutual funds with records of three years or longer and compared their risk-adjusted performance with that of conventional funds. The methodology I used is explained in detail in the appendix.

Star Ratings

The Morningstar star rating is a risk-adjusted measure of return that compares funds within four broad asset classes (domestic equity, international equity, fixed-income, and tax-free bond). Funds are awarded from one to five stars based on their risk-adjusted performance relative to other funds within their asset class. Stars are normally distributed within each asset class, as follows: five stars, 10 percent; four stars, 22 percent; three stars, 33 percent; two stars, 22 percent; one star, 10 percent.

Table 10.1 shows the distribution of star ratings for SRI funds compared to those for the normally distributed mutual fund universe. The results show that the distribution of SRI funds' star ratings is very close to normal and, if anything, is skewed toward the higher end of the star ratings. Specifically, 37.5 percent of SRI funds garnered ratings of four or five stars compared with one-third of the overall fund universe. And while 10 percent of the overall fund universe received the lowest, one-star rating, only 4 percent of SRI funds rated one star.

This showing confirms previous Morningstar studies from 1999 and 2000, which also showed SRI funds' star ratings to be normally distributed or skewed toward the high end of the ratings, and is especially notable in light of the recent market decline.[4] Many SRI funds were riding high in the late 1990s because a number of them were heavily invested in high-flying technology and other large-cap growth stocks. This focus raised questions about how these funds' performance would look in the aftermath of a market correction such as the one that began in March 2000. The answer appears to be that SRI funds have held up pretty well relative to conventional funds.

Table 10.1 SRI Funds vs. the Overall Fund Universe:
Morningstar Star Ratings

Star Rating	Number of SRI Funds	Percentage of SRI Funds	Percentage of All Funds
5 (Highest)	4	8.3	10
4	14	29.2	22
3	15	31.3	33
2	13	27.1	22
1 (Lowest)	2	4.2	10

Note: Ratings as of June 30, 2001.
Source: Morningstar Principia Pro Plus for Mutual Funds, July 2001.

The star ratings reported in Table 10.1 are based on performance through June 30, 2001, some 14 months after the stock market peaked. During that time, many funds, particularly those with significant exposure to growth stocks, posted their worst absolute returns ever. The Domini Social Equity Fund, for example, lost 19.4 percent for the 12 months ending June 30, 2001, and the more growth-oriented Citizens Core Equity shed 28.6 percent during the same period. In all, 19 of the 48 SRI funds in this study are categorized as large-cap growth and large-cap blend — two categories that suffered significant losses. The mean 12-month return for the 19 large-growth and large-blend SRI funds was only a few basis points below that of the mean for all large-growth and large-blend funds (-21.09 percent vs. –20.71 percent). As Table 10.1 shows, SRI funds continue to fare well on a risk-adjusted basis despite the recent downturn.

Star ratings can be misleading precisely because they rate funds within such broad asset classes. Often a fund's star rating can be as much a function of its investment style as its manager's ability. For example, when large-cap growth stocks outperform smaller-cap value stocks over a significant period, as they did in the late 1990s, large-cap growth funds tend to dominate the four- and five-star ratings, while many small-cap value funds languish in one- and two-star territory. This doesn't necessarily mean that large-growth managers are better investors than their small-cap value counterparts; it means simply that their investment style was in favor. For the 14 months from April 2000 through June 2001, the large-cap growth investment style was distinctly out-of-favor and many large-cap blend and large-cap growth funds saw their star ratings fall. Overall, though, the universe of SRI funds has held its own in the star ratings.

Table 10.2 SRI Funds vs. the Overall Fund Universe:
Morningstar Category Ratings

Category Rating	Number of SRI Funds	Percent of SRI Funds	Percent of Overall Fund Universe
5 (Highest)	5	11	10
4	15	32	22
3	12	25.5	33
2	12	25.5	22
1 (Lowest)	3	6	10

Note: Ratings as of June 30, 2001.
Source: Morningstar Principia Pro Plus for Mutual Funds, July 2001.

Category Ratings

Morningstar has a less well known risk-adjusted rating that makes more precise comparisons among funds. The Morningstar category rating compares funds within specific investment styles. Rather than making a broad comparison of all domestic equity funds, as the star rating does, the category rating compares large-growth funds with large-growth funds, small-value with small-value, and so on. Category ratings are based on the same calculation as the star rating and are normally distributed from one to five within each style-based category.

Table 10.2 shows how SRI funds compare to unscreened funds with similar investment styles. The answer: very well. SRI funds' category ratings are clearly skewed toward the higher ratings. While overall, one-third of funds receive category ratings of four or five, 43 percent of SRI funds did so. Highly rated SRI funds are found in a wide range of categories. A dozen different style-based categories are represented among the 20 SRI funds with category ratings of four or five.

A Look at SRI Fund Veterans

One objection to the comparisons made thus far might be that they do not really measure how well SRI funds have fared over long time periods. Morningstar's category ratings, in particular, cover only three years of performance (see the appendix for an explanation). Star ratings incorporate longer time periods, but only for those funds that have longer performance histories. A three-year old fund and a ten-year old fund both may receive the same star ratings, but the younger fund's star rating is based on a much shorter time frame and is therefore a less reliable indicator of long-run performance.

Table 10.3 Morningstar Ratings for SRI Funds with 10+ Years of History

Rating:	Current Star	Average Historical Star	Current Category
5 (Highest)	1	0	3
4	4	3	5
3	6	6	4
2	2	5	1
1 (Lowest)	1	0	1

Note: Ratings as of June 30, 2001.
Source: Morningstar Principia Pro Plus for Mutual Funds, July 2001.

Table 10.3 shows the current star rating, average historical star rating, and category ratings of the 14 SRI funds that have histories of 10 years or longer. The current star ratings and average historical star ratings for these funds have a distribution that is close to normal, an indicator that the SRI mutual funds that have been in existence for the past decade have performed on a par with nonscreened funds. These most seasoned of SRI funds have also done well versus their nonscreened peers lately. As the category ratings in Table 10.3 indicate, 8 of the 14 funds have category ratings of four or five, and only 2 have category ratings of one or two.

In summary, SRI funds appear to perform as well as, if not a little better than, nonscreened funds on a risk-adjusted basis, using Morningstar's star rating methodology. This holds for SRI funds overall and for veteran SRI funds that have been around for several market cycles. This also holds when SRI funds are compared to funds in their broad asset classes (star ratings) and to funds in their specific style-based investment categories (category ratings).

To be sure, individual fund performance for SRI funds is largely a function of investment style and manager performance, as it is with all mutual funds. Thus, we should expect a range of performance from SRI funds just as we would with any mutual fund. The evidence presented above, however, strongly suggests that there is no systematic cost being exacted from socially responsible investors who are putting their money in SRI funds. The finding that SRI mutual funds, in general, do just as well as nonscreened funds should strengthen the resolve of individual investors who want to invest according to their values and should provide additional evidence to institutional fiduciaries that a socially responsible investment is, in principle, one that is competitive with alternative nonscreened investments having similar risk profiles.

Appendix
Defining the SRI Universe

In the June 30, 2001, release of its Principia Pro Plus for Mutual Funds software, Morningstar categorized 117 mutual funds as "socially conscious funds." (To search for these funds in Principia, select the "Search" function, then "Special Criteria," then "Socially Conscious Funds.") Many of the listed funds represented different share classes of the same underlying portfolio. For example, Calvert Capital Accumulation was listed three times because it has A, B, and C shares. In these cases, only the oldest share class was included. Eliminating multiple share classes reduced the SRI universe to 67. A perusal of the list resulted in two funds being eliminated, GMO Tobacco-Free Fund and MFS Union Standard, because they are not broadly screened funds. Of the remaining 65 funds, 48 had three-year records and were thus eligible for a Morningstar star rating.

The following is a list of funds included in the study (Ratings and Net Assets as of June 30, 2001).

Table 10 Appendix

Fund Name	Morningstar Category	Morningstar Rating	Category Rating	Net Assets (Millions of Dollars)	Fund Inception Date
Amana Growth	Large Growth	4	5	26.4	1994–02
Amana Income	Large Value	3	3	23.2	1986–06
American Trust Allegiance	Large Growth	2	3	30	1997–03
Aquinas Fixed-Income	Long-term Bond	3	4	46.8	1994–01
Aquinas Growth	Large Growth	4	4	67.5	1994–01
Aquinas Small Cap	Small Growth	2	-	6.2	1994–01

Fund Name	Morningstar Category	Morningstar Rating	Category Rating	Net Assets (Millions of Dollars)	Fund Inception Date
Aquinas Value	Large Value	2	2	49.8	1994–01
Ariel	Small Blend	4	4	395.9	1986–11
Ariel Appreciation	Mid-Cap Blend	4	4	530.2	1989–12
Calvert Capital Accumulate A	Mid-Cap Growth	2	3	141	1994–10
Calvert Large Cap Growth I	Large Growth	4	4	6.2	1994–08
Calvert New Vision Sm Cap A	Small Growth	3	3	97.6	1997–01
Calvert Social Inv Bal A	Domestic Hybrid	3	2	600.7	1982–10
Calvert Social Inv Bond A	Intermediate-term Bond	3	4	81.9	1987–08
Calvert Social Inv EnhanEq A	Large Growth	3	3	34.4	1998–04
Calvert Social Inv Equity A	Large Blend	3	5	279.3	1987–08
Calvert World Value Intl EqA	Foreign Stock	3	2	194	1992–07
Catholic Values Eq Indiv	Large Blend	1	1	4.2	1997–05
Citizens Core Growth Stndrd	Large Growth	3	3	472.8	1995–03
Citizens Emerg Growth Stndrd	Mid-Cap Growth	4	4	283.8	1994–02
Citizens Global Eq Stndrd	World Stock	5	4	236.1	1994–02
Citizens Income	Intermediate-term Bond	3	2	71.6	1992–06

Fund Name	Morningstar Category	Morningstar Rating	Category Rating	Net Assets (Millions of Dollars)	Fund Inception Date
DEM Equity Institutional	Mid-Cap Growth	4	4	26.1	1998–04
Devcap Shared Return	Large Blend	4	3	14.3	1995–10
Domini Social Equity	Large Blend	3	3	1278.3	1991–06
Dreyfus Premier Third Cent Z	Large Growth	2	3	989.2	1972–03
Green Century Balanced	Small Growth	4	4	72.7	1992–03
IPS Millennium	Large Growth	4	4	276.7	1995–01
Meyers Pride Value	Mid-Cap Value	5	4	14.3	1996–06
MMA Praxis Core Stock B	Large Blend	3	3	149.8	1994–01
MMA Praxis Interm Inc B	Intermediate-term Bond	3	2	34.6	1994–01
MMA Praxis International B	Foreign Stock	2	2	25	1997–04
Neuberger Berman Soc Resp In	Large Value	3	2	91.7	1994–03
New Alternatives	Small Blend	2	4	54.5	1982–09
Noah	Large Growth	2	2	12.8	1996–05
Parnassus	Mid-Cap Blend	4	5	373.4	1984–12
Parnassus Income CA Tax-Ex	Muni CA Interm	5	2	17.8	1992–09
Parnassus Income Equity Inc	Large Value	4	5	61.3	1992–09
Parnassus Income Fixed-Inc	Intermediate-term Bond	2	1	11.3	1992–09

Fund Name	Morningstar Category	Morningstar Rating	Category Rating	Net Assets (Millions of Dollars)	Fund Inception Date
Pax World Balanced	Domestic Hybrid	4	5	1221.7	1971–11
Pax World Growth	Mid-Cap Growth	2	2	28.3	1997–06
PIMCO Total Return III Instl	Intermediate-term Bond	5	3	805.4	1991–05
Rightime OTC	Large Blend	1	1	3.1	1990–03
Security Social Awareness A	Large Blend	2	2	13.1	1996–11
Smith Barney Social Aware B	Large Blend	3	4	162.8	1987–02
Timothy Plan Small Value A	Small Blend	2	3	17	1994–03
Women's Equity	Large Blend	4	4	11	1993–10

The Morningstar Star Rating

Morningstar's Star Rating is a purely quantitative measure of a fund's risk-adjusted performance relative to its broad asset class, recalculated monthly. To determine a fund's star rating for a given period (three, five, or ten years), Morningstar subtracts a fund's risk score from its return score and then plots the results on a bell curve to determine the fund's rating for each time period.

A fund's Morningstar Return score is the fund's load-adjusted return minus the return of the 90-day T-bill over the same period, divided by the higher of the average excess return of the fund's broad asset class or the 90-day T-bill return. A Return score above 1.00 indicates that a fund has outperformed its broad asset class. A fund's Morningstar Risk score is a measure of downside volatility relative to its broad asset class. To calculate it, Morningstar plots a fund's monthly returns alongside the 90-day T-bill, adds up the negative amounts for the months in which the fund trailed the T-bill return, then divides by the total number of months in the period (36, 60, or 120). This number is then divided by the asset class average. A Risk score above 1.00 means that a fund is more risky than its broad asset class.

A fund's overall star rating is a weighted average of three time periods. For funds with ten years of history, the ten-year statistics account for 50 percent of the overall rating, the five-year statistics for 30 percent, and the three-year statistics for 20 percent. For funds with at least five years of history but not yet ten years, the five-year statistics account for 60 percent of the overall rating and the three-year statistics account for 40 percent. For funds with at least three years of history but not yet five years, the three-year statistics account for the entire star rating.

The Morningstar Category Rating

Morningstar's Category Rating simply compares a fund's three-year Morningstar risk-adjusted rating (or star rating) with a narrower group of funds in the same style-based category, rather than with the broad asset class. The Category Rating thus provides a more direct apples-to-apples comparison of funds than the Star Rating. The drawback of the Category Rating is that it only takes into account three years of performance, because many funds change categories over time. Although few funds change their investment objective over time, their style-based category can change because funds are placed in categories based on their actual portfolio holdings.

Notes

1. Amy Domini, *Socially Responsible Investing: Making a Difference and Making Money* (Chicago: Dearborn, 2001), pp. 13–14.

2. See for example, Ariel Mutual Funds, "Slow and Steady Wins the Race: An Advisor's Guide to Ariel Mutual Funds, 5; Citizens Funds, "Social Screening," CitzensFunds.com, www.citizensfunds.com/live/about/approach_social.asp.

3. Department of Labor Advisory Opinion 98-04A, May 28, 1998.

4. Emily Hall and Jon F. Hale, "How Do Socially Responsible Funds Stack Up?" Morningstar.com, September 17, 1999: see www.news.morningstar.com/news/MS/ Commentary/990917com.html; and Catherine Hickey, "2000 Update: How Do Socially Responsible Funds Stack Up?," Morningstar.com, October 5, 2000, www.news. morningstar.com/news/MS/Articles/0,1299,3717,00.html.

11

Factoring Out Sector Bets

By Christopher Luck

If you're a money manager with an SRI mandate, it's important to have an appropriate benchmark to measure how much your efforts are adding. For example, if you are managing for a client that does not allow you to hold tobacco stocks, you don't want to be measured against the S&P 500. Instead, you'd like to be measured against the tobacco-free S&P 500. The same is true of other socially responsible restrictions: If you are not "allowed" to hold a particular stock or class of stocks, that stock or class of stocks should not be included in the benchmark. In looking for an appropriate socially responsible index to function as a benchmark, I was struck by the simplicity of using such a benchmark to evaluate socially responsible investing itself. Much of the work I have done is to based on analysis of the performance of the Domini Social Index. Although there are other SRI indexes, like the Citizens Fund Index, the DSI has a longer history and more diversity.

When I look at the literature of socially responsible investing, I have always been struck by the focus on performance of SRI funds, particularly mutual funds. To summarize it briefly, the literature indicates that although there are some SRI funds with very strong performance, overall performance has not been particularly inspiring. Socially responsible funds have modestly underperformed the market, but they have underperformed by essentially the same amount as other active managers. What makes it difficult to evaluate social funds as a group is precisely the fact that most of them are actively managed. Hence, the performance of these funds says far less about the social aspect of the fund managers' approach than it says about the alpha generation and portfolio construction skills of the active managers themselves!

One obvious way around this problem is to look not at active managers but at an index fund like the Domini Social Index Fund, something that mimics the S&P 500 Index. Because the DSI is well diversified, has low index level turnover, and accounts for social issues, the difference between it and the S&P 500 more purely reflects the difference that social screens make, not a difference in active management skills. Since you're taking social issues and wrapping them in a passive indexing portfolio wrapper, social considerations, not active management skill or lack of skill, will determine performance.

The Domini Social Index itself is, like the S&P 500, a capitalization-weighted index. Turnover is consistent, albeit slightly higher than that of the S&P 500 (turnover in the S&P 500 is on average 4 percent to 5 percent per year; the DSI is 6 percent to 7 percent per year). The DSI is well diversified, with 400 companies. A great majority of those companies come from the S&P 500 itself, with the remainder encompassing larger capitalization companies that also fill out appropriate industry definitions. Of course, there are inevitably differences in defining the criteria for what qualifies as socially responsible. Definitions do matter, and the definitions that Domini uses may, for example, be different from those that Citizens Funds uses. *Socially responsible* thus clearly does introduce judgment calls about what is in fact socially responsible. However, it should be noted that there is far more agreement on the criteria used than there are differences. Although these differences are not unimportant, a very similar set of companies is used by all the SRI index funds.

For the investment world the DSI has a fairly long history of over ten years. And over that period the Domini Social Index has delivered a return of almost 20 percent per year, outperforming the S&P 500 by a little more than *1.5 percentage points* a year since the inception of the index. That is very strong performance, since it occurred in a decade when 90 percent of active managers could not outperform the passive S&P 500 index itself. This accomplishment was generated by taking only minimal risk, approximately 2 percent per year (standard deviation).

Let's take a more detailed look at that outperformance of 1.5 percentage points. Below is a summary of that performance. What we want to look at in more detail are the style and sector biases of this portfolio to determine as best we can the *sources* of that outperformance. The very act of screening out a class of stocks, like tobacco stocks, for example, introduces biases in the portfolio relative to the S&P 500. Some of those biases are that the DSI is a more technology-oriented and more growth-oriented than the S&P 500. It also focuses more on smaller cap companies than does the S&P 500, because Domini tends to exclude the large basic industries. Accordingly, the portfolio is less valued-oriented and has a slightly higher beta than the S&P 500.

Table 11.1 DSI Performance
(Returns and Risk Annualized)

	Return	Risk
Systematic timing premium	0.51	0.69
Residual components:		
Risk indices (style characteristics)	−0.27	1.22
Industries	0.60	1.68
Specific asset selection	0.69	1.61
Total residual	1.17	2.56
Total active	1.53	2.66

The key question is how much of that outperformance has been driven by biases introduced in the screening process, and potentially how much was driven by the social screens themselves. There have been several influences on performance. One has been simply the impact on performance of having a higher-beta portfolio. The market has been up strongly, so one area of outperformance has been the beta impact itself. Second, the style biases have had a positive contribution on return. Growth stocks, of course, have done very well over the life of the DSI, and the growth bias has led to a positive performance. Less fortunately, the small-cap bias has detracted from performance, since large-cap stocks have done much better than small-cap stocks in the US. When you put all that together, plus the impact of the other smaller style biases, the net impact of the style biases has been close to zero.

Third, the industry orientation of the DSI has clearly helped boost its performance, and its technology orientation in particular. Finally, we have the most intriguing component of value added, and that is stock-specific performance — the performance not explained by the style and sector biases of the DSI. That is intriguing because what the stocks in the index have in common, once their sector and style biases have been accounted for, is their social worthiness — evidence that the social screens themselves have contributed positive performance. We should note at this point that the result was not statistically significant, at least at the 95 percent confidence level (the usual confidence level for judging statistical significance for fans of statistics). The performance record encompasses more than ten years, which is a long time frame in the investment world but not in the world of statistics. Nonetheless, one-half percentage point of the outperformance of the DSI can be explained by stock-specific performance, which in any world is a reasonably compelling number over such a long time frame.

Although certainly not a definitive answer to the question of the contribution of social screens themselves, it is interesting to see this group of socially responsible companies performing better in the stock market than their peers. This certainly seems to suggest that a socially responsible orientation is a positive attribute for all companies. In other words, socially responsible investing is no different conceptually from any other screen that investors might use. It does not take that much of an intellectual leap to appreciate that social screens may very well serve as a proxy for strong management — for example, through superior employee relations or employee motivation.

Let's look at the issue of tobacco, which has become a sort of social responsibility litmus test over the last several years. One of the largest funds in the country, the Florida State Board of Administration, decided in June 1997 to divest tobacco stocks completely from its fund. As a manager for the State Board, we were told that we had a certain time period to divest all of the tobacco stocks we held, which is what we and the rest of the managers did. That again brought up the issue of appropriate benchmarking, since there was now a class of stocks that the managers could no longer hold. And to applaud Florida, the board then proceeded to construct tobacco-free indexes to more properly evaluate the managers.

I have that tobacco-free performance data, since that is how we are evaluated by our client. To summarize, although tobacco performance excelled through the 1970s and 1980s, it has been pretty miserable since then, except for quite recently. Interestingly, in the 1970s and 1980s, Philip Morris was one of the best-performing stocks in the entire US equity market. In the 1990s, although it has delivered positive overall performance, it has badly lagged the rest of the market. The Florida results shows that since June 1997 (when the State Board divested its tobacco stocks), the tobacco-free S&P has outperformed the S&P 500 by 20 basis points a year. That's not a large sum, but for a fund the size of the State Board that translates into a huge sum of money: a billion here, a billion there, and pretty soon you're talking real money.

An interesting question, given the poor performance of Philip Morris, is why that differential is only 20 basis points a year? The reason for that is the weight of Philip Morris in the S&P 500 itself. If you go back to the start of the prior decade the company represented more than 1 percent of the index; it now equals .5 percent. So in a sense there is a self-fulfilling component there — as Philip Morris struggles it matters less and less to the performance of the S&P 500.

There is a second component of tobacco divestment, which is the cost of selling the tobacco stocks themselves. The transaction cost associated with selling a large position is not trivial, although it is only a one-time cost. We estimated the cost of selling the Philip Morris stock we held at about 180 basis points round-trip on the stock. At the portfolio level that cost is not very large. Our holding in Philip Morris was about 1 percent of the portfolio at the time, about benchmark weight, and that, multiplied by a 180–basis point transaction cost, is approximately a 2–basis point up-front cost to the divestment. Compared to a positive 20 basis points in performance, it is easy to conclude that the divestment decision has been a profitable one for the state.

Let me summarize that there are certainly a number of different ways that SRI managers can exercise social considerations, from making investment decisions based on social criteria to using ownership to lobby corporations directly to effect social change. At First Quadrant we have been motivated by exit considerations, by making decisions in our socially responsible mandates to include or exclude stocks from our portfolio. We think of social considerations as no different than other types of investment considerations active managers use to differentiate stock selections. We think that it is feasible, and there is some very suggestive evidence for this, that social considerations are either direct or indirect proxies for better management, better labor relations, better use of resources, and a host of other factors. We've seen it in our own portfolios: We've been able to deliver very strong performance with a socially responsible mandate, and we have seen it with an index fund like the Domini Social Index. Social investing can pay. Social investing certainly pays in the moral sense, and it can pay better from a performance standpoint as well.

12

Can Universal Owners Be Socially Responsible Investors?

James P. Hawley and Andrew T. Williams

American corporate capitalism has entered its third phase since the modern corporation first emerged in the late nineteenth century. The first phase was entrepreneurial corporate capitalism, characterized by the large ownership stake held by founders such as Ford, Carnegie, and Stanford. The second era was characterized, as Berle and Means argued, by the separation of ownership from control in firms dominated by nonowning managers. Chandler called this era managerial capitalism. In our book *The Rise of Fiduciary Capitalism: How Institutional Investors Can Make Corporate America More Democratic,* we suggest that American corporate capitalism is entering a third phase, one of "fiduciary capitalism."[1] In this phase, ownership has become reconcentrated but this time into the hands of fiduciary institutions — primarily pension funds and mutual funds. The unintended origins of this reconcentration began during World War II with the rise of fringe benefits (most importantly pension funds) because of the need to compete for workers on dimensions other than wages. The massive growth of public pension funds began in the 1960s, and the domination of equity and debt markets by fiduciary institutions grew rapidly from the 1970s into the new millennium.

We suggest that a significant convergence is emerging between many of the overall aims of the socially responsible investing (SRI) community and the imperatives of what we call *universal owners,* which comprise the core of fiduciary capitalism. Briefly, a universal owner is a large fiduciary institution which by virtue of its size or its asset allocation strategy owns a cross-section of publicly traded equities. For example, such an institution might hold between 1500 to 4500 different stocks, in essence owning the economy.[2]

The term *fiduciary capitalism* is based on the fiduciary duties and legal obligations of financial institutions to manage their assets in the sole interest of investors or beneficiaries. These duties are often summarized as the duty of care — to act in a "prudent" manner — and the duty of loyalty — to act solely in the interests of the institutions' beneficiaries.[3] Thus fiduciary institutions are legally obligated to have the long-term interests of their beneficiaries as their only goal. In addition, most investments held by fiduciary institutions are long-term investments, and fiduciary institutions are ethically and legally obligated to maximize long-term return on a risk-adjusted basis, using the "prudent person" standards of fiduciary duty to evaluate risk.

However, while exercising many of the rights and responsibilities of ownership — buying and selling equity, voting for directors and resolutions submitted to shareholders, submitting proxies, monitoring investments, etc. - institutional investors are not owners in the sense that they benefit directly from ownership. Rather, they are the *agents* of beneficial owners — pensioners or mutual or fund investors. Thus, just as the earlier alienation of ownership from control led to the rise of the professional manager, the rise of fiduciary institutions has created a class of professional owners — individuals exercising by virtue of professional education and training the ownership responsibilities vested in fiduciary institutions. This development creates a long agency chain among different types of fiduciary agents.

Individual and Institutional Ownership

One of the most important characteristics of the new fiduciary capitalism is that institutional investors have come to own about 50 percent of
all US publicly traded equity, and also have significant stakes in numerous
other sectors as well. As a group, they effectively own a major part of the
US economy. The shift from individual to institutional equity ownership
has been dramatic. As recently as the early 1970s individuals owned as
much as 80 percent of US corporate equity, but by the middle 1990s
individual ownership had fallen below half. And by the late 1990s institutions — particularly pension funds, bank trust departments, mutual fund
companies, and insurance companies – owned a larger fraction of the equity of US companies than did US individuals. This shift in ownership is
clearly illustrated in Figure 12.1.

**Figure 12.1 Institutional vs. Household Share of Publicly Traded Equities:
1957–2000**

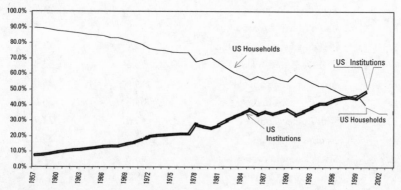

Note: Equity ownership is net of foreign holdings.
Source: Federal Reserve System, *Flow of Funds Accounts of the United States: Annual
Flows and Outstandings,* (Washington: General Printing Office, 1999), Series L.213
Corporate Equities. Available at the Federal Reserve Board of Governors website:
www.federalreserve.gov/releases/z1/current/data/htm.

The case of General Electric clearly illustrates the concentration of ownership of corporate equity into the hands of fiduciary institutions. Table
12.1 reports the percentage of all shares held by institutional owners in

Table 12.1 Equity Ownership of the Largest 25 Corporations

Rank	Corporation	Percent of Total Shares Held by All Institutions	Percent of Total Shares Held by Top 25 Institutions
1	General Electric Co.	48.8	25.4
2	Microsoft Corp.	35.1	20.1
3	Coca-Cola Co.	49.3	34.4
4	Exxon Corp.	41.7	23.3
5	Merck & Co.	52.8	27.3
6	Pfizer Inc.	56.3	29.3
7	Wal-Mart Stores	37.1	23.8
8	Intel Corp.	46.9	23.4
9	Procter & Gamble Co.	46.4	25.2
10	IBM Corp.	49.3	25.6
11	Bristol-Myers Squibb	57.4	30.9
12	AT&T Corp.	45.7	30.0
13	Lucent Technologies Inc.	39.9	22.6
14	Johnson & Johnson	54.5	28.7
15	Philip Morris Cos. Inc.	59.9	33.7
16	Berkshire Hathaway — CLA	15.7	13.5
17	E. I. Du Pont de Nemours	55.6	33.3
18	American International Group	54.6	28.0
19	Cisco Systems Inc.	64.8	36.6
20	Walt Disney Company	49.3	27.7
21	NationsBank Corp	49.7	29.2
22	SBC Communications Inc.	43.6	25.0
23	Bell Atlantic Corp	39.0	22.2
24	Travelers Group Inc.	63.9	37.5
25	Eli Lilly & Co.	61.3	43.5
	Average Ownership	48.7	28.0

Source: *Institutional Investment Report: Patterns of Institutional Investment and Control in the United States,* The Conference Board, Vol. 2, No. 2, August 1998, Table 20, p. 38.

Table 12.2ᵗ Institutional Ownership at General Electric, December 1997

Rank	Manager	Percent Held
1	Fidelity Investments	3.5
2	Barclays Global Investors, N.A.	2.9
3	Bankers Trust Company (New York)	1.8
4	State Street Corporation	1.6
5	Mellon Bank Corporation	1.3
6	College Retirement Equities Fund	1.2
7	Vanguard Group, Inc.	1.1
8	General Electric Investment Corp.	1.0
9	Putnam Investment Management, Inc.	0.9
10	Fayez Sarofim & Co.	0.9
11	Wells Fargo & Company	0.8
12	Northern Trust Corporation	0.8
13	Travelers Group Inc.	0.7
14	Equitable Companies, Inc.	0.7
15	Chase Manhattan Corporation	0.6
16	NationsBank Corporation	0.6
17	PNC Bank Corporation	0.6
18	American Express Financial Corp.	0.6
19	Wellington Management Company, LLP	0.6
20	First Security Corporation	0.5
21	First Union Corporation	0.5
22	California Public Employees' Retirement System	0.5
23	Fleet Financial Group	0.5
24	American Century Investments	0.5
25	United States Trust Company (New York)	0.5
	Total Held by All Institutions	48.8
	Top 5	11.1
	Top 10	16.2
	Top 20	22.9
	Top 25	25.4

Source: Institutional Investment Report: Patterns of institutional investment and control in the United States, *The Conference Board* 2, no. 2 (August 1998), Table 21A, p. 39.

the largest US firms in 1998 and notes the high level of concentration of ownership by the largest 25 institutional investors. Table 12.2 lists the 25 largest institutional owners in GE as of 1997.[4]

In addition to owning about 50 percent of the equity in the United States, institutions own about 21 percent of *all* assets, as shown in Table 12.3.

Table 12.3 Institutional Assets, 1999
(Billions of Dollars)

Pension Funds	8,823.3
Private Trustees	4,996.4
Private Insured	1,135.9
State and Local	2,690.9
Investment Companies	4,234.4
Mutual-open end	4,066.9
Closed End	167.5
Insurance Companies	2,819.0
Bank and Trust Companies	2,254.2
Foundations	442.0
TOTAL	18,583.7

Equals: 21.3 percent of ALL U.S. Assets

Source: *Institutional Investment Report, Financial Assets and Equity Holdings,* The Conference Board, vol. 4, no. 1, 2000, Table 2, p 16.

The term *fiduciary capitalism* suggests, however, more than simply changes in ownership patterns. Large fiduciary institutions have a different nature, respond to different incentives, and have different patterns of behavior than do other owners, even wealthy individual owners who exercise some degree of control over their portfolio companies. In addition to their fiduciary duties of loyalty and care, many of these institutions are so large and diversified that they effectively own a broad cross-section of the economy. Because of this breadth of ownership we call them universal owners. And because they effectively own the economy as a whole there is a commonality between many issues of significant concern to socially responsible investors and the fiduciary duty to which universal owners are legally and ethically obligated.

The Universal Owner

A universal owner is a large institutional investor that holds in its portfolio a broad cross-section of the economy, holds its shares for the long term and on the whole does not trade except to maintain its index. Most important, a universal owner's cumulative long-term return is determined not merely by the performance of each individual firm it owns, but by the performance of the economy as a whole. In short, its total long-term return is greater than the sum of its parts. This has a number of potentially important consequences. First, it means that when universal owners evaluate the behavior of the firms they own one significant dimension should be how each firm's activities affect the economy as a whole, and hence the returns earned by other firms in their portfolio. The universal owner — like the economy as a whole — captures positive externalities generated by firms and is harmed by their negative externalities.[5]

A second consequence is that universal owners come to occupy a quasi–public policy position as having an economic interest in the long-term health and well-being of society as a whole. The universal owner's unusual position suggests that it has an interest not only in standard macroeconomic policy issues, but more specifically in regulatory policy and the provision of public goods such as education and health, tort law, and infrastructure generally, both physical and human. Confronted with this potential, many universal owners have moved cautiously, not only for fear of stepping on politically sensitive toes over a variety of immediate "hot button" issues such as health or the environment but also due to their concern about exercising what has come to be a significant amount of economic power. Public pension fund managers do not generally conceive of themselves as public policy makers, in spite of their growing recognition that they often play such a role or may be forced by the logic of economic efficiency to do so. However, as the ultimate beneficiaries — pension fund participants, mutual fund owners, etc. — come to realize the importance of universal owners acting as such, more fund managers will find the political room to use the potential power that universal owners possess.

It should be noted that if universal owners come to act on public policy and investment issues, as we argue is part of their fiduciary duty, this is very unlikely to become a form of "backdoor socialism." Although large universal owners as a group own historically large percentages of stock, each individual institution owns a very small percentage of all outstanding equity. Thus, if institutions are to be effective, they must work in coalitions, much as they have done in the last decade with regard to corporate governance issues. Institutions currently do not see eye to eye on many of these issues, and the organizing of coordinated activities is complex, decentralized, and pluralistic — quite the opposite of centralized state ownership and direction.

A Profile of a Universal Owner

A typical universal owner is the Teachers Insurance and Annuity Association — College Retirement Equities Fund, better known as TIAA-CREF. It is one of the largest financial service organizations in the US and one of the largest retirement systems in the world. A look at its financial structure in general and its equity portfolio in particular provides insight into the nature of universal ownership. As of September 30, 1998, TIAA-CREF had over $222 billion under management. Of this total, $100 billion was in the TIAA portion (the annuity association) of the organization. The bulk of these assets were invested in bonds, commercial mortgages, and real estate. Almost all of the remaining $122 billion was in the CREF portion of the organization, the portion that would be characterized as a universal owner.[6] These assets were primarily invested in the equity of domestic and foreign firms.

CREF invested in 67 industry groups spread across some 4669 different equity issues.[7] Investments in most industry groups represented less than 2 percent of the total portfolio; however, six industry groups accounted for more than 5 percent each, and three — chemicals and allied products, communications, and depository institutions — each accounted for more than 10 percent of the portfolio. Of the total value of the stock account portfolio, most of the equity, 82 percent, was invested in US companies, while 18 percent was invested in the common stock of companies in 35 foreign countries.

Clearly, CREF's equity portfolio represents a broad cross-section of the industrial and financial wealth of the United States. In effect, it owns the economy, and as such, its return on its portfolio depends very heavily on the macroeconomic performance of the United States. If the economy does well, CREF does well. If the economy does poorly, CREF does poorly. Thus CREF has an interest — a purely financial interest flowing directly from its fiduciary obligations — to promote a healthy, efficient economy. It should support the reduction of negative externalities and the encouragement of positive ones since it will capture the benefits of these actions — even if only a small portion of the benefit is captured by each of its portfolio companies. It should inform itself on public policy issues such as education policy, trade, globalization, work place practices, and environmental policy that have the potential to affect the economy positively or negatively, and it should develop public policy positions on these issues as part of the exercise of its fiduciary duty of care.[8]

Universal Owners and Their Role As Socially Responsible Investors

Most socially responsible investors have traditionally avoided corporate governance issues, while until recently most large institutional investors have avoided or minimized their focus on "social" issues. However, both these stances may be changing. With more and more public funds like the California Public Employees' Retirement System (CalPERS) focusing on SRI issues (in additional to Taft-Hartley trade union funds, which have focused on many SRI issues in recent years) a very important intersection is emerging between SRI and some large institutional investors. This is true not only in the US, but in the UK and increasingly in continental Europe as well.[9]

The intersection of SRI, trade union funds, and state and local government funds is noteworthy because traditionally SRI has defined itself based primarily on moral and ethical and/or in political terms, while large institutional investors traditionally have defined themselves based exclusively on their legally obligating fiduciary duty — their duties of loyalty and care to their beneficiaries. Consequently, most pension funds have avoided both the language of SRI and an SRI orientation, viewing themselves, perhaps incorrectly, as trading ethically correct investing for higher returns.

SRI funds, on the other hand, have on the whole been screened and exclusionary and/or based on best practices rather than engaged with companies on more traditional corporate governance issues. However, strong returns by many SRI funds from the middle 1980s through the 1990s have increased the interest in SRI in many quarters.[10] It has also increased interest in the SRI community in bottom-line issues. Can doing good lead to doing well? And if so, what are the implications, over what time frame, and why has this occurred? Similarly, this has led trade union funds and state/local and cooperative pension funds to look more closely at SRI from a financial performance perspective.

The Need to Account for Externalities

As noted, one of the fundamental characteristics of a universal owner is that it cares about the performance of the economy as a whole as well as the governance and performance of the individual companies that comprise its investment portfolio. Simply put, the universal owner's concern with overall economic performance is based on the recognition that it "owns" the economy (typically, a highly representative cross-section of the economy) and therefore bears the costs of any shortfall in economic efficiency produced by negative externalities and reaps the rewards of any improvement as the result of positive externalities.

This approach complements the traditional approach of the finance model, which argues that investors should carefully monitor individual companies and, if their strategy allows, buy "winners" and sell "losers."

However, for institutions following an indexing strategy, buying and selling is ruled out by definition, except to maintain the index. Even very large fiduciary institutions that do not index cannot buy and sell freely for fear of disrupting the market due to the sheer volume of trades (in addition to the fact that most large fiduciary institutions have portfolios that mirror each other). Thus many of these institutions, such as the state public employee retirement systems, have actively tried to improve the performance of lagging companies though various types of intuitional investor corporate governance activism such as performance targeting, "just vote no" campaigns, etc. To date this has been the main thrust of corporate governance activities, both in the US and abroad. But universal owners should realize that this firm-by-firm approach will go only so far toward maximizing returns for beneficiaries and that they may therefore need to complement it with an analysis of the impact that externalities might have on the performance of their portfolios as a whole.

Externalities affect the return on investments by imposing costs or benefits on firms from areas outside their control. Externalities are often characterized as pecuniary and nonpecuniary. Pecuniary externalities impose costs (or provide benefits) that are readily measurable in monetary terms, often as a change in resource costs to a firm. An example of a negative pecuniary externality would be the dumping of effluent by a plant upstream. This negative externality would impose direct, measurable costs on downstream plants (and municipalities) as they made expenditures to clean up stream water for their use. Nonpecuniary externalities impose costs or confer benefits that are not initially measurable in monetary terms, though they may have important economic consequences. An example of a negative nonpecuniary externality would be the lost future productivity of a child who labors in a factory rather than going to school. The society loses the potentially higher productivity of its citizen, but the cost, while potentially quite large, is not easily or directly measurable in monetary terms.

The importance of externalities to universal owners is reinforced because of the size of their portfolios — which makes it difficult or impossible to avoid investing in particular sectors or firms — or because the institution has adopted an explicit indexing strategy that requires it to passively hold a portfolio that mirrors the economy as a whole. Some institutional investors already appreciate the position this places them in. For example, Kim Johnson, general counsel for the Colorado Public Employee Retirement Association (PERA) notes, "We look at environmental issues very, very closely. We know that aside from the ideal that it is socially desirable to have a healthy and long-term stable environment there are also some good economic reasons for our actions. We have suffered the consequences of holding property with environmental problems so we know the costs first-hand. But I also think our trustees are aware that in a macro sense this is a good thing to do."[11]

While the Colorado fund focuses on the direct monetary effects of environmental concerns on its portfolio returns, when the CalPERS weighed in on the controversy surrounding Maxxam Corporation and the Headwaters forest controversy, it was recognizing to some extent the nonpecuniary externalities involved.[12] CalPERS owned a substantial stake in Maxxam and was, of course, deeply interested in the economic implications of any settlement that Maxxam might make. While negative publicity and a disregard for the concerns of an important, organized, and potentially powerful group were economic issues concerning CalPERS, it also considered them to be possible contingent legal liabilities.

Education and worker training are other areas where universal owners should be concerned about externalities. The quality of the skills and the education of the labor force are widely recognized as crucial to the long-run economic growth of a country and, hence to the long-run profitability of investments in that country. It has also long been recognized that a company will tend to underinvest in the education and training of its own work force because it can not capture all of the benefits the training provides.[13] However, a universal owner *does* capture those benefits because it captures the benefit of enhanced education and training to the economy at large. These returns are likely to be quite substantial. Researchers have estimated that the social returns to education are from 1.6 to 1.7 times larger than the private returns.[14] CalPERS and the combined New York City Funds recognize this through their "High Performance Workplace" programs. CalPERS has a "workplace" screen that surveys companies about their human resource policies and publishes the results. New York and CalPERS have issued studies on workplace practices and economic performance.[15]

Finally, a telling example of the divergence between firm-specific self-interest and the interest of a universal owner can be drawn from high-tech industry. Research and development activities in high tech are crucial to success. But some firms might be tempted to underinvest because they cannot capture all of the returns, as the following story told by Gordon Moore, one of the founders of the Intel Corporation, illustrates.

Before forming Intel, Moore and Robert Noyce, the company's other cofounder, started Fairchild Semiconductor. The R&D department at Fairchild was quite successful at identifying a large number of important technical advances, but the company lacked the ability to commercialize many of these discoveries. As a result, Moore reports that numerous ideas developed at Fairchild actually ended up benefiting its competitors. When it came time to found Intel, Moore and Noyce made a conscious decision not to have a permanent R&D department. Rather, technical teams would be assembled on a project-by-project basis and disbanded when the project was completed. This was an explicit attempt to avoid the spillover benefits that Fairchild had contributed to other companies (and, of course, to the economy as a whole) and to better capture for Intel the benefits of its R&D expenditures.[16]

A universal owner should prefer the Fairchild model to the Intel model since it would almost certainly capture the benefits of any technical advances regardless of which company commercialized a particular discovery. In any case, while it may not be in the interest of any one company to push forward the frontiers of knowledge unless it can capture a substantial portion of the benefit, it is certainly in the interest of a universal owner – and of society as a whole – to do so. Universal owners may do this either by encouraging individual companies in their R&D efforts, by supporting industry-wide research and development consortiums, or through their political support for publicly funded basic research.

Two Important Public Policy Initiatives

An attempt to account for externalities and to recommend investor actions on the basis of that accounting is a paper titled "Climate Change: A Risk Management Challenge for Institutional Investors" by the third largest pension fund in the United Kingdom, Universities Superannuation Scheme (USS).[17] The paper argues that since the fund holds both equity and property that would probably be affected (and perhaps drastically so) by climate change, it should develop policies in this area. The negative externality of adverse climate change would likely force major costs onto companies in its portfolio, so as a universal owner the fund should adopt a pro-environmental position. To respond to these challenges the paper recommends a number of measures institutional investors should take (review portfolios for risk, engage with investee companies, etc.).

The USS paper also highlights the central role universal owners might play in responding to the risks presented by climate change. In the words of the report, "It is possible to argue ... that long-term universal investors have a substantial degree of common interest and purpose with the good of the economy as a whole. This implies that it may be in the narrow interest of institutional investors to press for actions that support the common economic good."[18] Thus the USS paper specifically draws on the idea that a universal owner's broad and long-term view places it in a unique position to engage with firms it owns and to weigh in on public policy issues, acting as a "...bridge between public policy, corporate governance and the well-being of individuals (especially beneficiaries)."[19]

In addition, the report notes that because they must be broadly interested in long-term economic efficiency and sustainability, universal owners also have an interest in assessing the impact of special-interest lobbying and influence peddling by many of the firms they own. Activity in the public policy process on the issue of climate change can help to offset such special-interest activity. Importantly, universal owners have the potential to "stand above short-term and vested interests and could play a powerful role in supporting policy-makers to address climate change in the optimal economic and environmental way." In conclusion, the USS paper strongly suggests that from a strategic universal investor perspective "… there is a case for institutional investors to adopt a more strategic approach to climate change risk. This is to intervene in the policy debate [nationally and internationally] to encourage governments to take action to address climate change."[20]

A second public policy initiative by a universal owner was the response of CalPERS to the California energy crisis. CalPERS owns about $5 billion of stock in energy companies. In June 2001 it took the unusual (and unprecedented) step of asking Willie Brown, the mayor of San Francisco and a CalPERS Board of Administration member, to direct face–to-face "questioning" of energy companies on behalf of CalPERS. Normally such discussions are undertaken by in-house professional staff. The proposal to CalPERS by the State Treasurer Phil Angelides (also a CalPERS Board member) was to investigate the effect energy companies' practices were having "on both their [own] long-term health and on the California economy." Angelides added, "This needs to be elevated above the normal corporate governance action. We wanted to send a message that the board considers this to be especially important." This response to the impact that energy prices have on the California economy (which has been to worsen an existing economic contraction) is a good example of universal monitoring because the externality effects are arguably quite large. The assessment of what long-term risks might face some energy producers themselves as a result of alleged price "gouging" is also a good example of risk management to monitor the potential political backlash and possible future court-imposed liability settlements or rebates.[21]

As the above examples illustrate, both pecuniary and nonpecuniary externalities can impact the returns institutional investors experience and will therefore directly affect their ability to discharge their fiduciary responsibilities to their beneficiaries. In addition, universal owners also need to be aware of the changing social environment, since the evolution of norms of behavior can directly affect the return of their portfolio companies.

Universal Owners and Universal Monitoring:
Norm Shifts and Externalities

A *norm* is a society's attitude toward a particular activity or practice, and a *norm shift* is a change in a society's attitude. For a large part of our country's history, for example, employing children in factories was considered an acceptable labor practice — an accepted norm. But the norm changed (though not without significant conflict), and today child labor is neither acceptable nor legal. While norms are not externalities, some norm shifts, like the shift to the prohibition of child labor, can have extremely important economic consequences and are often justified to some degree by their economic impact — in this case, the enhanced long-term productivity resulting from a more highly educated labor force. This development was made possible by the universal public education that accompanied the movement away from child labor and that was used as a partial justification for the change in norms related to employing children.

Recent examples of the interaction between norm shifts and scientific and technologically based externality issues can be seen in issues as diverse as tobacco and smoking, the environment, labor practices, animal testing standards, health and safety issues, human rights, and various types of gender, racial, and other forms of discrimination that are closely related to human rights. In the US many if not all of these may also become significant forms of contingent legal tort liability that may well have major financial impact, as in the case of Texaco's discrimination settlement, which resulted in more than $170 million in bottom-line damages.

Contingent legal liability (and the often closely related regulatory actions by Congress and the courts) come to define market boundaries — what is legally, ethically, and prudentially possible — in business practices. Norm shifts are best evaluated through standard risk analysis, in this case done for a universal owner's portfolio as a whole. Norm shifts usually present themselves to a firm in the form of legal (tort), market, good will, and/or other forms of potential firm-specific liabilities. Because of potential adverse consequences, fiduciary duty compels institutional owners to have in place a process for tracking and analyzing these developments — that is, some form of risk analysis.[22] They should be obligated to monitor and analyze their portfolios for interactive externality effects, as well as for "risk" factors based on norm shifts. This type of extended monitoring we call *universal monitoring*.

Since universal owners internalize positive and negative externalities of the firms in their portfolios and since they bear the consequences of firms' norm-based liabilities, their fiduciary duty requires universal monitoring of their portfolio. It is in their long-term interest and the interest (by definition) of their investors and beneficiaries to maximize the positive externalities of their holdings and minimize the negative externalities. This may create direct costs (for example, pollution abatement and product and process redesign) for some firms and sectors of the economy, but will generate gains that accrue to other sectors and firms. However, as a general proposition, negative externalities impose costs on affected firms that outweigh — sometimes greatly outweigh — the benefit to the polluting firms. Thus it is in the long-term interest of a universal owner that owns *all* firms to pursue externality monitoring that attempts to reduce negative externalities and to encourage positive externalities. This should be combined with portfolio-wide risk monitoring, resulting in universal portfolio analysis and universal monitoring.

Conclusions: A Turning Point?

Universal monitoring coincides in many important respects with most SRI issues. Most SRI issues are long-term sustainability issues — that is, issues concerning health and safety, the environment, global warming, and many aspects of global human rights (for example, wages and working conditions). These are issues involving long-term economic growth, the growth and nature of consumer demand, and the physical environment — all critical components for long-term sustainable economic development and growth. Many of these issues focus on the effects of a firm's (or many firms') economic activity that are not included in the direct and indirect costs of production, distribution, and/or consumption, yet which have immediate or longer-term social costs. As such they are classic negative pecuniary and nonpecuniary externalities.

Since a universal owner holds a portfolio broadly representative of the economy as a whole, it internalizes both negative and positive externalities. As such, a universal owner has a fiduciary obligation to use a variety of means (including public policy advocacy and the corporate governance processes) to encourage firms to produce positive externalities, and to minimize or eliminate negative ones. Universal owners have the opportunity and the fiduciary duty to monitor and analyze their portfolios as a whole — attentive to changing positive and negative externalities that firms generate and how these externalities are likely to be viewed by society's changing definitions of market legitimacy and risk.

In this regard, universal owners appear to be at a turning point in their relationship to SRI issues and perspectives. Traditional SRI can go only so far if it continues only or primarily to screen and thereby filter firms on a case-by-case basis. Ironically, although this form of SRI may produce both pressures on firms to change and possibly above-average returns, it is prevented by its own screens and selective "best practices" from maximizing its impact on the economy as a whole. This is so because best practices and SRI selective screens ignore externalities, thus leaving them in place, and on the whole do not engage the worst (or even average) offenders. Indeed, a financial analysis that does not analyze the portfolio as a whole in terms of both externalities and changing market definitional norms will not be able to achieve financial returns equal to those possible if universal owners exercised their ownership responsibility and influence in order to maximize long-term portfolio-wide returns.

Universal monitoring can bring large institutions closer to many SRI investor sensitivities. However, universal monitoring and the fiduciary nature of universal owners' perspectives suggests that they will continue to use a different language, and typically a different yet complementary approach to the SRI perspective. Universal owners will view many of these issues not as matters of ethics or morality as such, but in terms of sustainability and long-term portfolio-wide economic effects and financial performance. Yet this approach necessarily also redefines financial performance by linking it with sustainability, and in this sense is a significant break with traditional "bottom-line" financial analysis.[23]

In this regard, socially responsible investors may need to consider changing their thinking and also their language. They may need to move from an emphasis (and often an exclusive emphasis) on ethical and morality-based arguments to arguments incorporating externalities and broad-based financial analyses. Such an analysis can draw explicitly on risk analysis and universal monitoring while integrating ethical, political, and moral perspectives.

The consequence of universal monitoring by universal owners, often working in coalitions with SRI-oriented investors, fits squarely within the framework established in the last decade by many corporate governance activists. These institutions have come to realize that on they whole they must care because they cannot sell, either because they are too large and move markets, or because they are indexed. "Care" involves active and forceful engagement with the firms they own. As SRI investors become (or consider becoming) universal investors, they too must care, and shareholder engagement on the basis of universal, interactive portfolio analysis may well come to supplement (and possibly replace) SRI screens and selectivity as the basis for investment. Such a strategy would marry SRI perspectives with corporate governance approaches. Large institutional investors cannot select only the best-of-class investments — nor, if they are indexed, can they normally screen out the most egregious cases (such as tobacco companies). Thus, they must engage. This is the origin of corporate governance activism. The questions are how effective is the engagement and to what ends. These are the classic corporate governance issues. It is where corporate governance, fiduciary responsibility, and SRI can find common meeting grounds and agendas.

Notes

1. James P. Hawley and Andrew T. Williams, *The Rise of Fiduciary Capitalism: How Institutional Investors Can Make Corporate America More Democratic* (Philadelphia: University of Pennsylvania Press, 2000).

2. While many small institutional investors do not own widely diversified portfolios, the largest do, and as a group the largest institutions hold the vast majority of institutionally owned equity.

3. Fiduciary duties have their roots in English common law, where they are described as the highest duty of an agent to a principle — such as a guardian to a minor. Today in the US, fiduciary duties have been codified as Section 1104 of the Employee Retirement and Income Security Act (ERISA).

4. Most of these institutions are either pension funds (such as CREF or CalPERS) or financial institutions that act as money managers for pension funds (such as Fleet Financial or Barclays), or money managers directly (such as Fayez Sarofim & Co).

5. An externality is a spillover effect that is either a positive or negative effect that falls on a third party not immediately party to the contract.

6. *Semi-Annual Report: College Retirement Equities Fund* (New York: College Retirement Equities Fund, 1998). A small fraction of the total assets of TIAA-CREFF consists of three other entities: life insurance, mutual funds, and a trust company.

7. CREF is invested in a smaller number of companies since some individual positions represent different equity issues of the same company.

8. While large universal owners such as CREF may want to perform these functions in house, smaller fiduciary institutions may want to join coalitions or subscribe to services such as the Investor Responsibility Research Center (IRRC) or Investor Shareholder Services (ISS) in order to exercise their responsibility in a cost-effective manner.

9. See CalPERS' website, www.calpers-governance.org/principles, especially its global proxy voting guidelines adopted in March 2001.

10. See, for example, Moses L. Pave and Joshua Crausz, *Corporate Responsibility and Financial Performance: The Paradox of Social Cost* (Westport, Conn.: Quorum Books, 1995); and "The Domini 400 Social Index," *Statistical Review*, February 2001 (KLD and Co., Boston, Mass.).

11. Interview with Kim Johnson, general counsel, Colorado Public Employee Retirement Association, December 4, 1997.

12. The controversy arose out of Maxxam's desire to log old-growth redwood trees, which provoked strong opposition from environmental groups and other concerned citizens. The issue was presented to the board of the California Public Employee Retirement System as Agenda Item 16 on April 14, 1997. See also Mitchel Benson, "Fund Warns Maxxam Not to Log," *Wall Street Journal*, February 19, 1997, CA1.

13. In economic terms, the optimal investment for a firm occurs when the marginal private cost to the firm just equals the marginal private benefit the firm receives. When the benefit to the economy at large — the social benefit — exceeds the private benefit, as it does with education, firms will underinvest from the point of view of society at large.

14. Robert E. Lucas, "On the Mechanics of Economic Development," *Journal of*

Monetary Economics 22, no. 1 (1998): 3–42; and James E. Rauch, "Productivity Gains from Geographic Concentration of Human Capital: Evidence from Cities." *Journal of Urban Economics* 34, no. 3 (1993): 380–400.

15. CalPERS, press release, June 15, 1994, "CalPERS Adopts Study on Workplace Practices," Sacramento, Calif.; and The Gordon Group, " Report to the California Public Employees' Retirement System, High Performance Workplaces: Implications for Investment Research and Active Investing Strategies," Waban, Mass.: The Gordon Group, 1994); City of New York, Office of the Comptroller, "High Performance Workplace Practices: A Recommendation for institutional Investor Action," January 1995.

16. "The Changing Nature of Entrepreneurship," a conference sponsored by the Center for Economic Policy Research in association with the Chemical Heritage Foundation, Friday, May 30, 1997, at the Donald L. Lucas Conference Center, Ralph Landau Center for Economics and Policy Research, Stanford University. The title of the talk was "Regional Linkages, Silicon Valley and the Networked Firm." The most famous case of a company failing to capture the benefits of its R&D expenditures may be Xerox Parc, a basic research facility for the Xerox Corporation in Palo Alto, Calif., which invented, among other things, computer networking and the graphical user interface with a mouse as an input device.

17. "Climate Change: A Risk Management Challenge for Institutional Investors," a discussion paper by Mark Mansley and Andrew Dlugolecki (London, July 2001).

18. Ibid., p. 47.

19. Ibid., p. 12.

20. Ibid., p. 47.

21. John Widermuth, "CalPERS Taps Mayor for Energy Talks," *San Francisco Chronicle,* June 19, 2001, p. 1.

22. An example of monitoring for risk related to SRI issues is articulated in CalPERS' Global Proxy Voting Principles, adopted in 2001. The duty to monitor is part of the concept of prudence under Department of Labor ERISA guidelines since the 1988 "Avon Letter." CalPERS justifies its global corporate responsibility stance as a "collateral benefit" of long-term maximization of beneficiaries' return. It bases the monitoring of the global activities of firms it owns on the Global Sullivan Principles, although it does not limit itself only to those. CalPERS enumerates seven Sullivan principles as the basis of its future corporate governance activities, and notes that violation of these guidelines has often resulted in both litigation against firms it owns and a decline in the "good will" value of some firms (CalPERS, "Global Proxy Voting Principles," March 19, 2001, Sacramento, Calif.).

23. In recent years sustainable growth and some SRI analysts have focused on the triple bottom line (financial, environmental, and social) in an attempt to account for the financial, environmental, and social performance of firms. While triple-bottom-line accounting has the potential to pressure managers to "manage what you measure," triple-bottom-line accounting is still too limited a perspective if only applied on a firm-by-firm basis since it tends to be screened, and even if it does not screen it misses portfolio-wide externalities. The really significant impact of triple-bottom-line accounting and management will occur when large universal owners begin to *act* as universal owners, understanding that the financial, social, and environmental performance of each firm taken singly is suboptimal from an economy-wide perspective.

13

Crossing the Black Waters:
The International Dimension of SRI

By Geeta B. Aiyer and Steven Heim

Ancient Hindu law and practice prohibited travel across the "black waters" (seas) to foreign lands for fear the traveler would be "polluted" by contact with the outlandish practices of unknown peoples. Adventurous souls, such as Mahatma Gandhi, who ventured abroad and took on these "pollutants" had to perform elaborate penance to cleanse themselves upon return.

Until recently, social investors held international investing in the same uncomfortable light. Some shunned foreign stocks because of unfamiliarity, certain that the data didn't exist to conduct corporate social research. Others opposed international social research, because in the process we would be using our American standards for corporate conduct to judge companies that operated in vastly different cultural settings. To be fair, information of consistent quality and reliability on company social records is harder to find overseas. And definitions of good corporate citizenship do vary widely across nations. Nonetheless, in an investment sense, we have crossed the black waters. Walden Asset Management has offered international portfolio management for social investors since

1995. In June 1998, we created the first ever SRI international index portfolio based in the US. In August 1999, this commingled fund became a publicly traded mutual fund, the Walden/BBT International Social Index Fund (WISIX).[1]

In the six years we have spent developing and managing international social funds, we have observed that:

- Information on corporate social conduct is becoming more available, but much primary research is needed. We must continue to work to expand networks of information sources.
- The socially screened international index fund has tracked, and in the market conditions of the past few years, outperformed, the broad developed-country market indices, bearing out our experience from domestic social investing.[2]
- Shareholder advocacy and dialogue are even more critical internationally than they are in the US, not only because they help social researchers to overcome information shortfalls, but also because they are the primary means for non-US corporate managements to get feedback from US social investors. Using the well-honed domestic shareholder advocacy tools of proxy voting, dialogue, and shareholder resolutions, US investors can have an important impact internationally.

We hope that telling the Walden story is instructive to those considering international social investing.

Why an Index Fund?

Walden had several goals in launching the fund, both financial and social. We wanted the fund to have country and sector diversification while maintaining meaningful social standards, to be competitive with international equity markets, and to serve as a platform for meaningful dialogue and action between committed long term investors and international corporations. WISIX is designed to match the international markets with a socially screened universe of stocks, and to provide social investors with international diversification similar to that of international developed country market indexes, for example, Morgan Stanley Capital International's EAFE (Europe, Australasia and the Far East) Index and the Financial Times World Indices European Pacific Index (FT Euro-Pacific).[3,4]

Table 13.1 Percent of Market Value Eliminated in Industries with High Social or Environmental Impacts
(For Initial Investable Universe)

Aerospace	99%
Metals & mining	89%
Beverages & tobacco	87%
Chemicals	61%
Utilities (electric & gas)	61%
Building materials & components	53%
Energy sources	50%
Electrical & electronics	48%
Machinery & components	48%
Food & household products	43%
Automobiles	36%
Forest products & paper	26%

The fund serves as a core choice for social investors, neutral to portfolio manager style. Another goal was to quantify the "costs" of international social investing. Our experience with actively managed international portfolios showed that social investors did not need to sacrifice their financial goals for their social mission.

Walden's Investment Process

Matching broad developed country market indices with a socially screened universe of stocks proved to be a challenging assignment. In particular, we needed to adjust initially for about 200 of the approximately 1000 companies included in broad developed-country market indexes, representing approximately 30 percent of the market capitalization, that did not pass social screening criteria. While this investment prohibition is moderate relative to typical actively managed domestic portfolios with comprehensive screens, a significant portion of the market value of international markets is screened out in high-social-impact industries as illustrated in Table 13.1.

Figure 13.1 Country Weight Comparison
(as of December 31, 2000)

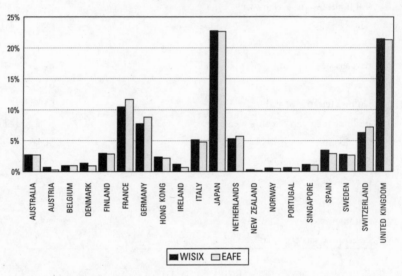

To fill the gaps in the screened universe of international stocks, Walden added acceptable companies from under-represented countries and industry sectors. To further round out the investable universe, we sought additional companies with exceptionally positive social records. For example, Holmen AB (formerly Mo ochs Domsjo AB, or MoDo), a Swedish forest products company was included for their early decision to eliminate elemental chlorine gas from the bleaching process. MoDo switched completely to oxygen, chlorine dioxide, and other safer paper bleaching agents.

The next task was to take the screened universe of international stocks and construct a portfolio that would match the investment performance of the broad developed country market indices. Fortunately, we know from experience with other stock market index funds that it is possible to track the market without holding every stock in a particular index.[5] This is especially important in composing an international index because high overseas transaction costs make it prohibitively expensive to hold the stocks of many smaller companies.

Figure 13.2 Sector Weight Comparison
(as of December 31, 2000)

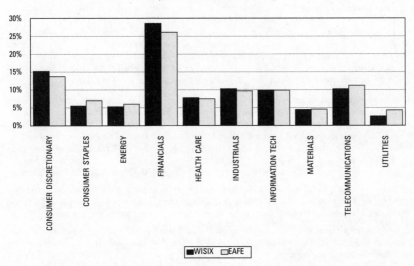

The stocks (currently about 700) chosen for the WISIX portfolio are selected using quantitative "optimization" techniques that maximize the portfolio's projected ability to perform in line with the international markets. This process also serves to minimize the sector and country biases introduced by our social screens. Figures 13.1 and 13.2 compare the sector and country weights for the Fund versus MSCI EAFE.

As noted above, since inception in June of 1998, the fund is ahead of the major market indices such as the MSCI EAFE Index and the FT Euro-Pacific Index. Since the conversion to a mutual fund in August 1998, we have met our objective of tracking the performance of developed country markets with a socially acceptable stock universe; see the performance comparison in Table 13.2.

Table 13.2 Performance Comparison

	One Year Ending Dec. 31, 2000	Since Inception August 26, 1999
Walden/BBT International Social Index Fund (WISIX)[a,b]	− 15.86%	2.12%
MSCI EAFE Index[c]	− 14.16%	1.33%
Financial Times Euro-Pacific Index[d]	− 14.77%	1.77%

a. Walden Asset Management (Walden) performs shareholder advocacy, proxy voting, screening services, and other social initiatives for Boston Trust Investment Management Inc. (BTIM). BTIM, a wholly owned subsidiary of United States Trust Company of Boston and an affiliate of Walden, assumed on May 12, 2001, Walden's responsibilities as investment advisor for the Walden family of mutual funds, including the Walden/BBT International Social Index Fund. Some of the activities noted in this chapter were done by Walden on behalf of the shareholders of Walden/BBT International Social Index Fund, pursuant to Walden's agreement with BTIM. Walden receives a fee for its services.

b. After all expenses at an annual rate of 1%, the Advisor's expense limitation. Results shown are past performance which is not an indication of future returns. Investment return and net asset value will fluctuate so that an investor's shares, when redeemed may be worth more or less than the original cost. International investing involves increased risk and volatility. Shares of the Fund are not deposits or obligations of Boston Trust, United States Trust Company of Boston, or any Bank and are not insured by the FDIC, Federal Reserve Board or any agency. The value of the Fund shares and returns will fluctuate and investors may have a gain or loss when they redeem shares. Distributed by BISYS Fund Services.

c. The MSCI EAFE Index is based on the share prices of approximately 1023 securities of companies listed on stock exchanges in the 21 developed market countries, not including the US and Canada, that make up the MSCI National Indices. An investor cannot invest directly in an index.

d. The Financial Times World Indices European Pacific Index is a dollar-denominated, market capitalization-weighted index comprised of securities in the European and Pacific regions. An investor can not invest directly in an index.

Difficult Tradeoffs

Walden wrestled with many complex tradeoffs in order to pick stocks from an international universe. After companies were excluded on the basis of product screens — alcohol, tobacco, gambling, weapons and nuclear power — those remaining were then evaluated for their performance on environmental, labor, and human rights issues. As part of our screening process, Walden developed its own databases using industry data sources and published information, and built networks of alternative information sources with activists and foreign shareholder groups (see the box on the next page for some examples of international resources currently available to social investors).

As with Walden's screened domestic portfolios, energy and materials companies were two sectors that were disproportionately excluded for environmental reasons, while labor and human rights screens reached across all sectors. Still, many companies with positive social or environmental records were selected for the portfolio. Examples include Novo Nordisk A/S, the Danish pharmaceuticals company noted for its advanced environmental management and reporting; Norske Skogsindustrier ASA, a Norwegian paper and forest products company with a zero emissions goal for its mills; Abbey National PLC, a UK bank with progressive home mortgage lending policies; and Carrefour SA of France, one of the world's biggest retailers that has banned genetically modified foods from its store-brand products until these foods are proven safe.

The norm, however, for an index type fund such as WISIX, is that many portfolio companies will not have exceptional social performance and some may be controversial. The Fund's investment in Novartis AG, the giant Swiss pharmaceuticals and chemicals company created in 1996 from the merger of Ciba-Geigy and Sandoz was a tough decision. It is illustrative of the difficult tradeoffs inherent in matching the performance

---

Sample Resources for International SRI

- Corporate Critic, online business ethics database by Ethical Consumer, www.ethicalconsumer.org.
- Corporate Watch (USA), web site providing information on activities of corporations, www.corpwatch.org .
- Global Unions, a web site that is run by several international trade union organizations, www.global-unions.org.
- Ethical Investor, published by Ethical Investment Research Service, www.eiris.org.
- nexis.com, online full-text news article databases by LEXIS-NEXIS, www.nexis.com.
- Multinational Monitor, published by Essential Information, www.essential.org.
- SIPRI Yearbook, published annually by Stockholm International Peace Research Institute, www.sipri.org.

and portfolio profile of developed country markets or indices with social screens. The large European chemical companies we researched had major environmental problems, but for portfolio diversity we still needed to find a number of suitable investments in the industry. Each of the component Novartis companies has a well documented, troubling legacy of product liability and environmental problems.

Nonetheless, Walden approved Novartis because it responded with a significant turnaround in internal environmental management systems and with openness to dialogue with its critics. Further, we approved it expecting to continue our dialogue with the company. For example, in response to concerns about its historical practice of exporting pesticide products that were not approved in industrialized countries to the nonindustrialized world, Ciba-Geigy adopted a policy of not manufacturing a product unless it was approved in at least one OECD country. At the time of our initial research, Novartis's Ciba unit was ranked the seventh-best environmental performer out of 50 chemical companies worldwide by the German environmental group, Hamburger Umwelt Institut. In Europe Novartis held public forums with critics of Novartis's genetically engineered crops business. In November, 2000 Novartis spun off its controversial agriculture chemicals and genetically engineered seeds business into a joint venture with AstraZeneca PLC's agricultural chemicals unit, to form a new company, Syngenta AG.

Beyond Screening: Our Social Change Approach

While Walden has confidence in its ability to continue to build a strong social screening capability in an international context, obstacles to obtaining reliable and comprehensive information on corporate social performance are indeed real. This is particularly true when one moves beyond product-related social criteria to more qualitative areas such as environmental performance and employment practices. For this reason, standards of acceptability in the context of an index fund are not currently as stringent as those possible in the United States. Where in the US "below-average performance" is a typical minimum threshold, in the international environment Walden generally seeks to rule out those companies that rate as "worst performers."

Yet it is precisely these research challenges, coupled with the direction of our US-oriented social investing focus, that have led Walden to move expeditiously into the realm of international shareholder advocacy. We have found that all the tools available to us domestically — proxy voting, shareholder dialogue, representation at annual meetings, and even shareholder proposals — can be adapted to foreign markets. In fact, the global perspective that we bring to discussions with management adds significant shareholder clout. As is the case in the US, the cutting-edge work in socially responsive investing internationally is in using shareholder leverage to exert a positive influence on corporate practices, often in collaboration with local shareholder coalitions and activist organizations.

Specifically, Walden's approach to international shareholder advocacy includes (1) proxy voting; (2) country-specific advocacy; (3) dialogue, letters, questionnaires, conferences, or on-site visits; (4) representation at company annual general meetings of shareholders; and (5) sponsoring shareholder resolutions.

Proxy Voting. Walden has developed country-specific proxy voting guidelines for its international equities, including those held in the Fund to be consistent with the Fund's financial and social objectives. With the proxy process abroad less developed than in the US, the Fund's voting guidelines emphasize independence and transparency in operations. Walden generally votes against board of directors slates with no disclosure of professional affiliation or ties to the company, such as in Italy or Japan, and in the UK, if the board consists of less than one-third nonexecutives.

Country-Specific Advocacy. In Japan, for example, Walden presses for increased board independence and more transparency and accountability to shareholders. In 1999, to gain insight and baseline information on existing corporate governance practices, Walden surveyed its top 20 Japanese holdings for director and statutory auditor independence, board size, and remuneration. We offered companies our questionnaire translated into

Japanese if they preferred. We were encouraged that 80 percent (16) of the companies responded.

Dialogue and Meetings. Advocacy initiatives may be industry-focused. For example, strong concerns about the rights of children and the use of child labor led Walden to pursue a letter-writing campaign that encouraged global retailers to join RUGMARK, a labeling program certifying that carpets are made without child labor. At other times Walden has addressed concerns about a specific company's conduct. In correspondence with Novartis, we helped reinforce the view that a constituency of investors, not only activists, cares about the environmental and human impact of improper pesticide use in developing countries and its marketing of genetically engineered seeds.

Further, an index fund approach provides an opportunity to engage leading companies in entire industries. For example, Walden has focused on financial services companies working with nongovernmental organizations (NGOs) to press banks to strengthen their lending and underwriting practices to incorporate environmental and social impacts. As part of this effort, Walden wrote to all portfolio banks that participated in a $500 million China Development Bank (CDB) bond issue. The CDB provides financing for China's Three Gorges Dam, a project with enormous social, economic, and environmental costs.

Walden has augmented advocacy on this issue through home country visits to leading global banks that are signatories to the United Nations Environment Program, including Credit Suisse, Deutsche Bank, and UBS. Discussions with environmental department officials and credit officers about policies and practices in integrating environmental and social criteria into core business activities have been well received.

Representation at Company Annual Meetings. As part of its international advocacy work, Walden seeks partnerships with local shareholder groups and NGOs, including trade unions, to bring issues before companies at their annual shareholder meetings. During the 1999 proxy season, we were represented at the ABN-Amro Annual General Meeting (AGM) through our

Dutch NGO partner to present our joint concerns over ABN-Amro's position as primary lender to the mining industry. We asked that the company include environmental and social criteria in its credit risk analysis and to encourage best practices among corporate borrowers. We also had representation at the HypoVereinsbank AGM through our German partner to ask it to reassess its involvement in the Maheshwar Dam project in India due to serious environmental impact and resettlement concerns.

In 2000 Walden had a trade union representative at the Imerys SA annual meeting in Paris to advocate for respecting workers' rights to unionize at an Imerys plant in Alabama. Imerys, an industrial materials company, is known for its good labor relations in Europe. Walden's intervention attracted major media coverage in France. Following the annual meeting, the company pledged not to retaliate against union supporters. According to the workers, this step allowed them to debate collective bargaining and union representation more freely without fear of company retribution. Soon after that, the workers voted in favor of union representation and in early 2001 they approved their first collective bargaining agreement.

Sponsoring Shareholder Resolutions. This tactic is used much more often in the United States than abroad. Shareholders in foreign countries usually have fewer rights than their US counterparts and face bigger hurdles in sponsoring shareholder resolutions on social issues. Walden has, however, begun to use this tool with foreign companies. In 2001 Walden helped lead a shareholder campaign to sponsor a resolution with BP Amoco PLC (BP) regarding its plans for drilling in the Arctic National Wildlife Refuge (ANWR) in Alaska. This is an extension of Walden's ongoing dialogue with BP that started in 1997 and has included discussions on plant closings in Lima, Ohio, to the company's involvement in ANWR and its commitment to renewable energy.

A Work in Progress

After more than two years of operation we are pleased that we launched the Walden International Fund and met our objectives. We have been able to develop sound methodologies to screen companies in conjunction with effective shareholder activism. Most important, the Fund's performance has been competitive with broadly diversified developed-country markets.

Although encouraged by the Fund's development thus far, we understand that it is a work in progress, to be improved upon as more information and tools become available. For many reasons, we believe that we have the wind at our back as we journey the black waters. More standards are being set. For example, we look forward to the wide adoption of ISO 14001 environmental management guidelines and to more regions harmonizing regulations and reporting within the European Union. We are also developing better contacts with global shareholder groups. Large institutional investors are making a concerted push for greater transparency and better reporting, including on issues of social concern. Social investors can take comfort from these trends as they contemplate diversifying their investments into international securities.

Notes

1. Walden Asset Management (Walden) performs shareholder advocacy, proxy voting, screening services, and other social initiatives for Boston Trust Investment Management, Inc. (BTIM). BTIM, a wholly owned subsidiary of United States Trust Company of Boston and an affiliate of Walden, assumed on May 12, 2001, Walden's responsibilities as investment advisor for the Walden family of mutual funds, including the Walden/BBT International Social Index Fund. Some of the activities noted in this chapter were done by Walden on behalf of the shareholders of Walden/BBT International Social Index Fund, pursuant to Walden's agreement with BTIM. Walden receives a fee for its services.

2. Results shown are past performance, which is not an indication of future returns. Investment return and net asset value will fluctuate so that an investor's shares, when redeemed, may be worth more or less than the original cost.

3. The MSCI EAFE Index is based on the share prices of approximately 1023 securities of companies listed on stock exchanges in the 21 developed countries, not including the US and Canada, that make up the MSCI National Indices. An investor cannot invest directly in an index.

4. The Financial Times World Indices European Pacific Index is a dollar-denominated, market capitalization-weighted index comprising securities in the European and Pacific regions. An investor cannot invest directly in an index.

5. Interestingly, we have found this to be true also for constructing equity portfolios for world (ex US) market indices that include emerging market stocks.

14

A Revolution in Energy

Samuel Case

Scenes from a Revolution

In Seattle, several buses in the city's fleet go about the streets quietly and with no exhaust, in marked contrast to their noisy, smoky diesel counterparts. In Chicago, a major bank, citing millions of dollars lost in downtime from blackouts, disconnects itself from the utility grid and employs a new source of power. These are examples of the first practical applications of fuel cells.

Near Sacramento, a thousand houses in a proposed new development will sport solar panels on their rooftops. In addition to generating their own electricity, these homes will require half the normal amount of heating and air conditioning. In California's Central Valley, Chevron Texaco is building a one-megawatt photovoltaic system — one of the largest solar arrays in the world — to power its oil field operations.

A large municipally owned utility purchases 141 microturbine power systems to supplement its larger power plants. These 30-kilowatt microturbines run on low-polluting natural gas and operate at efficiencies substantially higher than traditional generators. Across the country, a number of businesses are also purchasing microturbines to produce their own power and ensure against blackouts.

In Minnesota, farmers contract with utilities to place wind turbines in their fields, bringing in about $2,000 yearly for each turbine. Crops can be grown, or animals grazed, around the turbines, so the income is an addition, not a replacement, to agricultural income. Similar scenarios are beginning to catch on in windy areas throughout the Midwest.

These are scenes from a revolution in the making. During the next 25 years, this revolution will forever alter the way that energy is produced, distributed and utilized. Fossil fuels and nuclear power will be on their way out, and renewable sources will take their place.

This chapter will describe the key components of these changes and discuss how investors can both contribute to and reap benefits from the new technologies. Socially responsible investors have been naturally drawn to companies that work with efficient, low-polluting technologies, but up to now, most of these firms have been working on the margins, struggling against the status quo. This is changing rapidly: sustainable energy is going mainstream.

The economic environment is now beginning to favor those with foresight, environmental concerns — and pragmatism. Investors with any foresight at all know that unless the natural capital of the earth is preserved, there will be little left to invest in. But the energy revolution will not be powered solely by interest in sustainable environmental practices, though they will add impetus. This revolution will be driven by technologies that are cheaper, more effective, and more efficient than those currently in use.

For example, compared to a nuclear plant, a wind turbine farm is simpler to build and maintain, contains no hazardous materials, and is fueled by an inexhaustible supply of free energy. The cost of the power produced is already comparable to nuclear power in many areas, and will soon be cheaper. This chapter will look at the ways in which sustainable technologies already outperform conventional models. During the next decade, these will provide new, high-performing vehicles for socially responsible investors. Before we start with the new technologies, however, let's take a look at how energy is produced and consumed in the world today.

The Status Quo

At the start of the new century, the pattern of world consumption of energy remains roughly the same as in the last quarter of the 20th century. Oil is king, followed by natural gas and coal, then hydropower and nuclear power. Natural gas consumption surpassed coal for the first time in 1998; indeed, the use of coal has shown a slow decline since 1996. Overall, total worldwide consumption of fossil fuels increased only 0.1 percent in 1999.

In the US, power from biomass fuels (which includes methanol) surpassed hydropower in 1999; in the developing world, biomass in the form of wood remains a major fuel for cooking and heating. Renewable energy sources, such as wind and solar, while growing at a rapid pace, still account for a very small percentage of consumption.

Utilities with centrally based power plants and extensive distribution systems remain the dominant source of electric power and natural gas. Many of these utilities, however, have lost their status as regulated monopolies, as deregulation of the power industry proceeds in many states. These changes have proven to be disruptive to the power industry in several areas, most notably in California, where a botched deregulation led to dramatically increased prices for consumers and bankruptcy for at least one major utility.

Transportation, which is closely linked to energy use, has been largely fueled by petroleum for the last hundred years. While various experimental vehicles are now on the roads, virtually all autos, trucks, buses and trains are still powered by gasoline and diesel fuel.

As we suggested in the opening section, however, this stable picture is illusory. Vast changes are in the works, driven by market forces, environmental concerns and the adoption of innovative technologies. After a hundred years of mostly sustained development, oil companies, coal producers, independent power providers, utilities and automotive industries are highly vulnerable to new, disruptive technologies. We will discuss these technologies later on, but first, let's look in greater detail at the energy landscape as it appears today.

Petroleum

Petroleum products represent 40 percent of the total energy consumed in the United States, with consumption growing at a rate of 0.8 percent in the 1990s and accelerating. Petroleum products drive our transportation system. Ever since petroleum became a major source of energy, we have heard widely varying predictions on when the supply would run out. Now it appears that all these predictions have been erroneous: we will probably never run out of oil. Computer-based techniques have brought about a revolution in oil exploration to such a degree that industry experts now believe that new technologies will replace petroleum long before the supply gives out.

Natural Gas (Methane)

At present rates of usage, the supply of natural gas is projected to be sufficient for 200 years. As in the case of petroleum, new technologies are projected eventually to replace natural gas before the supply runs out. At present, natural gas supplies a little more than 20 percent of US energy.

Natural gas is fast becoming the fuel of choice in the US and throughout the world, in part because natural gas combustion produces much less pollution than other fossil fuels (it also creates only one-half as much carbon dioxide as coal). Consumption rose by 1.9 percent yearly during the 1990s and is accelerating; consumption is growing even faster in Europe and the developing economies. About 70 percent of new homes in the US are fueled by gas, and a growing number (a thousand, at present) of transit buses run on compressed natural gas. This growth is expected to accelerate, partly because of the promising fuel cell technology: the primary way of obtaining hydrogen for fuel cells, at present, is reforming methane into hydrogen and carbon dioxide.

Coal

After three centuries as a primary energy source, the use of coal is declining. Although it still provides 20 percent of the total energy consumed in the US, consumption declined in 1999 to 1987 levels. Consumption of natural gas surpassed coal for the first time in 1998. The environmental damage caused by coal mining and the pollution from burning the fuel has come under fire from environmentalists. Electricity generation is the largest source of pollution in the US, and the great majority of that comes from older, coal-fired power plants. While coal will remain an important fuel for a few more decades, natural gas is being employed for most new power plants.

There is experimentation going on with so-called "clean coal" technology. This involves "scrubbers" that clean the smokestack emissions, and various coal gasification techniques (the gas produced from coal burns more cleanly than the solid fuel). Although these technologies do reduce air pollution, mining is still necessary and carbon dioxide emissions continue to contribute to global warming. We cannot, therefore, recommend clean-coal technologies to socially concerned investors. There are much better things to invest in, as you will see further on.

Nuclear

Nuclear power is also moving towards a decline. During the 1990s, total global nuclear capacity rose only 4.7 percent, in contrast to a total growth of 140 percent in the 1980s. Nuclear power use is expected to peak in 2002 and then start to decline. No new reactors are under construction in Europe and North America and only a few in the rest of the world, while aging reactors are being taken offline. The Department of Energy estimates that 31 percent of total nuclear capacity in the US will be permanently shut down by 2015.

The inability of nuclear power to compete in a level marketplace is coming to light: nuclear has long been subsidized by national governments. This inability, combined with the dire consequences of a failure in containment and the difficulty in disposing of radioactive waste, have made utilities unwilling to invest in any new nuclear projects. At present, nuclear accounts for roughly 5 percent of total energy consumption in the US, all of it used to generate electricity.

The recent energy crisis in California, coupled with high prices in the oil and natural gas markets, have emboldened the nuclear forces to push their technology once again. The nuclear industry in the US argues that nuclear plants do not produce greenhouse gases or contribute to trade deficits in foreign oil. Various mini nuclear plants in the design phase are claimed to be safer and more cost-effective than the present technologies. The problem of radioactive waste disposal, however, is still not being addressed.

In addition, since the attacks of September 2001, there has been growing concern about the vulnerability of nuclear plants to terrorist attacks. In Russia and certain Third World countries, there is great concern that nuclear material could be stolen and converted into weapons by terrorist groups.

Hydropower

Although hydropower is a renewable, nonpolluting source of energy, some of the giant dams that produce it have come under fire as harmful to the environment. That, plus the fact that the best sites for productive dams have already been employed, means that hydropower will not be a growing source of energy. Environmental groups have even advocated the destruction of some smaller dams so that the rivers can return to their natural state. Hydropower supplies about 8 percent of total power consumed in the US.

Utilities and Independent Power Producers

At the beginning of the 20th century, Thomas Edison envisioned a widely distributed power system, with many small power plants and businesses generating their own electricity. And, indeed, by 1907, small, individual systems accounted for 60 percent of electricity generated in the US. Many of these plants employed waste heat from their steam-driven generators in an early version of cogeneration. The advent of alternating current and transformers, however, made it possible to transmit current over long distances, and the highly efficient steam turbine began to favor the economies of scale of larger generating plants. By the 1930s, large, monopolistic, utility systems had been established in most industrialized countries. The central power plants connected to an electrical grid steadily reduced the cost of power and provided reliable service. Industries involved in the generation and distribution of power continued to expand in an orderly manner with improvements in sustaining technology.

By the 1980s, however, the industry had reached limits in efficiency gains from size, and flaws had begun to show up in the system. For one, the high exposure of the system to fluctuations in fossil fuel prices became apparent. In addition, increased environmental awareness exposed the ecological disruption necessary to support the large-scale generation of electricity. Fossil fuel extraction and uranium mining, pollution from combustion, enormous dams for hydropower, and high-voltage transmission lines were perceived as disruptive and harmful to the environment.

During the 1990s, small-scale power technology began to surpass the grid system in efficiency and environmental friendliness. The trend is now toward the kind of small, distributed power generation we saw at the beginning of the 20th century. This trend will be discussed further in the next section.

Deregulation has hastened an already marked trend that is separating power production from distribution. Utilities are increasingly becoming simply distributors of gas and electricity, dependent on the independent power producers (IPPs) and the energy markets for the products they bring to consumers. The energy crisis in California revealed the downsides of this trend when an ill-planned deregulation allowed the IPPs to charge whatever the market would bear, while limiting the amount utilities could pass on to consumers. An unhappy outcome of this debacle has been sharply increased gas and electricity prices to consumers.

On the positive side, as prices rise and the threat of blackouts increases, alternatives begin to look better to consumers. In California, in particular, there has been an upsurge of interest in renewables and distributed power. "If the days of cheap, dependable power are gone," the thinking goes, "then I had better produce it myself for my home or business." Before we get to these new, promising models, however, we need to look at the hidden costs of conventional fuels.

Hidden Costs of the Status Quo

We hear a lot about how the cost of renewable sources has yet to compete with power from fossil and nuclear fuels. What we don't hear about are the hidden costs contained in the present technologies. These hidden costs are not paid for by the energy companies; they are paid by us as taxpayers through government subsidies, or by us as utility consumers. The costs may also manifest themselves as environmental damage or health problems. It has become common to view the harm done by fossil fuels and nuclear technologies as simply part of the costs of doing business. To fully comprehend the disruption and damage they cause, it can be useful to get out of the present for a minute and imagine a solar-powered world fifty years from now.

In this world, there are few oil wells on land — or offshore, where the dangers of spills are constant. There are no wells or pipelines in environmentally sensitive areas. There are no immense oil tankers plying the oceans and regularly spilling oil that devastates beaches and marine life. There are no polluting refineries. Coal strip mines no longer despoil the landscape, fouling the surrounding ground and water. Black smoke from coal-fired power plants no longer dirties the air.

The air is clear and healthy because there is virtually no pollution from fossil fuel combustion: no ozone, particulates, or nitrogen oxide causing health problems, no acid rain killing forests and lake fish. Human contribution to global warming has ceased. There are no military actions in the Middle East to preserve access to oil, no balance of payments problems caused by hundreds of billions of dollars spent for foreign oil, and no recessions caused by oil price shocks. The US no longer needs to support corrupt, repressive regimes in the interest of stable oil production and supply.

Nuclear plants no longer pose the threat of ruinous meltdowns, and nuclear material for these plants is no longer in danger of being converted to weapons. While there is still the problem and expense of storing nuclear waste from decommissioned power plants, at least no new waste is being created. In addition, governmental support of nuclear power no longer burdens the taxpayers.

The hidden costs of present technologies should be evident from their absence in the picture described above. The difficulties in placing a dollar value on these costs, however, should also be evident. How, for example, does one calculate the cost of the disrupted ecology of a wilderness area? How to compile the total damage from oil spills to wildlife — or to human endeavors, like fishing or tourism? How to price a human life lost to pollution-related illness? Nevertheless, some analysts have bravely attempted to compile certain of these costs — those expenses that eventually accrue to all of us. Here are their estimates:

Global Warming. The 1990s saw a exponential increase in the number of devastating storms, both in the United States and abroad, causing damage in the tens of billions of dollars. In 1992, for example, Hurricane Andrew caused $30 billion worth of damage, bankrupting nine insurance companies. These extreme weather conditions are caused by warmer water in the tropics, and are not expected to abate. By the year 2040, some analysts predict that the total cost of global warming in the US alone, including storms, drought, and disruption to agriculture and other industries, will approximate $260 to $400 billion each year. These figures do not include factors that are more difficult to measure, like loss of wildlife and damage to ecosystems.

Energy Costs. In the US, hidden expenses for conventional fuels (including nuclear fuels) are estimated at approximately $235 billion a year; worldwide, the figure is $600 billion. The true cost of gasoline is estimated to be $4.50 per gallon, when the real costs to American society are tabulated.

These costs come from a number of different places:

- Direct subsidies and tax breaks to energy companies, like the oil depletion allowance
- Indirect subsidies, such as utility consumers paying higher rates for the decommissioning of failed nuclear plants, or government assistance in storing the radioactive waste
- Expenses related to illness from air pollution, including lost work days
- Expenses related to land and water pollution — from mining, oil spills, etc.
- The costs of maintaining a military presence — especially in the Middle East — to stabilize the oil markets.

In developing countries, damage from combustion of coal and oil is even more serious. For example, during the early 1990s, one of every eight deaths in China was attributed to air pollution (mostly from the burning of coal).

Both the environment and human health have suffered greatly from activities relating to the use of fossil and nuclear fuel. While these costs might have been considered necessary evils when there were no viable alternatives, today they must be looked on as unacceptable. Even without considering the hidden cost advantages of conventional power listed above, the price of renewable energy is now comparable to fossil and nuclear fuels in several cases, like wind power, and is falling fast in others, like solar.

Several countries are already moving rapidly toward economies fueled by sustainable energy. For instance, Germany will decommission all of its nuclear plants by 2020, and is looking to wind power to fill the gap. Already, several German states get 20 to 30 percent of their electricity from wind turbines. Iceland has dedicated itself to creating the world's first hydrogen-based economy, with most of its energy coming from sustainable sources. In this next section, we'll take a closer look at these new, sustainable technologies.

Sustainable Energy Technologies

There are presently a number of technologies that contribute to the energy revolution. There is *synergy* at work here: The combination of innovative models is going to bring about greater change than the simple impact of each one separately. The trend to distributed power, for instance, will get a big boost as fuel cell technology improves — and as the price of renewables comes down. Together, these innovative models are creating a new architecture that will prove highly disruptive both to energy producers and distributors.

The energy revolution is progressing on five main fronts. These are:

- Renewable energy. Photovoltaic (solar electric) power will soon become competitive with fossil fuels (the best estimates are by 2010 or even sooner). Wind energy is already competitive in many areas and costs are continuing to fall.

- Fuel cells. This new technology uses fuel approximately three times as efficiently as the internal combustion engine, while producing zero pollution. The hydrogen that runs the cells can be produced from methane or other fossil fuels — or from renewable sources. Fuel cells hold the promise of nonpolluting vehicles and of better load-leveling for intermittent power sources, like solar and wind.

- Transportation. Initial changes will come from more efficient vehicles — hybrid vehicles, for example. More sweeping changes will come as improved storage technology and fuel cells come into general usage.

- Distributed generation of power. The utility model of centralized production and distribution of power is being challenged by the new technologies.

- Efficiency. By bringing efficient technologies into common usage, estimates are that we could cut our national energy bill by as much as 50 percent, with no loss of performance or convenience.

These are the technologies of the future. The next 25 years will see a gradual replacement of the old technologies with the new. The new models are more efficient, cleaner, and either are, or will become, significantly cheaper. They preserve the natural capital of the earth, in that they do not strain the regenerative capabilities of the ecosystem. By lowering or eliminating pollutants in the air, they contribute to human health. In short, they are smarter, better designs. Well-managed companies whose business models optimize these technologies will prosper, as will the investors who support them. These investors will have the further satisfaction of watching their investment dollars speeding up the worldwide revolution in energy.

There are two ways that individuals and businesses can profit from this revolution, while contributing to its progress. The first is in the equity markets — investing in the most promising companies working with the new technologies. The second is by direct investment — the actual purchase of photovoltaic panels or efficient technologies. This second alternative has recently become very attractive; investments in the new technologies not only provide a good return, but a safe and reliable one as well.

Renewable Energy

This section on renewable sources of energy covers those newer technologies that are likely to show rapid growth. Hydropower, for instance, is a renewable source, but will probably not grow appreciably over the coming decades. The same is true of geothermal power, which generates power by employing heat from deep in the earth to run vapor engines. Geothermal has great potential in certain areas of the world, but is unlikely to show much growth without further investment. So far, geothermal has not attracted the same attention and investment dollars as solar and wind technologies.

There are also a number of experimental technologies that attract small amounts of investment, such as tidal power, wave power, power from temperature differentials in the ocean, and small hydropower installations, and these may prove useful in certain areas. In particular, wave power — harnessing the energy in ocean waves — has attracted attention in the UK. For the foreseeable future, however, none of these appears to hold the potential of solar and wind technologies.

Solar Power

There is a point in the life of new technologies when their cost becomes attractive and their utility surpasses that of existing models. This is often a sudden shift, after a long period of marginal use and noncompetitiveness in most areas. Photovoltaics — which produces electricity from sunlight — is fast approaching that shifting point.

First invented in 1957 at Bell Laboratories, solar cells quickly found special use in the space program to power satellites and, later, manned space flights. As their high price gradually came down, the technology was employed for various remote power applications like road signs, navigational buoys, and small calculators. In the 1970s, photovoltaic modules began to appear on rooftops, particularly on houses where connecting to utility lines was prohibitively expensive. In conjunction with battery storage, homeowners could generate their own power apart from utilities.

Because utility power was still cheap and reliable, however, the high initial cost of the systems made them unattractive to most. Utilities experimented with a few photovoltaic installations and related technologies, including solar-powered heat engines to generate electricity, but high costs and cheap fossil fuel dampened their enthusiasm. The profit curves didn't look attractive to the large utilities, and most of their customers were not demanding solar power.

Several factors are now contributing to a new outlook for photovoltaics. First, the technology is a natural for distributed power systems. The fuel, after all, is distributed for free, and rooftops are a prime location for the modules. Second, after a few years of stagnation, the price is moving down once more. Its production cost is presently $3,500 per kilowatt; a further drop to $2,000 per kilowatt would make it competitive with conventional fuels. Research on improved photovoltaic cells has increased, and industry experts expect this drop in price to happen within the next ten years.

Even without technological breakthroughs, however, there is good evidence that economies of scale alone will make the technology competitive. For example, when photovoltaic arrays are installed on a number of houses at once, the price falls by as much as half. In California and other states with liberal tax incentives for solar power, there are plans for a number of solar housing developments, including a thousand-home project near Sacramento. The houses in these developments will get most of their electricity from the photovoltaic arrays on their rooftops. When the sun shines, the arrays will feed extra power into the utility grid; the utility will purchase this power, essentially running the meter backwards. On cloudy days and at night, the homes will purchase power from the utilities.

Solar homes are normally more efficient in their use of energy, incorporating such features as extra insulation, energy-saving appliances and low-heat-exchange windows. This further lowers the cost of the photovoltaic arrays by decreasing the amount of required power. This combination of economies of scale, efficiency and tax incentives already makes electric power from the sun competitive with fossil-fuel-generated electric power in many areas. By generating their own power, homeowners, businesses, and public agencies can lock in their electrical power costs for a number of years, thus avoiding future rate hikes.

When these figures become public knowledge, the photovoltaic industry will grow at a much faster rate than most analysts predict. Future energy hikes and oil shortages will only contribute to this growth. At present, production of photovoltaic modules is growing at an average rate of 30 percent a year, but this already phenomenal rate will almost certainly rise sharply over the next few years.

Photovoltaics has found new uses all over the world, particularly in developing countries where thousands of villages are not connected to any power grid. New models, like thin film solar technology, allow the devices to be incorporated into building materials like roofing shingles, siding and even windows, thus further reducing the installed cost.

Most analysts envision solar panels being connected to the existing power grid. This could change, however, if a cheap, reliable storage device — or "load-leveler" — comes onto the market. The existing storage technology consists of expensive, relatively short-lived battery systems. With a better way of leveling energy production during nights and cloudy days, many homeowners and businesses might opt for complete disconnection from the grid. Better batteries or high tech flywheels may accomplish this, but the fuel cell, described later on, appears to be the best candidate for leveling energy loads.

The slow development and downward price curve over 45 years has given businesses plenty of time to consider their options and prepare for the solar revolution. Unlike many disruptive technologies that are developed over periods of just a few years, photovoltaics has given the energy industry decades to get ready. Oil companies like Amoco, Shell, and BP are now investing in the technology. Chevron Texaco has constructed a large photovoltaic array to power one of its California refineries. Many oil producing countries are likewise aware: even Sheik Yamani, the Saudi Arabian oil minister, speaks of the need to prepare for renewable sources of energy.

Wind

Wind power is growing even faster than solar at present. Wind turbines are being installed all over the world, particularly in northern Europe where strong coastal winds are put to good use. In Denmark (the industry leader) and in Germany, there are large wind turbine farms placed in coastal areas and offshore, where the ocean winds are strong and steady. Wind power reached a total installed capacity of over 16,000 megawatts in 2000, and the capacity installed each year is increasing by 65 percent to 70 percent. If the present growth rates are sustained, wind power could supply 10 percent of the world's electricity by 2020. In actuality, it will probably be significantly greater, because wind power keeps outrunning analysts' projections.

According to the US Department of Energy, electricity produced by wind turbines is now competitive with electricity produced by gas and coal-fired plants and, as the turbines increase in size and efficiency, the price is continuing to drop. Although there is also a small market for home or ranch-sized wind machines, the bulk of investment is going into large, utility-based turbines.

Biomass

Biomass is a poor cousin to solar and wind in terms of publicity, but surpasses both of them in total power. Producing electrical power and useful heat from the combustion of agricultural crops, agricultural waste, sewage sludge, and organic industrial waste is a fast-growing technology. Some analysts project that the growth of biomass energy worldwide could surpass that of both wind and solar over the next twenty years, particularly in the developing world. In China, for example, many villages employ simple composting digestors of animal waste to produce methane gas, which then fuels small electric generators.

Burning organic material no longer needs to be a smoke-producing operation. New technologies gasify the waste and burn the resulting methane as cleanly as natural gas. Another biomass product — methanol — is mixed with gasoline. A further environmental benefit of this renewable fuel is that it is carbon dioxide neutral in terms of emissions (the growing plants absorb carbon dioxide, then give it up when they are burned).

Fuel Cells: The Hydrogen Economy

There has been a lot of talk about the "Hydrogen Economy," but what exactly does that mean? At present, we have an economy based mostly on fossil fuels, but hydrogen could replace them in most areas. Hydrogen can power our homes and businesses, run all our vehicles, ships and, possibly, aircraft. It can be burned to provide heat and used for cooking, just like natural gas and propane. It has the advantage of being the most ubiquitous and plentiful element in the universe and it produces zero pollution when burned. The only by-products of its combustion are heat and water.

Hydrogen can be extracted form natural gas, gasoline, or methanol; this process is cleaner and more efficient than burning those fuels in internal combustion engines. Hydrogen can be reformed from natural gas at the well head; carbon dioxide is a by-product of this process, but this can be re-injected into the gas field to provide continuing pressure (which helps bring more gas to the surface). The hydrogen is then transported by pipeline or in liquid form, just like natural gas.

Hydrogen can also be split from the oxygen in water (H_2O) through the process of electrolysis; this involves a simple process of applying an electric current to water and collecting the released gases. When the electricity for this reaction comes from renewable sources, like wind or solar, the entire process is even more ecologically friendly than extraction of hydrogen from fossil fuels.

In terms of safety, hydrogen is very similar to natural gas in its combustibility. This is a technology we are used to dealing with in our stoves and furnaces. Although the storage of hydrogen for fuel cells in vehicles is still being worked out, hydrogen use in buildings presents few new challenges or dangers.

Hydrogen Fuel Cells

If you can imagine a battery that, instead of being recharged, can be re-fueled, you have a basic understanding of fuel cells. Fuel cells produce power by reversing electrolysis — recombining hydrogen and oxygen into water and creating heat and an electric current in the process (the oxygen is present in the ambient air). This electric power can be used to power a building, or run a vehicle. While the technology is still in the experimental stage, it is garnering large amounts of investment for many different models. The size and weight of the cells need to be reduced for vehicles and a better storage system for hydrogen created.

Fuel cells promise reliable, non-polluting power for individual buildings. As the technology is perfected over the next decade, it will boost the already strong trend towards distributed power. The First National Bank of Omaha, mindful that a one-hour power outage can cost it $6 million in loss of transactional ability, has invested in a fuel cell–based power system. The cells supply 800 kilowatts to the mainframe of the data center and operate in the "high nines" in reliability (99.9999 percent availability).

Projections vary as to the speed with which fuel cells will come into general use, but there is general agreement that the technology has arrived and is presently being perfected. Allied Business Intelligence estimates a US market of $10 billion by 2010, representing 10,000 megawatts of electricity.

Transportation

The vehicles we use to transport ourselves will also undergo radical changes during the next twenty-five years. The trend is toward low-polluting, quiet power systems, with efficiencies three times greater than internal combustion engines. The first commercially available vehicle in this trend is already on the roads: the Toyota Prius combines a small, gasoline-driven engine with an electric motor, resulting in an average 50 miles per gallon. This is more than double the fuel efficiency of the present automobile fleet in the US. Honda produces a smaller version of a hybrid — the Insight — with an average of 65 mpg.

The electric car has been around since the 1890s. It has many good qualities, like low pollution, quiet operation, reliability, and low maintenance, but has suffered because available batteries have had insufficient storage capacity. Consumers have been unhappy with the 50- to 100-mile range allowed by current battery systems. The hybrid solutions replace battery storage with a fuel-driven power source, but retain the electric motor. Whether this power source is a conventional, gasoline-driven engine, an advanced microturbine, or a fuel cell, the result is a vehicle that includes the advantages of an electric but offers a range comparable to present-day vehicles. Fuel efficiency is increased and emissions are sharply reduced.

Advocates of battery-driven electrics protest that hybrid vehicles still produce emissions. But, since most battery-driven electrics are charged from the utility grid, which is powered by fossil or nuclear fuel, they cause indirect pollution, though much less than conventional vehicles. Only when batteries are charged from renewable sources can a vehicle truly be said to produce zero emissions.

In line with our argument that the most profound changes will be the result of new technologies working in synergy, there is research under way on a so-called Hypercar. This vehicle would incorporate the latest in lightweight, polymer composite materials, aerodynamics, regenerative braking and motive power systems. The Hypercar will be an advanced hybrid design, with power generated by fuel cells. All these technologies working together will produce as much as 150 miles per gallon without compromising on power or amenities.

Distributed Power

Earlier, we noted the difficulties facing the utility model of centrally generated power distributed over a vast electrical grid. At the same time, technologies are being introduced that make a more distributed form of power generation attractive. Advanced microturbine technology is one, and the growth of renewables like solar and wind is another. These are termed "micropower" systems because of their small size compared with the enormous, utility-sized generating plants.

There are several forces driving the trend toward distributed, micropower systems:

- Increased costs of utility power resulting from fuel price increases and fallout from deregulation policies.
- Greatly increased reliability and efficiency of small systems, coupled with lower costs.
- Perceived drawbacks in large-scale generating systems, including unreliability, the high cost of maintenance, and environmental considerations.
- Environmental benefits of small-scale systems, including the use of renewables.

The new microturbines, especially when fueled by natural gas, emit roughly half as many harmful gases and particulates as do existing central generating stations. Their efficiencies are also higher, partly because the heat from exhaust gases can be used for space heating — or cooling, with absorption coolers (cogeneration). This dual use sends efficiency ratings into the 85 percent to 90 percent range, compared to 35 percent to 70 percent at central power stations. In addition, there are no power losses from transmission lines over long distances — and the costs of maintaining the grid are eliminated.

Efficiency

The energy crisis of the 1970s led to an increased supply of fossil fuels as government encouragement and high prices led to expanded exploration and production. The crisis, however, also prompted significant gains in the efficient use of energy by the private sector. As a result of this increased efficiency, between 1979 and 1986, US gross domestic product rose 20 percent while total energy use *fell* by 5 percent. This pattern confounded most energy analysts and led to a supply glut that in 1986 crashed energy prices, particularly in the oil industry. Unfortunately, the resulting lower energy prices also discouraged users from instituting more energy-saving programs.

Growth in efficiency waned for ten years, then reappeared in 1996. Since 1996, energy savings in the US have averaged 3.2 percent per year, more than in the 1980s. This trend has been given a big boost recently by increased energy prices and deregulatory efforts that have brought higher prices to end users. At the same time, the present administration is supporting increased production, creating the possibility of a reprise of the energy crash of 1986.

Efficiency can be a powerful force, especially in a time of high prices when small improvements can translate into large monetary gains. Amory Lovins of the Rocky Mountain Institute was among the first to emphasize that increased efficiency is, in effect, a cheap energy "source" (Lovins calls this source "negawatts"). Regardless of whether energy is saved or produced, the result is more available energy. Potential savings from efficiency is a vast resource; some estimates place it at half the country's present energy usage. More efficient vehicles, buildings, industrial electric motors, lighting, and appliances can add up to tremendous energy savings at a fraction of the cost of increasing energy supply (Lovins estimates one-sixth the cost).

The Synergy of New Technologies

Earlier, we mentioned that it would be the synergy of new technologies employed together that would be most likely to bring disruption to the energy sector. The scenario described below will be brought about by several of the new models working together. Here is how a renewable and hydrogen-based economy might appear in the microcosm of your home in the year 2025.

The photovoltaic cells built into the roofing material of your home generate electricity that powers the home during the daylight hours. Some of the electricity is used to separate hydrogen from water by electrolysis. This hydrogen then runs a fuel cell that provides power for the house at night and on cloudy days. Enough hydrogen is stored (in a tank outside the house) to power the house for a week of cloudy weather; in a pinch, you can have a tank delivered to your door in the same manner that propane is delivered today. The stored hydrogen also provides fuel for your car — which uses very little, being a super-efficient Hypercar. In addition, the gas is piped to your stove, furnace and water heater.

The photovoltaic system is affordable, both because installed costs have come down and because the house employs the latest in efficient technology. As such, it requires very little heat or air conditioning, and the lighting and appliances use one-third the power of today's houses. Thus, efficiency is added to renewable energy, fuel cells and the trend towards distributed power to produce a home that is effectively energy independent.

This synergistic model can be repeated with variations in business establishments. One scenario has the fuel cells in automobile fleets providing power for buildings or feeding current into the utility grid when the cars are parked. Whatever the variations, though, it's easy to see that a scenario like this would, by eliminating the need for any other fuel or distribution system, be highly disruptive to the whole energy sector. Energy independence might bring lower costs and greater reliability to individual users, but it would bring revolutionary changes to the entire energy industry.

Conclusion

The coming revolution in energy presents a unique opportunity to socially responsible investors. As pioneers in these new technologies, they stand to profit from their investments while furthering the cause of sustainable power. The benefits to the environment and to human society will come in many areas.

- Benefits of sustainable energy not accounted for in standard accounting procedures:
- Reduced strain on the ecosystem; preservation of natural capital
- Reduced pollution, with resulting health benefits
- Diversity of fuel supply leading to economic benefits and greater national security by lessening dependence on foreign oil
- Solution to the human contribution to global warming
- Elimination of the risk from nuclear plants — whether from accidents or terrorist attack

The main risk to energy investors may be over-enthusiasm. There are a growing number of small firms in the field, each with its own version of the new technologies. Inevitably, some will succeed while others will be left behind; it's up to the individual investor to perform the necessary due diligence.

Right now, the safest and most profitable way of investing in the new technologies is the direct method. While this too requires due diligence, the returns from purchasing and installing efficient technologies and renewables look very good. This is a win-win-win situation: The sustainable industries are strengthened, the ecosystem benefits, and the home or business owner reaps the rewards of cheaper energy.

In terms of personal benefit and public good, the new energy solutions present unparalleled opportunities to the socially responsible investor. With care and proper due diligence, social investors should handily outperform investors in conventional energy.

15

Foundations and Mission-Related Investing

By Stephen Viederman

All investments have effects. That is a simple fact. If, however, you were to ask your personal money manager, or the people who have fiduciary responsibility for your pension fund, or your church's endowment, or other institutional investors like the trustees of foundations and of educational institutions you would be hard pressed to find someone who considers it important to consider these effects in the investment process. For example, some years ago London financial analysts were asked about the environment and their responsibilities. The majority reported that the environment was a moral and ethical issue and, therefore, not relevant to their work.

The president of a subsidiary of BP Amoco observed in an article in the *Wall Street Journal* in March 2000 that the environment was on the table at every corporate boardroom discussion. The public cares about the environment, and a well-governed company pays attention to its shareholders and its customers. An effort to be more environmentally sensitive has become for many companies a part of their license to operate. The corporate boardrooms of America are considering the environment as a business issue; as a way of reducing costs by reducing waste; and as a source of new opportunities for new products and services. They also believe that trying to be good stewards enhances their reputation. Why is it, therefore, that most money managers and institutional investors continue investing the old-fashioned way, largely oblivious to the social and environmental consequences of their investments?

For nearly a decade I have been engaged in efforts to help social institutions, especially philanthropic foundations, reduce the dissonance between the ways they invest their endowments, and the social purposes those endowments serve. The results have been sobering. Fiduciaries are supposed to act as prudent persons, under the law. The original meaning of the word *prudent* is farseeing. But these fiduciaries look backward through rear-view mirrors at the past, rather than through the windshield to the future.

The Jessie Smith Noyes Foundation, from which I retired as president in March 2000, is one of a very small number of foundations that align their investment practices with their philanthropic purposes. The foundation, with assets of about $90 million, supports community organizing and advocacy on issues of the environment and reproductive rights. Particular attention is paid to the intersections between these issues and economic and social justice. We coined the term "mission-related investing" to describe our efforts.

The discussion began in earnest in the early 1990s when new finance committee members joined the board. They were people skilled in financial matters who shared the values of the foundation, and who were committed to exploring ways that the foundation's endowment could be used as an instrument of change in addition to making grants. The discussions that ensued required that all of the board members, not just the members of the finance committee, become knowledgeable about investment issues, to ensure that the links between program and investment were made, and so that the board as a whole could exercise its fiduciary responsibility. English rather than "financese" became the lingua franca.

The program that emerged was like a stool with three legs: screening, shareholder activity, and mission-related venture capital.

Screening

The first board effort to define screens left us with a long list of concerns on newsprint pasted on the wall of the boardroom. A cursory review of the cumulative concerns of the individual members of the board suggested that there was nothing publicly traded that the foundation might hold in its portfolio. As individuals the concerns of the members of the board were comprehensive.

Further discussion led to a set of positive and negative screens around the environment and women's issues, reflecting the foundation's programs and its mission. Both the equity and fixed-income portfolios were invested with managers who had long experience in screening investment portfolios. The financial rates of return for the decade were competitive. As Peter Camejo argues, there was no reason to accept lower rates of return, nor did we receive lower rates of return. In fact, the foundation believes there was some outperformance in comparison to benchmarks.

Does screening make a difference? Since most trading is in secondary markets, inclusion or exclusion of a particular stock is not likely to have much, if any effect on the cost of capital to a company. The research efforts of organizations such as KLD, CEP, and IRRC in the 1990s to identify the social and environmental impacts of corporate behavior did raise awareness of these issues. This does in part explain the greater attention to social and environmental reporting we now see. But until very recently, the argument for screening was largely to maintain a sense of personal or institutional integrity.

Recently, however, there is some admittedly anecdotal evidence that screening is making a difference. Innovest Strategic Value Advisors provides information to the financial world on the environmental performance and management capacities of corporations, and has recently been approached by CEOs of a number of Fortune 100 companies asking what they needed to do to obtain higher Innovest ratings. Some of the other organizations that provide ratings of companies, including KLD, report similar approaches.

It is striking, however, how few institutional investors see screening as a fiduciary responsibility, even when they are informed that there is no cost in terms of return, or, as Peter Camejo suggests, there may even be some outperformance. Though data are hard to obtain, the best estimates suggest that fewer than 15 percent of foundations screen any part of their portfolios, and much of that screening involves only tobacco. But even most health funders do *not* screen for tobacco, despite the fact that it causes 10,000 deaths per day worldwide when "used according to manufacturer's instructions," and that continuing to hold the stock costs the funds hundreds of thousands of dollars in lost net asset value. Funders that support efforts to expand human rights around the world do not consider the human rights records of the companies in their portfolios. Most environmental philanthropies and nonprofits passively hold stock in some of the very companies that their grants and campaigns are directed against. The firewall between investments and grantmaking or program seems almost impenetrable. These groups tell the world to be aware of a particular problem or issue, but they are in denial about ways that they can use their assets to further their programmatic goals.

Screening is, of course, not the only way for an institution to use its portfolio in support of program. It can hold the stock in a company whose behavior it finds egregious and become an active shareholder. Many religious orders and a few pension funds and foundations, including Noyes, have chosen to follow this route with portions of their portfolios. This admittedly requires an expenditure of time but can be very effective.

Shareholder Activity

The foundation's managers had always voted the foundation's proxies. But the decision was made in the 1990s that the foundation had to take on the responsibility directly. It had to inform itself about the issues and vote according to its mission. The foundation could not be a passive bystander.

In 1993 the SouthWest Organizing Project (SWOP) prepared a report on Intel's expansion in New Mexico fueled by huge state financial incentives. SWOP argued that the returns for the people were minimal, while the costs were considerable. Intel refused to talk with SWOP, a community organization in Albuquerque. Noyes discovered it held Intel stock (all of 100 shares) and asked SWOP how it, as a shareholder, could help them, as stakeholders. When Intel failed to respond to our request for them to meet with the community, Noyes filed a shareholder resolution to be voted in 1995, asking the company to change its Environmental, Health and Safety (EHS) Policy, committing them to share information and be responsible to the community. This brought Intel to the table with SWOP on the issues of their concern, and with the foundation on issues of transparency and accountability. The first resolution received enough support from stockholders to make it possible for Noyes to refile our resolution the next year, which the foundation did, while discussions continued. However, in December 1995 Intel proposed an acceptable revision of its EHS Policy, and the resolution was withdrawn. The process strengthened the hand of SWOP in their negotiations and gained them greater standing in the state. It demonstrated conclusively that a foundation could add value to its grants through shareholder activity.

In order to encourage other foundations to become more involved shareholders, Noyes collaborated with the Interfaith Center on Corporate Responsibility (ICCR) to form the Foundation Partnership on Corporate Responsibility. ICCR's thirty-year history of social shareholder activity and experience is now available to foundations. In 1999 a dozen foundations cofiled shareholder resolutions. Though a seemingly small number, it is a significant increase over just a few years earlier, when the number was zero. Now about 150 foundations receive information to guide their proxy voting. Again, that is a small number compared with the tens of thousands of foundations — but it is a beginning.

Mission-Related Venture Capital

The third leg of Noyes' investment stool is mission-related venture capital. Setting up its own partnership, the foundation sought investments in young companies that provided commercial solutions to the problems that the foundation supported through its grantmaking. A good example of the venture capital investments is Stonyfield Farm. Based in New Hampshire, Stonyfield produces yogurt that is organic and/or made from milk from family farms that follow sustainable agricultural practices. Since the foundation has a major grantmaking program in sustainable agriculture, the investment and the grants are supportive.

If We're So Smart, Why Aren't Others?

William McKeown, a leading lawyer specializing in nonprofits and foundations, suggests that foundations and nonprofit groups may not be fulfilling their fiduciary responsibility if they do not consider the consequences of their investments on their missions. Even if the boards of these organizations groups felt that their only responsibility was to maximize their returns, they would have to consider social or mission-related investing, as Peter Camejo shows. The financial performance of social funds has demonstrated over the last five and more years that taking into account the social and environmental consequences of an investment is an important adjunct to financial analysis.

There are a number of reasons, based upon almost a decade of work in this area, that I believe keep the finance committees and boards of institutions from considering social investing.

The culture and psychology of finance focuses on a single bottom line, which is what members of the committees have been trained to do. Furthermore, their institutional connection is secondary to their primary occupational role, and "being social" may raise issues in that portion of their life. Citizenship in corporate life, all too often, seems to be exercised in the evenings and on weekends, like going to the gym. Consultants and other gatekeepers reinforce this culture. Within the institutions, finance staff claim it is not part of their job description, nor do they have the core competencies.

The politics of boards must be accounted for. Experience suggests that a strong advocate must be present, one who is knowledgeable and committed and willing to give up some of her political capital if action is to be taken. Interest alone is not sufficient.

Intellectually what is taught in economics departments and business schools discourages thinking about mission-related investing. The environment is considered an externality. The dollar is discounted, thus placing less value on the future than on the present. Equity is ownership, not justice. Any effort to reduce the opportunity set of a portfolio is considered a drag on financial performance, even though no one holds the entire market.

Legal impediments are assumed to exist, even though the best legal advice argues that if fiduciaries follow generally accepted rules of due diligence, no legal barriers prohibit them from practicing mission-related investing.

"We aren't big enough to make a difference" is a lament often heard — even from foundations with many billions of dollars in assets.

Is the Glass Half-Full or Half-Empty?

As an impatient person, I wish that I could report a groundswell of enthusiasm for mission-related investment among institutions. Yes, we are much further along than we were a decade or even five years ago. The subject is at least becoming part of the agenda. I have spoken at many conferences of trustees and staff of foundations and endowments with more people expressing great interest and follow up. Trade associations at state and national levels are putting the issue on the agenda, often for the first time. The press has become interested with articles appearing, for example, in the *New York Times* (June 11, 2000) and the *San Jose* (California) *Mercury* (June 23, 2000). Students for the Reform of Corporations is very active on campuses. While some higher educational institutions remain obstinate even on tobacco, Columbia University has, for example, formed an advisory committee to its trustees on social investing. Contra Costa County's pension fund is leading the way in California, joining a few other funds like the New York City pension fund.

It has been suggested that the obscure takes a while to see, the obvious even longer. Schopenhauer believed that all truth passes through three stages: first it is ridiculed; second it is violently opposed; and third, it is accepted as being self-evident. For most institutional investors, social investing is somewhere between stage one and two. All in all, there is reason for hope despite there being a long row to hoe. But the journey has begun.

16

Community Investing:
An Exploration of the Strategy

By James Nixon

A substantial and growing gulf divides communities across the United States, separating those that have benefited from the high-tech and stock markets booms of the 1990s from those that have been left out. *The Double Bottom Line: Investing in California's Emerging Markets,* issued in May 2000 by California State Treasurer Phillip Angelides, describes the emergence of two Californias: "Despite all its successes, California has the greatest gap between rich and poor of all but four states and the gap widened during the last decade. The level of poverty, particularly among children, remains stubbornly high…. In the 1990s, the poorest 20% in California saw their real incomes drop by 10% to just over $12,000 per year."[1]

Two generations of community investing use a double-bottom-line strategy — investing for both financial return and social progress — to address this growing disparity in resources and standards of living. The first generation has attempted to supplement market forces in addressing poverty. The newly emerging second generation of community investing seeks to guide the market in ways that create wealth for the residents of economically disenfranchised communities.

The First Generation of Community Investing: Supplementing the Market

During the past 30 years, the community investment paradigm has been for relatively small funds (under $15 million) to offer investment(s) at below-market cost to clients and below-market financial returns to investors. These funds have been used to address poverty in poorer families and communities.

The vision for the first generation of community investing is well articulated by the National Community Capital Association:

> Our vision is a world where all people experience social, economic, and political justice and so have the opportunity and ability to act in the best interests of their communities, themselves, and future generations. For economically disadvantaged people, lack of access to capital with which to pursue economic opportunities is a primary barrier to social engagement, economic well-being, and political participation. As a catalyst for lasting social, economic, and political justice... [community investments] provide capital that increases resources and opportunities for economically disadvantaged people and communities.[2]

The Field

To accomplish this vision, the field of community investing works to provide capital, technical assistance, and development services to support the revitalization of economically disadvantaged communities. The field has grown and diversified during the last 30 years. According to the *Social Investment Forum 2001 Trends Report,* community investing grew by 41 percent between 1999 and 2001. Assets held and invested locally by community development financial institutions (CDFIs) totaled $7.6 billion in 2001, up from $5.4 billion in 1999.[3]

As its major community investing initiative, the Clinton administration sponsored legislation to create the CDFI Fund. This fund has certified 334 CDFIs and in 1999 invested $122 million in 250 CDFIs, a 30 percent increase over 1998. Since 1996, the CDFI Fund has invested more than $300 million in CDFIs nationally, which leveraged $1 billion in overall investments. According to the *Directory of Community Development Financial Institutions,* there are approximately 500 CDFIs currently in operation in the United States. They fall into five main categories:

1. Community Development Banks (CDBs), with 24 banks and $2.9 billion in assets, offer the same types of services available at conventional banks, including savings and checking accounts. Like their conventional counterparts, they are federally insured. They provide capital to rebuild economically distressed communities through targeted lending and investment.

2. Community Development Loan Funds (CDLFs), with 198 loan funds and $1.7 billion in assets, aggregate capital from individual and institutional social investors, often at below-market rates, and lend this money primarily to nonprofit and for-profit housing and business developers in economically distressed urban and rural communities.

3. Community Development Credit Unions (CDCUs), with 170 credit unions and $601 million in assets, are membership-owned and controlled nonprofit financial institutions that promote savings and provide affordable credit and retail financial services to low-income people, with special outreach to minority communities. Members receive all the services available at conventional credit unions and are covered under the National Credit Union Share Insurance Fund.

4. Community Development Venture Capital Funds (CDVCFs), with 45 venture funds and $150 million in assets, use the tools of venture capital to provide equity and debt with equity features for community real estate and medium-sized business projects. Their goal is to create good jobs, entrepreneurial capacity, and wealth to improve the livelihoods of low-income individuals and the economies of distressed communities.

5. Microenterprise Development Loan Funds (MDLFs), with 340 organizations and $25 million in assets, foster social and

business development through loans and technical assistance to low-income people who are involved in very small nonprofit and for-profit businesses or self-employment and are unable to access conventional credit.

CDFIs typically use some or all of the following social criteria to determine investment recipients:

- Construction of affordable housing
- Creation of livable-wage jobs for low- and moderate-income community residents
- Ownership by minorities and women
- Beneficial social and environmental impact of the product/service and the business operation
- Use of good business practices, including positive employee relations, 401(k) plans, and workplace safety

The Clients

CDFIs provide financing for many different kinds of undertakings. Again according to the Directory of Community Development Financial Institutions, the number of CDFIs involved in different types of financing are as follows:

Type of Financing	Number of CDFIs Involved
Homeownership	119
Rental housing	72
Cooperative housing	43
Micro-businesses	134
Small businesses	147
Medium/large businesses	52
Childcare facilities	61
Healthcare facilities	41
Other community facilities	43
Individual Development Accounts (IDAs)	43
Personal loans	76
Checking/savings accounts	70

To a large degree, CDFIs serve community development corporations (CDCs). According to the National Congress for Community Economic Development there are 3600 CDCs in the United States that have:

- Produced more than 550,000 units of low-income housing
- Developed more than 71 million square feet of commercial, industrial, retail, and community space
- Created or retained more than 247,000 permanent, nonconstruction jobs
- Provided job training, emergency food assistance, childcare, and other services to residents

A Handbook

The Social Investment Forum has published a handbook on the first generation of community investing — *Increasing Investment in Communities* — as an aspect of the Forum's 1% in Community Investing campaign. This initiative is "designed to help move a total of one percent of actively managed social investment dollars into community investing by the year 2005 ... If just 1% of the total managed assets involved in socially responsible investment were targeted to community investing, it would triple the total dollars directed towards low-income communities, from $5 billion to $15 billion."[4] The handbook, available online at www.socialinvest.org, looks at the five basic types of community investment institutions — community banks, community credit unions, community loan funds, community venture capital, and micro-enterprise lending — as well as surveying:

- International funds
- Pooled approaches
- Investment managers and trusts
- Mutual funds
- Institutional securities
- Legal and administrative issues
- Implementation strategies

In addition, the www.socialinvest.org site offers brief descriptions of the 12 community investment organizations that the Community Investing Campaign has recognized for "best exemplifying the building of economic opportunity and hope for individuals through community investing." One of the best ways to get a flavor for community investing is to look through these descriptions of Accion International, Boston Community Capital, the Calvert Social Investment Foundation, Cascadia Revolving Fund, Community Bank of the Bay, Levitcus 25:23 Alternative Fund, Manna, Inc., Mercy Housing, Self-Help Credit Union, Shorebank, Shared Interest, and Southern Development Bancorporation,

A Comprehensive Investment Vehicle
Since 1990, the Calvert Social Investment Fund and other funds in the Calvert Group have pioneered the "1% in Community Investing" idea — investing over $12 million in approximately 70 community-based organizations.

The success of this investment program led the Calvert Foundation to launch Calvert Community Investments in 1995. Through this community development finance intermediary, the Calvert Foundation raises funds from socially responsible investors in order to reinvest the funds in community development finance institutions and other community development corporations and nonprofits. Major foundations have provided subordinated debt to the Calvert Foundation as a credit enhancement to increase the safety of the Calvert Community Investments, making this vehicle a safer, more convenient way for investors to target funds to rebuild local communities.

Offering an annual interest rate of 4.5 percent, the Calvert Foundation has raised over $13 million that has been reinvested in over 100 organizations, including community development and affordable housing loan funds; nonprofit facilities funds; community development corporations and intermediaries; micro-finance institutions; community development banks and credit unions; nonprofit entities and cooperatives; and international financial intermediaries.

The Calvert Foundation invests in organizations that:

- Focus on low-income communities and individuals that do not have access to traditional sources of capital
- Expand the local economy by expanding opportunity and promoting work-related activities, homeownership, and nontraditional business owners
- Support diverse communities in urban and/or rural areas, domestically, or internationally
- Demonstrate a consistent track record and the organizational management capacity to repay the investment

The Calvert Foundation has partnered with other investment organizations to offer specialized versions of their community investment vehicle. For example, the Calvert Foundation has joined with Progressive Asset Management, Inc. to offer the Progressive Asset Management (PAM) Community Investment Notes.

The Second Generation of Community Investing: Guiding the Market

A second generation of community investing is now emerging. This second generation is expanding beyond the strategy of supplementing the market, seeking now to guide the market into new areas.

To an increasing degree, economically poorer communities are seeing themselves and being seen from the perspective of their assets rather than their liabilities. According to *The Double Bottom Line* by California State Treasurer Phil Angelides:

> Beyond the fact that many of these neighborhoods are defined by quality housing stock, strong community design, and historic strength, they also contain inherent market strengths.
>
> Many of these communities sit at strategic locations within their regions — proximate to major transportation corridors, downtown business districts, regional business clusters, and significant consumer markets, with underutilized infrastructure that can support business expansion.

These communities offer the advantage of an available and growing workforce in an era in which labor supply will be a critical factor in continued economic growth. Population increases will further strengthen already underserved consumer markets in many of these communities. Coupled with already relatively high densities, this will translate into significant economic power in the years ahead.[5]

However, according to Glenn Yago of the Milken Institute, domestic emerging markets continue "to be overlooked and untapped due to misperceptions and lack of information. Demand for capital remains unsatisfied."

If the 1% in Community initiative of the Social Investment Forum is completely successful, $15 billion of capital will be engaged in first-generation community investments by 2005. Significant as this would be, it would not begin to meet the needs for capital required for revitalization of urban core and inner ring suburban communities throughout the United States. In the US market economy, capital flows to where economically viable rates of return can be obtained. The first generation of community investment has sought to generate social returns by supplementing the market, acquiring capital primarily from public, nonprofit, and generous individual sources, offering financial returns that are well below market rates. These efforts are important, but they have remained small.

The second generation of community investment is seeking to guide the market to accomplish double bottom line results by raising the rates of return and the size of the developments and deals. To move large amounts of capital to accomplish double-bottom-line results, economically viable rates of return must be offered.

From the perspective of the second generation of community investing, domestic emerging markets, whether defined by location, income level, ethnicity, or gender, result from market imperfections. Since the market has not recognized the outstanding investment opportunities that these domestic emerging markets offer, intelligent investing can produce outstanding financial results. It is important, however, to maintain a double-bottom-line orientation, linking the financial returns with substantial social and environmental returns.

Place-Based Examples of the Second Generation

Although the second generation of community investing is relatively new, there are already a number of suggestive successful examples, a few of which are discussed below, beginning with examples that are place-based, followed by examples that are ethnicity- and gender-based.

Genesis L.A. Genesis L.A. is a new, "smart growth" private-public partnership between the City of Los Angeles and private investors. Genesis L.A. grew out of the difficulties encountered by Rebuild L.A., a loose consortium of private and public interests, and the L.A. Community Development Bank, a public sector initiative. The goals of Genesis L.A. include:

- Development of blighted, underutilized urban core sights
- Creation of livable wage jobs, based on local hiring
- Production of ancillary economic benefits for surrounding neighborhoods
- Expansion of the capacity of community organizations to partner in and eventually initiate developments
- Creation of the financial and social infrastructure, including a guiding nonprofit organization and a family of investment funds, to organize and coordinate the effort

Between the fall of 1998 and spring of 1999, the Mayor's Office of Economic Development of the City of Los Angeles analyzed more than 75 projects with a total estimated project value in excess of $2.5 billion. By April 1999, this list was reduced to 15 keystone projects sponsored by Genesis L.A., with the goal of generating $250 million of private sector investment and 5000 jobs by May 2001.

By May 2000, one full year ahead of schedule, 5 of these 15 Genesis L.A. keystone projects had already exceeded their goals, generating $293.5 million in private capital investment and 5324 jobs. These are livable-wage jobs with a high percentage of workers being hired from the local communities. Genesis L.A. includes local hiring and community wealth creation criteria in the developments.

There is a Genesis L.A. nonprofit at the center of the Genesis L.A. Initiative. According to Joanne Halbert, the point person in the Mayor's office for the Genesis L.A. Initiative, the Genesis L.A. nonprofit has received $1 million in funding and has begun to function as a collaborator with community organizations in the neighborhoods where keystone projects are located. Typically, the Genesis L.A. nonprofit will partner with a leading community organization and then bring in a mainstream lead developer. The community organization becomes a partner in the development with an equity stake and takes responsibility for building community support. At the same time the community organization receives training so that it will be able to play an even stronger role with a larger equity stake in the next developments that take place in that neighborhood. One goal of Genesis L.A. is for the community organizations ultimately to acquire the capacity to become the lead developers for developments in their neighborhoods.

As a result of the early success of Genesis L.A., 6 new Keystone Projects have been added. Total private sector capital investment in the 21 keystone projects is expected to exceed $1.5 billion. To further catalyze these keystone projects, a group of leading private sector banks, private investors, foundations, and pension funds has held a first closing for the Genesis L.A. Real Estate Investment Fund, raising $71 million. The Genesis L.A. Fund will invest in urban smart growth, mixed-use, mixed-income projects. The investors include Bank of America, Wells Fargo, Washington Mutual, California Federal, Union Bank, Far East Bank, US Bank, Citibank, Shamrock Capital Advisors, Nehemiah Corporation, California Community Foundation, and CalSTRS. Independent due diligence by these investors anticipates an investor return of at least 15 percent.

DVCRF Ventures. DVCRF Ventures, a $10 million equity investment fund organized by The Reinvestment Fund in Philadelphia, has made investments in ventures that have created more than 800 high-quality livable-wage jobs for local residents. DVCRF Ventures has links with the Reinvestment Fund's Workforce Development Group to fill those jobs. As of the summer of 2000, returns were running at above 15 percent.

DVCRF Ventures is a part of The Reinvestment Fund family of funds and programs — including The Sustainable Development Fund; the Affordable Housing Loan Program; the Small Business Loan Program; The Community Resources Group, making loans to community service, educational, and child care institutions; and the Workforce Development group.

DVCRF Ventures is an example of what can be characterized as a second-generation Community Investment fund growing up from the foundation of a set of first-generation funds.[6]

Examples Based on Ethnicity and Gender

The concept of emerging domestic markets not only applies to urban core, inner ring suburban, and rural contexts, it also applies to the emerging markets created by ethnicity and gender. Minority-owned businesses are the fastest growing segment of the US economy. Yet less than 2 percent of all private equity investments are in minority businesses. A number of investment firms and investment funds are now beginning to serve this emerging domestic market.

Fulcrum Ventures. Fulcrum Ventures has actively invested in minority businesses since 1977, with the vast majority of businesses located in urban communities. Fulcrum provides capital to assist successful businesses to expand, focusing on traditional, fragmented, and consolidating sectors of the economy in the service, light manufacturing, retail, and communications industries. Fulcrum was chosen by Merrill Lynch to manage a portion of the fund Merrill Lynch set up in response to the Orange County bankruptcy settlement.

Fulcrum makes mezzanine capital investments in the form of pure equity and subordinate debt. From 1992 through 2000, Fulcrum recorded a 55.7 percent internal rate of return on a portfolio with a value of $24 million.

Opportunity Capital Partners. Opportunity Capital Partners also serves this market, operating three funds with a total of $35 million, providing debt and equity financing to minority owned businesses, primarily in the areas of telecommunications, industrial manufacturing, and health services. OCF has achieved a 35 percent return on investment.

NewVista Capital Fund. NewVista Capital Fund is a $21 million early-stage venture capital fund that invests in women and minority entrepreneurs in the field of information technology. After two years of operation, returns are in excess of 75 percent.

The Two Generations Working Together in Massachusetts

In Massachusetts, the two generations of community investment organizations are working together to create an emerging statewide community economy.

The Massachusetts Community Economic Development System. The Massachusetts Community Economic Development System has a 26-year track record of successful, market-driven urban economic development by local, place-based community development organizations. This system has integrated the two generations of community investing to form a relatively mature full-scale community economy.

The Massachusetts Community Economic Development System includes 28 private-public community development financial institutions, 68 community development corporations and affordable housing organizations, and a set of large-scale financial institutions. During its 26-year history, the Massachusetts Community Development Finance System has financed close to $20 billion of development. The system placed more than $2 billion in investment capital in 1998: $1 billion was invested in commercial, industrial, and business finance, and $1 billion was invested in affordable housing and mixed-income projects. This $2 billion of community development finance in 1999 in Massachusetts served a total state population of 6.17 million.

The goals for the Massachusetts Community Economic Development System can be formulated as

- Creation of a community economy that has the power and scale to be able to make the communities full participants in the evolution and direction of the mainstream economy
- Establishment of an infrastructure that can receive $2 billion in investment capital annually to build affordable housing, complete mixed-use commercial and industrial developments, and create thousands of local livable-wage jobs
- Building the capacity of communities CDCs and CDFIs to be players in the economy
- Defense of the economic interests of the members of the various communities

The Massachusetts Capital Resource Company (MCRC) is one of the large-scale financial institutions at the heart of the Massachusetts Community Economic Development System. William Torpey, president of MCRC, describes an impressive record. Over 22 years, through 1999, MCRC has invested close to $430 million in over 230 companies in 101 communities, resulting in the creation of over 15,000 new jobs, with approximately $260 million in cities and towns designated as Economic Target Areas by the Commonwealth of Massachusetts. Average returns have been estimated to exceed 20 percent — with recent-year results even stronger.

The CDC Production and Pipeline Report for 1999, a publication of the Massachusetts Association of Community Development Corporations, reports these results:

- 52 CDCs have developed or improved 16,205 units of affordable housing, with 412 units in the pipeline
- 36 CDCs have completed 62 commercial projects, totaling 1,259,715 square feet, with 42 commercial projects, totaling 905,847 square feet, in the pipeline

- 29 CDCs completed 61 open space projects covering 774,562 square feet, with 6 projects covering 300,360 square feet in the pipeline
- 36 CDCs are involved in business development assistance, 14 CDCs are involved in workforce development, and 22 CDCs have a community organizer on staff[7]

The Massachusetts Housing Investment Corporation. In 1990, the Massachusetts Housing Investment Corporation (MHIC) was formed to make profitable urban investments in mixed-use, mixed-income affordable housing, commercial and industrial projects in partnership with CDCs and affordable housing organizations. In the last decade, MHIC has invested more than $400 million and generated a 15 percent return, according to *The Double Bottom Line: Investing in California's Emerging Markets* issued by California State Treasurer Phil Angelides. Over 60 percent of the jobs created by MHIC financed projects employ minorities, and over half of the contractors and suppliers on those projects are minority owned.[8]

Similar to the experience of many affordable housing developers throughout the United States, the Massachusetts Housing Investment Corporation (MHIC) uses a "layer cake" approach to financing. For example, the research for this paper looked at 1997 deal summaries for 8 deals financed by MHIC. Four deals included straight equity and debt. The other four deals also included tax credits. In this layer cake approach, public and nonprofit sources of finance make capital available at lower rates of return (in the low single digits) in order to leverage investment of MHIC capital that obtains the MHIC return objectives (with returns in the mid teens). The community development corporations have a cost of capital for the whole project that is in the mid to high single digits.

The Life Initiative. In 1998, the Massachusetts life insurance industry created the $100 million Life Initiative to invest 50 percent of its assets in urban, community-based commercial, industrial and business ventures and 50 percent in affordable housing projects. The industry was confident about the viability of investing this $100 million, based on its successful 22-year experience with the Massachusetts Capital Resource Company. In its first year of operations, the Life Initiative committed $40 million.

The "Double Bottom Line" Initiative in California

In California, State Treasurer Phil Angelides is calling for a "Double Bottom Line" initiative for the state. According to his report *The Double Bottom Line,* the financial bottom line means attaining a market rate of return so that the fiduciary responsibilities of financial decision-makers are upheld. According to Angelides, the social bottom line means:

- Improving the quality of life and stability of neighborhoods for current and future residents
- Making better use of existing urban fabric through higher density, quality development and through reuse of abandoned sites
- Increasing opportunities for homeownership and decent rental housing
- Enhancing economic viability and competitiveness — strengthening not only at-risk communities, but also regional economies
- Creating new economic opportunities — from quality jobs at wages that can support families to business ownership — for neighborhood residents and those outside the mainstream
- Creating value — from a sense of pride to broader wealth creation — not just for the neighborhood as a physical entity, but also for the people who have made it their home
- Directing new attention to the quality of community design and to the quality of services — from healthcare to retail — available to neighborhood residents
- Infusing new energy into and restoring hope in communities that have struggled hardest in this time of prosperity
- Recognizing and building on the rich and growing economic, social, cultural, institutional, and physical assets that already exist

The "Double Bottom Line" initiative is encouraging public pension funds and investment pools to make more than $8 billion of new double-bottom-line investments that achieve successful investment results and broaden economic opportunity. The "Double Bottom Line" initiative also seeks to broaden the pool of investment managers used by public funds in order to leverage additional capital investment in economically struggling communities, to fund new market research, and to encourage public partnerships with private sector and foundation capital to invest in California's struggling communities. The California Public Employees Retirement System (CalPERS) has already established a $500 million asset allocation for double bottom line investments.

Challenges

The central challenge for all of these initiatives is to encourage new economic activity in communities with high levels of poverty in ways that generate livable wage jobs and create wealth for current residents while avoiding displacement. If these initiatives were to encourage investment in one-sided or problematic development, the results could include poor jobs, loss of community capital, environmental problems, and displacement. Business development that offers low-wage jobs without benefits, job security, or opportunity for advancement produces some economic benefits, but does not create significant wealth and economic advancement for community residents.

A business transaction with a multinational corporation that has a location in a targeted community may result in the money leaving the community instantly. In order to produce a multiplier effect with a powerful positive economic impact on the communities, the money from transactions needs to stay in communities, recycling many times through payments to workers, suppliers, service providers, and subcontractors.

Pollution-intensive development and development that produces adverse impacts on jobs–housing balance and transportation can lead to a serious decline in community environmental quality. Upscale office, plant, commercial or housing development can lead to a dramatic increase in commercial and residential rents and comparable increases in the cost of home ownership. This, in turn, can produce gentrification and displacement of the current residents of the targeted communities.

If developments in communities are not to lead to displacement, then forms of community equity participation need to be utilized to create wealth for homeowners, renters, and community organizations and institutions. This means investment in developments and business deals that include community wealth creation forms such as:

- Livable-wage jobs with local hiring programs
- Minority, women, local CDC, and worker ownership
- Community partners
- Local contracting and local sourcing
- Donation of stock to community organizations

The Bay Area Family of Funds

The Bay Area Family of Funds and the related Community Capital Investment Initiative (CCII) are being organized to engage market forces in accomplishing the related goals of poverty reduction and smart growth. This initiative is particularly interesting because it is being organized explicitly as a second-generation community investment attempting to address all of the issues by drawing on the full range of national and international experience with second-generation efforts. CCII is structured as a Business Council, a Community Council, and a Government Advisory Council that form a Community Investment Roundtable.

The Bay Area Council, a regional business-sponsored, CEO-led public policy organization, is the lead organization for the Business Council. The Bay Area Council has joined with corporate, community, environmental, and government leaders to form the Family of Funds, including a real estate fund, a business equity fund, and an environmental remediation and redevelopment fund.

The National Economic Development and Law Center, PolicyLink, and Urban Habitat Program are the lead agencies for the Community

Council, which proposed an initial set of social equity criteria that, after negotiation and modification, are being used to guide investment.

Target Communities. The Bay Area Partnership study, *A Guide to the Bay Area's Most Impoverished Neighborhoods by County,* identified 46 communities in the San Francisco Bay Area with concentrated, persistent, and, in many cases, increasing levels of poverty. Although significant amounts of capital flow in and through the Bay Area, not enough capital flows into these communities in ways that produce larger scale developments that generate livable-wage jobs for local residents and community wealth creation while avoiding displacement.

Objectives. The objectives the Family of Funds and CCII are to produce a double bottom line combining financial and social returns by:

- Offering economically viable rates of return
- Reducing poverty, producing high-quality jobs, and promoting community wealth creation, while avoiding displacement and mitigating adverse impacts
- Encouraging smart growth, decreasing pressure to develop at the region's edge

New Development Paradigm. The Family of Funds and CCII are based, in part, on the recognition that a new "smart growth" sustainable development paradigm is needed and is emerging. According to this paradigm, successful development involves all the relevant stakeholders and produces a combination of economic prosperity, social equity, and environmental responsibility (the "three E's of sustainable development"). The Family of Funds and CCII will integrate:

- "Place-based" strategies promoting neighborhood-serving development
- "Sector-based" strategies connecting communities to the regional economy

- "People-based" strategies strengthening community development capacity

One goal for these strategies is to build partnerships linking business, community, environmental, and public leadership. These partnerships can reduce conflict and expedite the desired types of development that are in the interests of all the stakeholders.

The Family of Funds. The Family of Funds includes three funds:

The Bay Area Smart Growth Fund invests equity in real estate developments, including mixed-use and mixed-income projects and commercial, housing, and industrial uses, that can be made commercially viable but are not yet sufficiently attractive to private developers. The fund projects returns in the mid to high teens and above and has a capitalization of $75 million to $100 million in equity investment. As of January 2002, the fund had raised $57.5 million. The Managing Member for the fund is Pacific Coast Capital Partners and it is sponsored by the Bay Area Council, which also serves as a Special Member for the fund.

The Bay Area Community Equity Fund is designed to invest equity in profitable growing businesses capable of generating substantial job and wealth creation in the 46 target neighborhoods. The fund projects returns in the high teens to low twenties and will have a capitalization of $75 million to $100 million in equity investments. The Community Equity Fund is managed by JPMorgan H&Q and is sponsored by the Alliance for Community Development, which includes representatives of community-based development and development finance organizations throughout the Bay Area. The Alliance for Community Development will serve as a Special Member.

The California Environmental Redevelopment Fund (CERF) is being established to invest in the cleanup of brownfields throughout California. Investors will invest $50 million to $75 million in debt and equity in the fund, which will in turn be invested, primarily in the form of debt, in environmental cleanup activities. This fund projects high single-digit annual returns.

Each fund will operate guided by financial, social, and environmental investment criteria that are consistent with the CCII criteria. However, each fund has its own organizational structure and professional fund managers, who will make all investment decisions.

A Few Conclusions

The first and second generations of community investing are not in competition or in conflict with each other. As the Massachusetts example demonstrates, the two generations can work together synergistically to the great benefit of each. However, the first generation needs a clear focus on establishing high financial standards so that the craft of business can become the vehicle for building economic, social, and environmental justice. Below-market financial returns cannot be an excuse for shoddy business practices. Programs to upgrade industry standards, such as those undertaken by the National Community Capital Association and the Community Development Venture Capital Alliance, are crucial to the health of this field

For its part, the second generation needs a clear focus on establishing and implementing clear, measurable social criteria to ensure that current community residents actually benefit from the development taking place. As the Community Capital Investment Initiative in the Bay Area has stated: "The stakes are high. Without smart growth, farmland and open space will continue to be consumed at the edge of regions, traffic and air quality will worsen, and, ultimately, the economies of regions will degrade. Smart growth means that development needs to be focused in the urban core and inner ring suburbs. However, if this development is not to produce displacement of current residents, it must also address poverty reduction through private, public, and community partnership in keystone developments that provide livable wage jobs and community wealth creation opportunities for local residents."[9]

A new smart growth development paradigm is emerging that includes criteria to guide and expedite development that avoids displacement and produces a combination of economic prosperity, social equity, and environmental responsibility.

As the new smart growth paradigm takes shape, new types of development are also emerging, such as mixed-use in-fill developments, transit villages, growth-sector-oriented business incubators and incubator-without-walls programs, and eco-industrial parks. For this new paradigm to function, it must channel market forces to accomplish social objectives and to produce market rates of financial return — in short, a double bottom line. The first and second generations of community investing are key to the accomplishment of this vision.

Appendix

Social Equity Criteria

Through an extensive process of collaboration among the Bay Area Council, the CCII Community Council organizations — Urban Habitat Program, National Economic Development and Law Center, and Policy Link — and lead investors in the fund, the following social equity criteria have been developed to guide the funds in making double-bottom-line investments. Because they are among the most developed social equity criteria in the field, it is useful to present them in their entirety. The Social Investment Objectives of the Smart Growth Fund are to:

- Build healthy and self-reliant communities.
- Create and recycle wealth for residents, community organizations, and institutions.
- Reduce poverty, increase household income, and produce high quality jobs.
- Increase the number of community-serving and region-serving businesses.
- Create new and improved services and amenities, including a contribution to increased affordable rental housing and home ownership.

The purpose of the Social Equity Criteria is to promote economic prosperity, social equity, and environmental quality while generating appropriate rates of financial return from the mid to high teens and above. The Criteria are designed to assist the Investment Manager in making investment decisions. While it is not expected that all projects that receive investment will meet all of the Criteria, it is expected that the investments will:

- Demonstrate substantial compliance with the Criteria;
- Contribute to the accomplishment of the Social Investment Objectives of the Fund; and
- Avoid impacts that are detrimental to those Objectives.

The intent of these Social Equity Criteria is to establish the context for a good faith effort by all parties working in the spirit of collaboration to achieve the double bottom line objectives of the fund in ways that:

- Facilitate deal flow.
- Streamline transactions financially.
- Encourage timely achievement of the purpose of the Fund.

It is expected that these Social Equity Criteria will assist in attracting and encouraging the best developers to undertake projects in the 46 neighbor-'hoods. It is also expected that these Criteria, with support from the Executive Coordinating Committee and the Community Capital Investment Initiative, will enhance the financial and social performance of the projects. At its periodic meetings, the Advisory Board of the Fund will review the performance of the Fund to assess the financial and social performance of the Fund and to recommend ways to enhance that performance.

Category One — Geographic Targeting
Is located in one or more of the 46 target neighborhoods of the nine county Bay Area — as defined by the Bay Area Council and the Bay Area Alliance for Sustainable Development — or is contiguous to one or more of the 46 neighborhoods, or is a brownfield site, or is a closed military base, and benefits the residents of one or more of the 46 neighborhoods at the time of the investment. For the Investments to be located in areas contiguous to the 46 neighborhoods, the investments shall have the support of a majority of the Advisory Board.

Category Two — Composition of the Development Team
Is led by a non-profit developer or a for-profit developer or a joint venture of both types of developers, and exhibits community support and incorporates community participation that adds demonstrated financial and social value to the project. Examples of community participation may include among other economic relationships economic/housing development corporations or other community-based service organizations as owners,

developers, designers, organizers, sources of gap financing, service providers, or property managers.

An effort will be made to include a community partner that adds demonstrated financial and social value to the project as part of the development team. The Executive Coordinating Committee will offer assistance, when requested, in identifying qualified community partners.

Category Three — Community Benefits Plan

Includes an explicit plan to produce measurable benefits for community residents. Examples of such community benefits may include programs for:

- Hiring local residents.
- Contracting with locally owned and minority and/or women-owned business enterprises for project design, construction, and ongoing operations.
- Building community equity through opportunities for ownership/profit-sharing for community residents and/or community-based institutions.
- Obtaining funding from the development and/or other sources of public or private funding to build the infrastructure of community-based institutions in the target neighborhood in ways that add financial and social value to the project.
- Using green design and construction processes, and pollution prevention technologies.
- Creating or expanding parks, open space, and other environmental amenities.
- Increasing transit, healthcare, and childcare services.
- Expanding of access to technology.
- Improving affordable housing and/or job opportunities.

Category Four — Strategies for Community Involvement

Includes a community input/oversight structure, which is expected to be established through the local entitlement process, or, if the local entitlement process does not include such a structure, through some other means. This process could include a plan for project-specific community outreach and education and may result in letters of endorsement for the project from community residents, neighborhood leaders, and public, private, and nonprofit proponents of the project.

Category Five — Connection to Existing Local Initiatives

Fits into a larger existing or proposed neighborhood strategic plan, initiative, collaborative planning process or revitalization program, wherever such a plan or program exists. Fits into an overall regional strategy for smart growth, by incorporating mixed income, mixed use development strategies that are conducive to transit and other self-sufficiency services.

Category Six — Monitoring and Evaluation Plan

Includes a plan for monitoring, evaluation and mid-course adjustment to ensure that the project is meeting the financial and social objectives of the Fund.

Notes

1. Philip Angelides, *The Double Bottom Line: Investing in California's Emerging Markets* (Sacramento: California State Treasurer's Office, 2000), p. 3.

2. National Community Capital Association, mission statement, adopted September 17,1998.

3. Social Investment Forum, *2001 Trends Report,* available at www.socialinvest.org.

4. Social Investment Forum, www.socialinvest.org.

5. Angelides, *The Double Bottom Line,* p. 13.

6. Information on DVCRF Ventures is from an interview with Jeremy Novack, president and CEO, The Reinvestment Fund.

7. Massachusetts Association of Community Development Corporations, CDC Production and Pipeline Report (Boston: MACDC, 1999).

8. Angelides, *The Double Bottom Line,* p. 16.

9. See statement at www.bayareaalliance.org.

Appendix A

SRI Investment Consultants

The following financial consultants participate in the Progressive Asset Management Network, offering expertise in socially responsible investing as well as financial matters in general.

Terry Atzen	Steve Fahrer	Pil Hwang
Aline Autenrieth	Tim Farley	Brian Laverty
Jack Bradin	Don Fecher	Eric Leenson
Hunter Brownlie	Georgette Frazer	Michael Lent
Scott Buttfield	David Gordon	Robert Libon
Peter Camejo	George Gorman	Hal Masover
Catherine Cartier	Barry Goldwater	Joan Masover
Donna Clifford	Deborah Granger	Gary Matthews
J. Chris Cogswell	Pam Harding	Joyce Moore
Douglas Conrad	Linda Homsey	Tom Moser
Rachelle Davey	Michael Honig	Allan Moskowitz
Belinda Duran	Jeff Howell	James Nixon
John Ernst	Mecky Howell	Eric Packer

Scott Pryor	Will Thomas	Alison Wise
Tim Rich	Richard Torgerson	Sara Yaeger
Catherine Scheib	Stuart Valentine	Mark Zoidis
William Stant	Jeff Weber	
Amy Tang	Susan Whalen	

The PAM Network is doing business in 48 states and has locations in the following states:

California	Minnesota
Illinois	New Hampshire
Indiana	New Jersey
Iowa	New York
Kentucky	Ohio
Maryland	Oregon
Massachusetts	Pennsylvania
Michigan	Wisconsin

For a free consultation with PAM SRI consultant, please contact:

PAM National Headquarters
800-786-2998

Appendx B

CCCERA's Social and Environmental Issues Voting Policy

In keeping with the Board's fiduciary responsibility, CCCERA Policy is to vote in favor of resolutions that come before the shareholders for a vote in regard to the social justice and environmental protection issues where the resolution's objectives are as listed below:

(a) Elimination of child labor

(b) Elimination of sweat shops or other abuses of labor laws and standards, including the use of foreign and domestic suppliers with such practices

(c) Elimination of slave labor

(d) Promote equal employment opportunities

(e) Elimination of discrimination due to race, religion, national origin, or sexual orientation

(f) Promote diversity for management and Board of Directors

(g) Promote corporate respect for laws both national and international

(h) Adoption of the CERES Principles

(i)   Adoption of the McBride Principles

(j)   Promote respect for environmental laws

(k)   Provide for disclosure of environmental liabilities

(l)   Eliminate or reduce toxic emissions

(m)   Promote product and marketing integrity

(n)   Provide for a smoke-free environment in company facilities

(ADDED 02/08/94)

(AMENDED 02/08/00)

Appendix C

Progress Is Possible:
Hawaii Capital Stewardship in the
New Millennium

By Ian Chan Hodges

There is a growing movement within the state of Hawaii to explore the real possibilities of achieving "double bottom line" returns from the state's primary sources of institutional capital. Two of Hawaii's largest institutional investors, the Hawaii Employees Retirement System (ERS) and Kamehameha Schools (KS), are currently being motivated by key policy shifts to move in this direction.

The Hawaii Employees Retirement System (ERS) had assets pegged at $9.78 billion by *Pensions and Investments* at the end of 2000, placing it among the top 200 institutional investors in the US. Kamehameha Schools reported in 2000 that it held assets of $5.65 billion, ranking the trust among the top educational endowments in the nation.

Adopted by the Hawaii Legislature in spring 2001, Senate Concurrent Resolution 13 (the full text of which appears later in this appendix) defines socially responsible investing (SRI) as the approach of "basing investment decisions on considerations of societal values and concerns as well as financial returns, thus balancing the investor's financial aims and needs with an investment's impact on society by the operations of the corporation or entity in which the investment is made" and encourages Hawaii's "financial institutions, financial advisors, banks, trust companies, trustees of our State's funded and landed trusts, trustees of the State of Hawaii Employee's Retirement System, and all other individuals and entities handling and managing financial investments, to become more familiar with the principles of SRI and to apply those principles to their financial advice and decisions." SCR 13 also requests the Legislative Reference Bureau (LRB) to "conduct research on SRI by examining the laws and practices in other states, and current reports and studies in the field."

In another policy shift pointing to Hawaii's growing interest in meshing social issues with investment goals, Kamehameha Schools recently adopted as part of its new Strategic Plan a specific goal: "Kamehameha Schools will *malama i ka 'aina:* practice ethical, prudent and culturally appropriate stewardship of lands and resources." A corresponding strategic objective for the school's multi-billion-dollar endowment is to "[m]anage the portfolio of resources to derive an overall balance of economic, educational, cultural, environmental and community returns."

The Hawaiian community is clearly recognizing the importance of developing an investment strategy that seeks more than just a single-bottom-line return. Diverse constituencies in Hawaii are seeing the value of this approach to the stewardship of institutional capital. Real potential exists for a homegrown double-bottom-line strategy to serve as a unifying policy focus in Hawaii. Labor unions, native Hawaiians, environmentalists, public officials, and small businesses can all be enthusiastic about the economic, social, and environmental benefits of double-bottom-line investing and have an opportunity to work together in implementing the various opportunities that this comprehensive approach to investing provides.

Labor unions are showing increasing leadership nationally in double-bottom-line investing. Hawaii is no exception. Approximately 25 leaders from Hawaii unions attended a breakfast meeting organized by Responsible Markets held in December 2000. Contra Costa County Trustee Peter Camejo gave a talk that resulted in increased interest in "double bottom line" investing among the participants and a desire to move forward with a summit on the topic.

In February 2001, a double-bottom-line investment summit sponsored by Responsible Markets was held at the state capitol building. The summit sought to provide an interactive venue to explore and weigh strategies for investing local capital in ways that include social, cultural, and environmental factors within the context of financial performance and fiduciary responsibility. The goal of the summit was to develop a "double bottom line" approach to investment that capitalizes on Hawaii's future economic opportunities while preserving what is special about the islands and communicating the values of Hawaii's people to the world. Members of the public were welcome to participate in the summit and there was no charge for the event.

Dennis "Bumpy" Kanahele and other key Hawaiian leaders played active roles in the summit. Kanahele and Responsible Markets associate Scott Crawford greatly assisted summit participants in recognizing a common vision of shared values that could potentially reconnect Hawaii's people to their rich heritage and inspire a desire to make prudent and proactive investments in a sustainable economic future. In August 2001, as a follow up to the summit, the Hawaii Capital Stewardship Forum was created.

Responding to a request from Forum organizers, Hawaii's Lieutenant Governor Mazie Hirono agreed to assist in convening an advisory board to assist the Hawaii Capital Stewardship Forum in its mission. On August 9, 2001, the lieutenant governor wrote a letter to a number of key individuals who have acquired a working knowledge of the various capital stewardship strategies currently under way at pension funds, foundations, universities, faith-based organizations, and unions across the nation. Lieutenant Governor Hirono's letter read in part:

> As Lieutenant Governor of the State of Hawaii, I am committed to Socially Responsible Investments (SRI)... I am writing to ask you to help me build a stronger Hawaii by serving as an advisor to the Hawaii Capital Stewardship Forum. The mission of the Forum is to provide an ongoing venue where those responsible for Hawaii's public and private institutional funds, as well as key community policy-makers, fund

beneficiaries, and other stakeholders, can develop a body of knowledge, skills, tools, and resources for investing Hawaii's institutional capital in a manner consistent with the spirit of SCR 13, which the Hawaii legislature adopted this year (see attached).

By the end of August, the following individuals had agreed to serve as advisors to the Hawaii Capital Stewardship Forum:

Peter Camejo, Trustee
Contra Costa County Employee Retirement Association

Thomas Croft, Executive Director
Heartland Labor Capital Project

Rich Koppes, Former General Counsel
California Public Employees Retirement System (CalPERS).

Melissa Moye, Chief Economist, Trust and Investment Services
Amalgamated Bank

Damon Silver, Associate General Counsel
AFL-CIO

Anne Stausboll
Chief Deputy Treasurer
California State Treasurer

Stephen Viederman, Past President
Jessie Smith Noyes Foundation

The advisory board provided valuable assistance in the drafting of Senate Bill 2983 which was introduced on January 25, 2002, in the Hawaii state Senate by Sen. Kalani English. If it is signed into law, SB 2983 will:

- Allow the Employees' Retirement System to invest in protected intellectual property which, in the informed opinion of the Board of Trustees, it is prudent to invest funds;
- Require the Employees Retirement System to invest a certain percentage of its investment portfolio in economically targeted investments, including venture capital enterprises and funds, with the intent to assist in the improvement of the economic well-being of the state, its localities, and residents; and

- Require the Employees Retirement System's Board of Trustees to execute all shareholder proxies and voting instructions in a manner that supports corporate governance, social justice, and environmental protection issues unless such a vote would result in long-term harm to the company.

The capital stewardship advisory board continued to provide critical guidance as SB 2983 was reported from two Senate committees with recommendations for passage by the full Senate. Responsible Markets provided pro-bono staffing assistance to the Forum during this period. On March 5, 2002, the Senate adopted SB 2983 and transmitted the bill to the House for consideration. As of this writing, SB 2983 has been referred to the House Labor and Finance Committees. SB 2983 thus represents a concrete step by the Hawaii legislature toward putting into practice the principles set forth in Senate Concurrent Resolution 13.

Report Title:
Socially Responsible Investment
THE SENATE S.C.R. NO.   13
TWENTY-FIRST LEGISLATURE, 2001   S.D. 2
STATE OF HAWAII

SENATE CONCURRENT RESOLUTION
ENCOURAGING, AND REQUESTING A REPORT ON, SOCIALLY RESPONSIBLE INVESTMENT.

WHEREAS, Socially Responsible Investment (SRI), also known as double-bottom line investment, mission-related investment, and natural investing, is the rapidly growing practice in the United States of basing investment decisions on considerations of societal values and concerns as well as financial returns, thus balancing the investor's financial aims and needs with an investment's impact on society by the operations of the corporation or entity in which the investment is made; and

WHEREAS, distinct but related aspects involved in an SRI strategy are: (1) avoiding companies whose record conflicts with the investor's values; (2) seeking out companies whose record is consistent with the investor's values; (3) targeting investments directly into communities; and (4) taking an active role as a shareholder in influencing corporate policies; and

WHEREAS, socially conscious investors will often include in their investment portfolios corporations with positive records on product quality, consumer relations, environmental performance, corporate citizenship, and employee relations, while screening out corporations involved in industries such as alcohol, tobacco, gambling, military weapons, and nuclear power; and

WHEREAS, investments that are sound from a fiduciary standpoint and which also promote equality of opportunity, environmental protection, and other causes critical to Hawaii's long-term future, have what is known as a "double bottom line" return; and

WHEREAS, SRI has its roots in the colonial era when abolitionist Quakers refused to invest in any business associated with slavery, and blossomed in the 1970's, influenced by strong social movements focusing on the environment, fair employment practices, the military-industrial complex, and the rights of minorities and women; and

WHEREAS, in the 1980's, anti-apartheid activists brought the idea of socially responsible investing into full public view by insisting that their schools and churches stop investing in companies which did business in South Africa; and

WHEREAS, this very successful campaign to remove foreign capital from South Africa marked a powerful new era for SRI; and

WHEREAS, the SRI movement has rapidly increased its strength since the early 1990s as the financial world became more aware of the force of social movements; and

WHEREAS, the Social Investment Forum, a Washington group that surveys the investment landscape, has indicated that in 1999, about $1 of every $8 of investments under professional management—some $2 trillion overall—was directed toward socially responsible investment, which is eighty-two per cent above 1997 statistics; and

WHEREAS, a large number of new SRI mutual funds have been created as increasing numbers of investors have chosen to put their money into socially screened funds; and

WHEREAS, the growth of SRI among the union pension funds, educational endowments, and not-for-profit foundations which control substantial resources has been hampered by lingering false perceptions that socially responsible investments will not fulfill the trustee's fiduciary responsibility to achieve a reasonable rate of return on the fund's corpus; and

WHEREAS, as SRI funds have become well established, they have demonstrated their financial soundness over the last five years, showing that not only are social and environmental concerns not a handicap in investing, but that social and environmental values and standards can actually correlate with superior financial performance; and

WHEREAS, studies by investment firms ranging from Spare, Kaplan, Bischel & Associates, to Merrill Lynch demonstrate that, in recent years, SRI stocks have outperformed non-SRI stocks by up to two per cent per year; and

WHEREAS, SRI can have significant beneficial consequences for the State of Hawaii in that SRI can help promote the growth of mercantile entities presently doing business here and who engage in business practices that enhance and promote Hawaii's fragile environment and contribute to the well-being of Hawaii's population, and can also be helpful in attracting other businesses that engage in similar practices; and

WHEREAS, the Legislature of the Twenty-First Legislature of the State of Hawaii, wishes to encourage our State's financial institutions, financial advisors, banks, trust companies, trustees of our State's funded and landed trusts, trustees of the State of Hawaii Employee's Retirement System, and all other individuals and entities handling and managing financial investments, to become more familiar with the principles of SRI and to apply those principles to their financial advice and decisions; and

WHEREAS, Responsible Markets LLC and the Native Hawaiian Advisory Council sponsored a Summit on Double-Bottom Line Investing in Hawai'i, 'Aha Ho'opuka Pono, at the State Capitol in Honolulu on February 26, 27, and 28, 2001, in which nationally known experts in the field of investments, and particularly in SRI, discussed its principles, merits, and benefits; and

WHEREAS, the Legislature of the Twenty-First Legislature of the State of Hawaii appreciates and recognizes the value of SRI to the State, and wishes to foster and encourage wider discussion, understanding, acceptance, and practice of SRI in the community; now, therefore,

BE IT RESOLVED by the Senate of the Twenty-First Legislature of the State of Hawaii, Regular Session of 2001, the House of Representatives concurring, that the Legislature encourages the Chief investment officer, administrator, and trustees of the State Employees' Retirement System to apply the principles of SRI in their investment practices and decisions, and encourages other investment counselors and money managers to also apply SRI to their investment portfolios; and

BE IT FURTHER RESOLVED that the Legislative Reference Bureau is requested to conduct research on SRI by examining the laws and practices in other states, and current reports and studies in the field; and

BE IT FURTHER RESOLVED that the Legislative Reference Bureau is requested to submit a report of findings and recommendations to the Legislature no later than twenty days prior to the convening of the 2002 Regular Session; and

BE IT FURTHER RESOLVED that certified copies of this Concurrent Resolution be transmitted to the Governor, the Employees' Retirement System, the Department of Business, Economic Development, and Tourism, the Office of Hawaiian Affairs, the Chamber of Commerce of Hawaii, Responsible Markets, the Native Hawaiian Advisory Council; and the Director of the Legislative Reference Bureau.

About the Authors

Peter Camejo

Peter Camejo is the founder and chair of Progressive Asset Management Inc. (PAM) a broker/dealer and research firm coordinating a network of financial consultants specializing in socially responsible investments. PAM opened its doors right after the 1987 stock market crash with one office in San Francisco. Today it has registered representatives functioning in 16 states. In 1990 he created the Eco-Logical Trust for Merrill Lynch, the first environmentally screened fund of a major Wall Street firm. The Eco-Logical Trust was a UIT for five years resulting in the second-best performance of all Merrill Lynch UITs. Camejo served as a county-appointed trustee of the Contra Costa County Employees Retirement Association for three years. Appointed by the Lt. Governor of Hawaii, he is presently serving as an advisor to the Hawaii Capital Stewardship Forum. He also serves on the board of the Council for Responsible Public Investments (CRPI), which he founded to advise elected officials and institutional investors. He also helped form the Environmental Justice Fund, uniting the environmental networks of people of color.

Peter Camejo served for five years on the board of Earth Share, a federation of 41 major environmental organizations. An organic farming firm, Earth Trade, that Camejo helped found turned Nicaragua into the world's largest producers of organic sesame. On Earth Day 2002 Camejo launched a new marketing firm, California Green Light Inc., to make solar energy cost-effective for homeowners in California.

Camejo has long been politically active, starting with civil rights movement of the 1950s and 1960s. He marched with Martin Luther King in Selma, Alabama, in 1965, and was active in the campaign against the war in Vietnam. On November 14, 2001, he announced his candidacy for governor of California on the Green Party ticket.

A Venezuelan-American born in New York, he is fluent in Spanish. In 1960 he competed in the World Olympics representing Venezuela in sailing with his father Daniel Camejo Octavio, a well-known resort developer in Venezuela. He lives with his wife, Morella, in Walnut Creek, California.

Geeta Bhide Aiyer

Geeta Bhide Aiyer is president and senior portfolio manager of Walden Asset Management, Boston, Mass., the socially responsive division of the United States Trust Company of Boston (USTC), an independently operated subsidiary of Citizens Financial Group (The Royal Bank of Scotland PLC). Walden Asset Management is a global investment manager with $1.2 billion in social assets under management (about one-third of the $3.4 billion managed by USTC). Working as a portfolio manager for socially responsible individuals and institutions allows Aiyer to combine her commitment to social justice issues with her training and background in investment theory and finance. Walden is committed to preserving investment opportunity while remaining true to its clients' social purpose.

Geeta Aiyer was a senior vice president and portfolio manager with USTC from 1988 to 1994 before she left to found Walden Capital Management, a socially responsible investment firm specializing in global social investing. Prior to joining USTC, she was a consultant with Cambridge

Associates, Inc., a leading endowment consulting firm. She has an M.A. and B.A. from the University of Delhi, India, and an M.B.A. from Harvard Business School. She is also a Chartered Financial Analyst. Before coming to the US in 1983, she worked in public administration and rural development in India.

Aiyer serves on the Advisory Board for Greenpeace Fund's Planned Giving Program and is a board member of Mount St. Joseph Academy in Boston and Cambridge Ellis School in Cambridge, Mass. She was previously on the board of Crittenton Hastings House, a Boston-based not-for-profit serving women and children. She is the founder of East India Spice, makers of Instant India curry pastes, a critically acclaimed line of all-natural seasonings sold through gourmet and natural foods stores nationwide. She lives with her husband and two daughters in Brookline, Massachusetts.

Samuel Case

Samuel Case is the author of three books on investing. *The First Book of Investing* (Prima Publishing, 1994) is a bestseller in its field. *The First Book of Small Stock Investing* (Prima, 1998) covers the best ways to invest in small company stocks, and is presently out in a new edition. *The Socially Responsible Guide to Smart Investing* (Prima, 1996) deals with investing in small companies whose products or services aid the environment (such as renewable energy and recycling). The book covers the technologies in some detail and also describes the social changes that the adoption of such technologies would bring.

Samuel Case is a Registered Investment Advisor with a business centered in the San Francisco Bay Area, and has written articles on finance and investment, including pieces for the 1998 Microsoft Encarta Encyclopedia. In addition to business and finance, he has specialties in the fields of sustainable technology and energy technology and policy. He is presently working on a book about the ways in which individual action can help to bring about a sustainable energy future.

Ian Chan Hodges

Ian Chan Hodges is managing director of Responsible Markets LLC, a Maui-based venture catalyst that he founded with San Jose–based entrepreneur Roy Goble with an overall mission of leveraging market imbalances profitably for long-term good. He has more than a decade of experience in community development finance and has played an instrumental role in a number of community development finance projects in Hawaii, including the development of a rural micro-enterprise loan program as well as the creation of a statewide community loan fund. In 1994, Chan Hodges secured a commitment from Bank of America to provide $150 million in financing for Hawaiians on their homelands. During Bank of America's merger with NationsBank, he negotiated a multimillion-dollar commitment from BofA to fund the creation of a Native Hawaiian Bank.

Since 1990 Chan Hodges has worked in various capacities to create an environment supportive of independent inventors. In 1999, working with the office of Hawaii's governor and a number of prominent independent inventors, he spearheaded an initiative to create an "island refuge" for intellectual property with the ultimate goal that Hawaii would become for independent inventors what Delaware is for the Fortune 500. Most recently, in 2001 he played an instrumental role in the community-friendly buyout of the Hotel Hana Maui.

Involved in the environmental movement since childhood and social justice issues since high school, Ian Chan Hodges grew up in a family very active in Hawaii politics. He lives on the island of Maui with his wife, Shay, and two sons, Liam and Keane.

Jon F. Hale

Jon Hale came to Morningstar in 1995 as an analyst covering closed-end funds and began covering open-end funds the next year. As a fund analyst, he covered funds across the full range of investment categories while developing an expertise in socially responsible investing. From 1998 to 2000, he helped launch Morningstar Institutional Investment Consulting. He joined the management team at Domini Social Investments LLC in 2000, and rejoined the consulting group in November 2001 as a senior consultant. Hale has taught at several universities, including Virginia Tech, the University of Oklahoma, Northern Illinois University, and the University of Chicago. He has a B.A. from the University of Oklahoma and a Ph.D. in political science from Indiana University.

James Hawley

James Hawley is a professor in the School of Economics and Business Administration, at Saint Mary's College in Moraga, California. Previously he held the rotating Transamerica Professorship in Business Policy and Strategy. He received his B.A. from the University of Wisconsin, his M.A. from the University of California, Berkeley, and his Ph.D. from McGill University in Montréal, Canada. He is the author of two books, the first on international banks and the global monetary system, and the most recent (co-authored with Professor Andrew T. Williams) on US pension funds and the ownership of US corporations, titled *Fiduciary Capitalism: How Institutional Investors Can Make Corporations More Democratic,* published by the University of Pennsylvania Press in 2000. In addition, he is the author (or co-author) of more than 15 articles on a variety of topics, including corporate governance, the international monetary and financial system and environmental issues, as well as numerous papers and reports.

Steven Heim

Steven Heim is a research analyst at Walden Asset Management, Boston, Mass., the socially responsive division of the United States Trust Company of Boston. Heim is a global research analyst and is the primary researcher for non-US companies for Walden and has worked for Walden since 1995. He served previously as director of research at Good Money Publications. Heim also works closely with the family farm and environmental group Rural Vermont and has served on the board of the Vermont Public Interest Research Group for 13 years. He holds two B.S. degrees from the Massachusetts Institute of Technology.

Matthew Kiernan

Dr. Matthew Kiernan is founder, principal, and executive managing director of Innovest Strategic Value Advisors, Inc., an environmental investment advisory firm with offices in New York, Toronto, and London. Prior to founding Innovest, Dr. Kiernan served as director of the Business Council for Sustainable Development in Geneva. Previously, Dr. Kiernan had served as a senior partner with KPMG Peat Marwick, one of the world's largest business advisory and financial consultancies. Dr. Kiernan has also lectured on environmental finance in senior executive programs at the Wharton School, Columbia Business School, and Oxford University. He holds advanced degrees in political science and environmental studies, as well as a Ph.D. in strategic environmental management from the University of London.

Christopher Luck

Christopher Luck joined First Quadrant in 1995. He currently manages the Equity Portfolio Management group, which is responsible for $6 billion in US and international equities. Prior to joining First Quadrant, Luck spent eight years at BARRA, most recently as director of sponsor services. He has published a number of articles in various journals, including research on socially responsible investing, international diversification, style management, and tax-efficient investing. Luck received his M.B.A. from the University of California, Berkeley, in 1988 with an emphasis in finance and graduated *summa cum laude* with a B.A. in economics from the College of the Holy Cross in Worcester, Massachusetts. He became a Chartered Financial Analyst (CFA) in 1994, and is currently an instructor for the CFA Review Course of the Los Angeles Society of Financial Analysts.

James Nixon

James Nixon is chair of the board of Sustainable Systems, Inc., which manages the Communications Technology Cluster, a successful business incubator in downtown Oakland, California. The firm also serves as initiative building consultant to the Bay Area Council for the Community Capital Investment Initiative and the Bay Area Family of Funds. He is also chair and CEO of ProgressiveTrade Securities, Inc., an online socially responsible investment brokerage.

Nixon served as co-coordinator of three Building the Sustainable Economy international conferences, two in New York City, and one in Havana, Cuba. He drafted *Building the Sustainable Economy: An Opportunity for Oakland*, a policy framework unanimously adopted by the Oakland City Council, and he chaired the Working Group that produced the Oakland's Sustainable Community Development Initiative, also adopted unanimously by the Oakland City Council. Prior to Sustainable Systems, James Nixon was for 12 years senior vice president for social research and network services with Progressive Asset Management, Inc., the first socially responsible investment broker/dealer in the US, where he coordinated social research, network services, shareholder advocacy, and community investments.

Steven J. Schueth

Steve Schueth is president of First Affirmative Financial Network, LLC, which specializes in serving socially conscious investors nationwide. He also serves as a director and spokesperson for the Social Investment Forum, the nonprofit trade association for the $2 trillion socially responsible investment industry in the US. He lives in Boulder, Colorado.

Stephen Viederman

Stephen Viederman is an internationally recognized speaker, consultant, author, and activist on the issues of the limits of corporate social responsibility, strategic philanthropy, sustainability, and environmental and economic justice. Until April 2000 he was president of the Jessie Smith Noyes Foundation, with an endowment of $90 million. He serves on the boards of the Council for Responsible Public Investment (CA); the Foundation for Business and Sustainable Development (US); the Tzedec Community Development Fund of the Shefa Fund; the Center for Labor and

Community Research; the Global Greengrants Fund; the Needmor Fund; and the Foundation Partnership on Corporate Responsibility, which he co-founded. Most recently he has been working with a Latino community in San Antonio, and with pueblos in northern New Mexico to help them define for themselves what is culturally sensitive, environmentally sound, and economically viable community development. He serves on a number of for-profit boards, including two ethical mutual funds from Friends Ivory & Sime (US) — the European Awareness Fund and US Social Awareness Fund — and the Technical Advisory Committee of Innovest Strategic Value Advisers.

Andrew T. Williams
Dr. Andrew T. Williams is the Transamerica Professor of Business Policy and Strategy in the Graduate Business Programs, School of Economics and Business Administration at St. Mary's College of California. He holds a B.A., M.A. and Ph.D. in economics from Stanford University and has published extensively in the area of corporate governance with an emphasis on institutional investor activism. Along with Professor James Hawley he has consulted on corporate governance topics for the Organization for Economic Cooperation and Development, co-authored a number of papers and written a book titled *The Rise of Fiduciary Capitalism: How Institutional Investors Can Make Corporations More Democratic,* published by the University of Pennsylvania Press.

Index

A

AFL-CIO SRI fund, 32–4, 92
Alpha. *See* Social screens, alpha
Aquinas Equity Growth Fund, 26
Asset allocation, 97–9, 101, 103–4, 106–8, 110–12, 152, 230

B

Backdoor financial screen, 47
Bay Area Family of Funds, 231, 233
Beta. *See* Social screens, beta
Bridgeway Social Responsibility, 27
British FTSE, 65

C

California Public Employees' Retirement
System (CalPERS), 32, 56, 89–90, 159,
162–3, 165, 230
California State Teachers Retirement
System (CalSTRS), 56, 224
Calvert Capital Accumulation Fund, 109,
139
Calvert Community Investment Notes,
113, 220
Calvert Foundation, 113, 220–1
Calvert Group of Funds, 25, 34, 69, 109,
113, 220
Calvert New Vision, 109
Calvert Social Investment Foundation, 113
Calvert Social Investment Fund, 220
Citizens Core Equity, 135
Citizens Fund Index, 20, 145–6
Citizens mutual funds, 21, 109
Coalition of Environmentally Responsible
Economies (CERES), 112, 243
Colorado Public Employee Retirement
Association (PERA), 162
Community Capital Investment Initiative
(CCII), 231–2, 234
Community Development Banks (CDB),
217
Community development corporations
(CDCs), 219–20, 226–8, 231
Community Development Credit Unions
(CDCUs), 217
Community development financial
institutions (CDFIs), 216–9, 227
Community Development Loan Funds
(CDLFs), 217
Community Development Venture Capital
Funds (CDVCFs), 217
Community investing, 118, 122, 215–6,

219–23, 225, 235
See also Pension funds, community
    investing
See also Socially responsible investing,
    community investing
Contra Costa County Employees'
    Retirement Fund, 58, 76, 213
Corporate citizenship, 80, 124, 212, 250
Corporate crime, 31, 79–80, 82, 93
Corporate governance, 159–61, 164, 169
Corporate social responsibility, 67, 130
Council for Economic Priorities (CEP),
    67, 209
Council for Responsible Public
    Investments (CRPI), 86–7

D
DJGI World Index, 17–18
DJSGI World Index, 18
Domini 400 Social Index (DSI), 12–17,
    19, 21, 38, 63, 91, 104, 109, 145,
    147–8, 150
Domini Social Equity Fund, 118, 122,
    146
Double-Bottom-Line initiative, 34, 117,
    215, 222, 229–30, 232, 235, 245–7,
    249–50, 252
Dow Jones Industrial Average (DJIA), 11,
    65
Dow Jones Sustainability Global Index
    (DJSGI), 17
Dow Jones Sustainability Group Index, 21
Dreyfus Premier Third Century Fund, 27
DVCRF Ventures, 224–5

E
Eco-Logical Trust, 30, 64
Employee Retirement Income Security Act
    (ERISA) (USA), 74, 85
Environmental concerns
    and energy, 186, 190–2, 194, 200, 203
    as externalities, 133, 159, 162, 164,
        166–7
    and foundations, 206–10, 230–6

in international investing, 179–80,
    182–3
in pension funds, 78, 85–7, 89, 93–4
in SRI, 1–2, 42–5, 47–9, 52, 70, 97,
    106, 115, 117, 123–7, 130–1
voting policy for, 243–4, 251
Externalities, 7, 160, 164, 213
See also Environmental concerns,
    externalities
See also Universal ownership,
    externalities

F
Fiduciary capitalism, 151–3, 156
Fiduciary duty
of institutional investors, 152, 160
Fiduciary responsibility, 65, 82, 85, 88,
    138, 157, 165, 229, 243, 247
See also Foundations, fiduciary
    responsibility
See also Pension funds, fiduciary
    responsibility
See also Socially responsible investing,
    fiduciary responsibility
Financial Times & Stock Exchange (FTSE)
    19, 100
Financial Times World Indices European
    Pacific Index (FT Euro-Pacific), 175,
    177
Florida State Board of Administration
    (fund), 149
Forbes 1000 Index, 19
Foundation Partnership on Corporate
    Responsibility, 211
Foundations, 207, 213, 224, 247
    fiduciary responsibility of, 208, 210,
        212–13
    and mission-related investing, 207–8
    and screening, 209–10
    and shareholder activity, 208, 210–11
Free market, 70, 78
Free trade, 53
FTSE4Good indexes, 20
Fulcrum Ventures, 225

G

Genesis L.A. Real Estate Investment Fund, 224

Global warming, 167, 189, 192–3

Green Century Balanced Fund, 26–7

Green Growth Fund, 109

H

Hawaii Capital Stewardship Forum, 92, 247–8

I

Independent power producers (IPP), 190–1

Indexes, 1, 11, 67
international, 177
socially screened, 19–20

Index funds, 146, 179–80, 182
international, 174

Index notes, 103–4, 110

Indexing strategy, 161–2

Interfaith Conference for Corporate Responsibility (ICCR), 79, 87, 211

Investing, community. See Community investing

Investing, international, 173

Investing, socially responsible. See Socially responsible investing

Investment decision-making, 117

Investment portfolios, 118, 120, 133

Investor motivations, 116

Investors Responsibility Research Center (IRRC), 91, 209

Investors Shareholder Services (ISS), 78, 86–7

IPS Millennium Fund, 27, 29

K

Kyoto Protocol, 130

L

Lehman Aggregate Bond Index, 33

M

Market volatility, 110

Massachusetts Association of Community Development Corporations, 227

Massachusetts Community Economic Development System, 226–7

Massachusetts Financial Services Union Standard Equity Fund, 93

Massachusetts Housing Investment Corporation (MHIC), 228

McBride Principles, 244

Microenterprise Development Loan Fund (MDLF), 217

Mission-driven investing, 94–5

Mission-related investing, 213, 249
See also Foundations, mission-related investing

Mission–related venture capital, 208, 211–12

MMA Praxis International Funds, 109

Modern Portfolio Theory, 52

Morgan Stanley Capital International's EAFE Index, 175, 177

Morningstar Star rating, 6, 26–9, 31–2, 121, 134–7, 139, 142–3

MSCI World (index), 17

Mutual funds, 67, 151

Mutual funds, nonscreened, 28, 32–3

Mutual funds, socially screened, 1–2, 28–30, 32–3, 42

N

NAFTA, 92

NASDAQ, 28–9, 108

National Congress for Community Economic Development, 219

New Economy, 3, 8, 127

New Vista Capital Fund, 226

New York City Funds, 163

Non-SRI funds, 30, 32

Non-SRI indexes, 21

Norm shifts, 166–7

O
Old Economy, 8, 44, 127

P
Parnassus Fund, 26
Pax World Fund, 27, 41, 100, 109
Pension fund beneficiaries, 85
Pension fund trustees, 8, 79, 92
    fiduciary obligation of, 73, 85
Pension funds, 75, 78, 82–4,106, 123,
    210, 213
    and community investing, 224, 230
    fiduciary responsibility of, 7, 42, 66, 73,
        87, 89, 124, 207, 251
    as universal owners, 76, 86–9, 151, 153,
        157, 160, 164
Photovoltaic power, 185, 195–9, 205
Political action committees (PACs), 81
Portfolio management, international, 173

R
Responsible Engagement Overlay, 86–7
Risk, company-specific, 15, 47
Risk, degree of, 14, 16–17, 44, 47, 97,
    105, 111
See also Socially responsible investing, risks
Risk measurement, 16
Russell Indexes, 14, 20, 34, 65

S
Shareholder accountability, 181
Shareholder activism, 89, 130, 183–4
Shareholder advocacy, 117–18, 122, 174
Shareholder advocacy, international, 181
Smith Barney Concert Social Awareness
    Fund, 27
Social audits, 94
Social investing, 214
Social investing, international, 174–5
Social Investment Forum, 28–9, 87, 90,
    112, 118, 121, 219, 222, 250
Social issues, 66, 85, 146
Social reform movements, 48–50
Social responsibility, 1, 52, 116

Social screens, 12, 15, 104, 112, 116–18,
    121, 133, 146, 208, 250
    alpha (performance), 50, 53, 62–3, 123,
        126
    beta (volatility), 14–17, 63, 148
    and fund performance, 25–6, 29, 48–51
    in international investing, 175–7,
        179–80; See also SRI screens
Socially conscious equity funds, 31
Socially responsible firms, 67–8
Socially responsible investing (SRI),
    1, 111, 115, 117, 121–2, 206, 245,
    249–50
    as community investing, 113
    and fiduciary responsibility, 74
    as financial screen, 63
    history of, 24
    as investment goal, 92
    in mutual funds, 28, 32, 42, 54, 60, 65,
        133, 145
    outperformance by, 1, 4, 6, 8, 11,
        13–15, 19–21, 52, 54, 60, 66–7,
        70,94, 97,210
    in pension funds, 73, 75, 91
    performance of, 4, 37, 95, 120, 130
    risks of, 64, 70, 73
    and universal ownership, 152, 159, 169
SouthWest Organizing Project (SWOP),
    210–11
SRI balanced funds, 100
SRI fund management, 25, 41
SRI funds, 32, 69, 111, 160
SRI index funds, 11, 20–1, 104, 145–6
SRI, international, 179
SRI international index portfolio, 174
SRI issues, 159, 167–8
SRI mutual funds, 2–3, 11, 19, 26, 38, 62,
    93, 97, 106, 108, 120, 251
    outperformance by, 23–4, 27, 30, 34,
        37, 41–3, 47–8, 59, 63–4, 109, 127,
        130, 147–8
    performance of, 26, 28–9, 61, 111, 121,
        127, 134, 138, 145
    underperformance of, 146

SRI screens, 4, 8, 15, 37, 47–9, 61–2, 65, 86, 111, 160, 168–9; *See also* Social screens
Standard & Poor's 500 Index (S&P 500), 11–16, 19–20, 25–7, 31, 44–5, 58–9, 91, 102–3, 110, 127, 145–7, 149–50
Standard & Poor's Barra Value Index, 14
State Association of County Retirement Systems (SACRS), 90–2
Sullivan Principles, 90
Sustainability, 4, 19, 167–9
Sustainability, corporate, 17–19
Sustainable energy technologies, 194–5, 206
Sustainable industries, 119

T
Teachers Insurance and Annuity Association – College Retirement Equities Fund (TIAA-CREF), 158–9
Technical Assistance Legal Center (TALC), 91
Tobacco industry, 7, 54–9, 70, 81, 166, 169, 213
Tobacco screens, 2, 15, 178, 210, 250
Tobacco stocks, 91, 93, 147, 149–50

U
Universal monitoring, 165–7, 169
Universal ownership, 74–5, 82, 95, 151–2, 156–60, 163–6, 168–9
and externalities, 77, 161–2, 165–8
fiduciary obligation of, 168
See also Socially responsible investing, universal ownership

V
Vanguard/Calvert Index, 19
Vanguard Index, 65
Volatility, *See* Market volatility; *See* Social screens, beta (volatility)
Voting shares, 84, 95, 97

W
Walden/BBT International Social Index Fund (WISIX), 174, 176–83
Walden International Index, 19
Wilshire Large Cap Value Index, 14
Winslow Balanced Fund, 100
World Bank, 92
World Health Organization, 57
World Trade Organization (WTO), 50, 92

If you have enjoyed *The SRI Advantage*, you might enjoy other

BOOKS TO BUILD A NEW SOCIETY

Our books provide positive solutions for people who want
to make a difference. We specialize in:

• Conscientious Commerce • Progressive Leadership
• Sustainable Living • Ecological Design and Planning
• Natural Building & Appropriate Technology • New Forestry
• Educational and Parenting Resources • Environment and Justice
• Resistance and Community • Nonviolence

New Society Publishers

ENVIRONMENTAL BENEFITS STATEMENT

New Society Publishers has chosen to produce this book on New Leaf EcoBook 100,
recycled paper made with 100% post consumer waste, processed chlorine free, and
old growth free.

For every 5,000 books printed, New Society saves the following resources:[1]

35	Trees
3,125	Pounds of Solid Waste
3,349	Gallons of Water
4,485	Kilowatt Hours of Electricity
5,681	Pounds of Greenhouse Gases
24	Pounds of HAPs, VOCs, and AOX Combined
9	Cubic Yards of Landfill Space

[1]Environmental benefits are calculated based on research done by the Environmental Defense Fund and
other members of the Paper Task Force who study the environmental impacts of the paper industry.

For more information on this environmental benefits statement, or to inquire about environmentally
friendly papers, please contact New Leaf Paper – info@newleafpaper.com Tel: 888 • 989 • 5323.

For a full list of NSP's titles, please call **1-800-567-6772** *or check out our web site at:*

www.newsociety.com

NEW SOCIETY PUBLISHERS

**New Society Publishers' books provide positive solutions
for people who want to make a difference.**

❑ Please mail me a hard copy of your catalogue.

Please notify me via email as new resources become available
in the following areas of interest:

❑ Sustainable Living
❑ Ecological Design and Planning
❑ Environment and Justice
❑ New Forestry
❑ Conscientious Commerce

❑ New Economics
❑ Making a Difference
❑ Progressive Leadership
❑ Educational and Parenting Resources
❑ All of the above

Name _____

Address/City/Province _____

Postal Code/Zip _____ Email Address _____

toll free 1-800-567-6772   **www.newsociety.com**

New Society Publishers

We would greatly appreciate hearing your comments,
suggestions, and personal stories about your successes
with socially responsible investing.

Please visit Progressive Asset Management's website at

www.progressive-asset.com

Or give us a call at 1-800-786-2998

Let's keep in touch. Please send me an occasional update. I would also like the following information:

❑ I want my investments to make a difference. I'm interested in working with a financial consultant who specializes in socially responsible investing. Please send me more information, or call or email me to set up a free initial consultation.

❑ I am an investment professional. Please send me information about how I can join the Progressive Asset Management Network of investment consultants who specialize in socially responsible investing, or call or email me to discuss opportunities

Name: _____   Address: _____

_____

Phone: _____   Email: _____

**New Society Publishers
P.O. Box 189
Gabriola Island, B.C.
V0R 1X0
Canada**

BOOKS TO BUILD A NEW SOCIETY

Progressive Asset Management
1010 Oak Grove Road
Concord, CA   94518

Now that you know about the SRI Advantage

Let's Stay in Touch.